Joseph Henry Lumpkin

Joseph Henry Lumpkin

Georgia's First Chief Justice

PAUL DeFOREST HICKS

The University of Georgia Press

Athens and London

© 2002 by the University of Georgia Press

Athens, Georgia 30602

All rights reserved

Set in 10.5 on 14 Bulmer by Bookcomp, Inc.

Printed and bound by Thomson-Shore

The paper in this book meets the guidelines for
permanence and durability of the Committee on
Production Guidelines for Book Longevity of the
Council on Library Resources.

Printed in the United States of America

06 05 04 03 02 C 5 4 3 2 1

Library of Congress Cataloging-in-Publication Data

Hicks, Paul DeForest, 1936–

Joseph Henry Lumpkin : Georgia's first Chief Justice
/ Paul DeForest Hicks.

p.   cm.

Includes bibliographical references and index.

ISBN 0-8203-2365-9 (hardcover : alk. paper)

1. Lumpkin, Joseph Henry, 1799–1867.

2. Judges—Georgia—Biography.

I. Title.

KF368.L847 H53 2002

340'.092—dc21   2001008407

British Library Cataloging-in-Publication Data available

CONTENTS

Acknowledgments *vii*

Introduction *1*

ONE. The Early Years *5*

TWO. Bright College Days *14*

THREE. Making His Mark *22*

FOUR. Riding the Circuit *29*

FIVE. Evangelical Benevolence *37*

SIX. Sounding the Trumpet *51*

SEVEN. Aristocracy of Talent *63*

EIGHT. Paterfamilias *73*

NINE. Establishing the Court *86*

TEN. First among Equals *98*

ELEVEN. The Front Rank *107*

TWELVE. Spirit of Improvement *114*

THIRTEEN. From Slavery to Secession *124*

FOURTEEN. A Flaming Sword *136*

Notes *153*

Bibliography *167*

Index *177*

ACKNOWLEDGMENTS

I am indebted to my grandmother, Louise Lumpkin Upson, for kindling my interest in Joseph Henry Lumpkin. She was a great-granddaughter of Georgia's first chief justice, and, like many matriarchs of her generation, she took her job as the family's chief genealogist seriously. I am also grateful to my mother, Mathilde Lumpkin Upson Hicks, for making me aware of Lumpkin's important judicial role, which she discovered as a student at the University of Georgia Law School in the class of 1926.

Most of my research was done at the University of Georgia in Athens, primarily in the law school library and at the Hargrett Rare Book and Manuscript Library. There were many individuals at the law school who aided me, including Dean David Shipley, who is a worthy successor to Lumpkin and his cofounders as head of what was known in its early years as the Lumpkin Law School. Among others, I am particularly grateful to Jill Coveny Birch, Director of Alumni Programs, who provided me with many creative suggestions, and to Sally Askew, Reference Librarian, who steered me to the law school's collection of Joseph Henry Lumpkin letters, which are now in the care and custody of the Hargrett Library along with other Lumpkin papers. I have the highest praise for Mary Ellen Brooks and her staff there. Their professionalism and breadth of resources, including the latest technology, were of great help to a novice in the field of historical research.

I received useful research suggestions from a number of historians, including Nash Boney, Thomas Dyer, John Philip Reid, and Erwin Surrency. Kermit Hall and Paul Finkelman, who read the entire manuscript, helped me sharpen the focus on Lumpkin's jurisprudence, especially with respect to his decisions on issues other than slavery. Timothy Huebner deserves my special thanks for his generous assistance throughout the project in sharing his deep knowledge and appreciation of Lumpkin.

I am grateful for the valuable assistance of Scott Henwood, who, as Reporter of Decisions for the Georgia Supreme Court, currently occupies the position once held by Thomas R. R. Cobb. I am also indebted to the late Lawrence Custer for his insights into the early days of circuit-riding lawyers and judges in Georgia.

Among the many residents of Athens and its vicinity who were helpful to me, I am particularly grateful to Beverly and David Montgomery for useful information about Oglethorpe County history and Lumpkin's early home in Lexington and to June and Milner Ball for all their assistance. Lastly, I dedicate this book to my wife, Barbara, with great appreciation for her constant support and many thoughtful contributions throughout the project.

Introduction

Roscoe Pound, a former dean of the Harvard Law School, described the period from the Revolution to the Civil War as the "golden age of American law," when the bar was led by illustrious lawyers like Daniel Webster and Rufus Choate and the judiciary claimed such eminent judges as John Marshall and Joseph Story on the United States Supreme Court as well as James Kent of New York and Lemuel Shaw of Massachusetts. More recently, however, Peter Karsten has noted the tendency "of those who have written of this Golden Age of American Law . . . to focus on a relatively small number of well-known jurists and jurisdictions." Of the ten judges who were ranked by Pound "first in American judicial history," eight were from northern states (five from Massachusetts and New York combined) and only two, John Marshall of Virginia and Thomas Ruffin of North Carolina, were southerners. Similarly, the six individuals named by Charles Warren in *A History of the American Bar* as "the Chief Justices who have left a marked impress upon the course of legal development" were all northerners.[1]

Until recently, there has been little written about the southern appellate judges who also influenced our country's legal history during that formative period. Timothy Huebner's useful book, *The Southern Judicial Tradition*, has begun to fill in some of the missing pieces by examining the lives and work of six individuals who headed the highest court in six different southern states during the antebellum period, including Joseph Henry Lumpkin, Georgia's first chief justice. After earning a distinguished reputation as a lawyer and orator, Lumpkin played a major role in the development of Georgia's jurisprudence while heading its supreme court for more than twenty years (1845–1867).

It would seem that those accomplishments alone would have made Lumpkin an excellent subject for a full biography before now. Moreover, his remarkable energy and evangelical Presbyterian convictions helped him gain broader regional and even national prominence as a leader of numerous benevolent reform

causes. At the same time, his intellectual interests and commitment to education made him an important contributor to the early growth of the University of
Georgia as a teacher, trustee, and founder of its law school.

Although Lumpkin was directly involved in politics only briefly, as a promising young member of the state legislature, he maintained an active interest in
state and national political issues throughout his years as a lawyer and during
his service on the judicial bench. In commenting on his approach to politics in a
letter to his daughter Callie, Lumpkin described himself as basically a Whig but
also a "trimmer," because he did not adhere dogmatically to one political party
or doctrine. As a result, he was able to enjoy close ties over the years to major
figures in opposing political camps, such as William H. Crawford, George M.
Troup, Howell Cobb (brother of his son-in-law Thomas R. R. Cobb), Joseph E.
Brown, and his brother, Wilson Lumpkin.

He applied the same independent approach as a participant in some of the
important political developments that affected the course of Georgia's history
in the antebellum period. As a young legislator in the 1820s, he stood up for
states' rights against the "intermeddling" of the federal government, but in the
1830s he was not willing to join with John Calhoun of South Carolina and his
Georgia allies in threatening disunion during the Nullification crisis. By the late
1840s he was ready to support dissolution of the Union but was persuaded to
support the Compromise of 1850 and did not finally conclude that secession
was the only choice for the South until shortly before outbreak of the Civil War.

The position held by Lumpkin in Georgia society was probably best described by Alexis de Tocqueville in *Democracy in America*: "In America there
are no nobles or literary men, and the people are apt to mistrust the wealthy;
lawyers consequently form the highest political class and the most cultivated
circle of society. . . . If I were asked where I place the American Aristocracy,
I should reply without hesitation, that it is not composed of the rich, who are
united by no common tie, but that it occupies the judicial bench and bar."[2]

Along with leading lawyers and judges in other states, Lumpkin was able to
achieve the status and influence identified by de Tocqueville because the social and economic changes occurring throughout the country in that era put a
premium on those with the greatest legal expertise. From 1800 to 1860 the population of Georgia grew from 162,000 to well over one million, including nearly
500,000 slaves, through whose labor cotton production increased from 20,000

lived at Newington ————— Col. Jacob Lumpkin (1644-1708) fought in 1676 for VA

George Lumpkin - capt. during Revolution
(1723 - in King & Queen County, VA
(Old Petersburg)   Bacon's
                                    Rebellion
(Fr. VA.) → Long Creek (Broad River)
                        Ogl. Co

~~John~~   John Lumpkin
                                    m. Lucy

        Wilson   Joseph Henry
        gov. of GA   1st Chief Justice of
                                    State Supreme Court

                                            James Cody (Fr. Kilkenny,
                                                            Ireland)
            George Lumpkin (m) Mary Cody   John George
                                                Robert
                    moved w. George to GA, 1784 w 2 sons

            Wilkes Co (renamed Oglethorpe Co in 1793)
    John's 1st home w. log cabin on Long Creek

784 moved to   George Lumpkin m. Mary Cody
GA w- John + Lucy + sons   1723
bought 1250 acres

    Robert   George   John Lumpkin m. Lucy   Mary
                                        Hopson
            Wilson   Joseph Henry   Thomas
                                1799 -   Jefferson
                                    m. Callender Grieve
                    Marion   Lucy

to 701,000 bales in the same period. By the time of the Civil War cotton had been crowned "king" in Georgia, but the state's economy had also diversified into manufacturing and commerce from its earlier dependence on agriculture. Moreover, Georgia's 1,200 miles of railroad tracks made its transportation system one of the best in the country and helped support the claim that it was "The Empire State of the South."

Despite such economic progress, Georgia had the dubious distinction of being the only state in the Union without a supreme court for nearly sixty years, an interesting story in its own right. When the Georgia Supreme Court was finally established in 1845 Lumpkin was made the senior member and served in that capacity until his death in 1867, becoming the first chief justice when the position was officially created in 1864. He wrote more than one-third of the nearly four thousand opinions that are found in the first thirty-five volumes of the *Georgia Reports*, and he has been widely recognized, at least within Georgia, for his important contributions to the early development of the state's jurisprudence. In the view of Neill Alford, a former dean of the University of Georgia Law School, the industrial development of the South can be traced in part to "Judge Lumpkin's astute molding of the banking and business law of [Georgia] in accordance with sound economic principles."[3]

Chapter 12 includes examples of Lumpkin's opinions, which support Alford's view that Lumpkin's pragmatic decision-making helped corporations prosper in the "spirit of improvement." His view of the law was not entirely pragmatic and utilitarian, however, as shown by other opinions that indicate his concern for balancing interests and protecting the poor and uneducated against corporate abuse of power. Lumpkin often dealt progressively with economic issues, but he was far more conservative when deciding cases that involved divorce and other family issues. His evangelical and patriarchal beliefs are even more evident in a number of his significant slavery opinions that are examined, along with the commentary and criticism of legal historians, in chapter 13.

On the subject of slavery and most other important issues, Lumpkin's views were often closely allied with those of his son-in-law Thomas R. R. Cobb. Among his many accomplishments, Cobb was the author of *An Inquiry into the Law of Negro Slavery*, which Paul Finkelman recently described as "the most comprehensive antebellum restatement of the law of slavery and the only treatise on slavery written by a southerner." Anyone seeking to explore more deeply into Lumpkin's views on slavery will find interesting insights in Cobb's treatise, which he dedicated to Lumpkin, describing him as "the profound lawyer, the eloquent advocate, the irreproachable judge, and the Christian philosopher."[4]

Even though he was convinced that preservation of slavery provided the best choice for the South, Lumpkin was slow to embrace secession. As late as August 1860, he warned in *Choice v. State* about the "upas of humanism, which has so pervaded and poisoned the northern mind of this country, and which, I fear, will cause the glorious sun of our union to sink in the sea of fratricidal blood." As Timothy Huebner observed, "Southern state appellate judges were both sectionalists and nationalists, political figures and legal expositors, southerners and Americans. As such, a study of their public lives offers insights into both the nature of southern distinctiveness and the development of American legal culture."[5]

Of equal interest are the differences, especially regarding slavery, that existed among the southern states during the antebellum period. Lumpkin acknowledged such differences in *Bryan v. Walton* (1853) when he noted that "the condition of the African race is different in every slave State; and is less favorable in the extreme Southern, than in the more Northern slave States; and that consequently . . . we must have recourse to our own local laws, to find the rule for our determination, and to such principles as are dictated by the peculiar genius of our people, and policy of our institutions." By astutely applying that philosophy, Lumpkin managed to maintain the trust of his fellow Georgians during the more than two decades that he headed the supreme court, while also earning a reputation as a legal, social, and economic reformer.[6]

CHAPTER ONE

The Early Years

━━━▷◦◁━━━

Not all of the Broad River settlers were Virginians . . . and some, even Virginians, were hardly a part of the close-knit clan. There was John Lumpkin, who settled on Long Creek, a tributary of Broad River, and who was important in Oglethorpe and Georgia officialdom. His son Wilson became governor of the state, and another son, Joseph Henry, became the first Chief Justice of the State Supreme Court.

E. MERTON COULTER, *Old Petersburg and the Broad River Valley of Georgia*

On June 7, 1867, an obituary in the *Savannah Daily News and Herald* reported the death of Joseph Henry Lumpkin three days earlier and commented that, among his other qualities, "He had a most happy faculty of seizing the right moment to make an impression." It seems that Lumpkin was born with that faculty, arriving just in time to qualify as a child of the eighteenth century. Moreover, his birth, on December 23, 1799, in Oglethorpe County, Georgia, occurred during a period of national mourning for George Washington, whose death at Mt. Vernon on December 14 symbolized the end of an era for many Americans. The Revolution was, nonetheless, still very fresh in the minds of the war veterans and other settlers in the upper Piedmont area of northeast Georgia near the new county seat of Lexington, which had been named for the historic Massachusetts town.[1]

Among those early settlers was George Lumpkin, grandfather of Joseph Henry. As a captain during the Revolutionary War, George had commanded a company of Virginia troops and was granted land by the Commonwealth of Virginia as a reward for his military services. However, he was not the first Lumpkin to serve in combat as a military officer in the new world. His ancestor Colonel Jacob Lumpkin (1644–1708) fought on the side of the colonial governor of Virginia, Sir William Berkeley, during the civil war of 1676, known as Bacon's

Rebellion. Jacob is buried in the graveyard of the Mattapony church in King and Queen County, Virginia, along with relatives of Carter Braxton, a signer of the Declaration of Independence, whose birthplace, Newington, had once been Jacob's home.[2]

George Lumpkin, who most likely was a grandson of Jacob, was born in King and Queen County in 1723. At the age of twenty-five he married Mary Cody, whose father, James, had come from county Kilkenny, Ireland. They raised one daughter, Mary, and three sons, John, George, and Robert, during the years they lived in Halifax and Pittsylvania counties, Virginia. Yet when George and Mary moved to Georgia in 1784, not long after the American army disbanded, the only family members to join them were their son John, his wife, Lucy, and their two young sons, William and Wilson.[3]

John Lumpkin, who had also served as a soldier of the Virginia line during the Revolution, settled with his father on 1,250 acres near Long Creek in a part of Wilkes County, which was renamed Oglethorpe County in 1793. It is likely that they were attracted to Georgia by the land grants offered to war veterans. These bounty inducements brought a tide of new settlers into the north Georgia frontier, especially from Virginia and North Carolina. The land bounties were part of an overall "headright" system, which provided that each free white head of a family could receive land from the state. Under a law passed in 1783, a family head was entitled to 200 acres by paying only the office and surveyor fees and could acquire up to 1,000 acres by paying as little as one shilling an acre. Georgia's liberal policy of land distribution resulted in the filing of over 1,600 headright applications in Wilkes County during 1784 alone. The system became so disorderly that by 1789 warrants had been issued for far more land than was available, and in 1803 it was replaced by a land lottery system.[4]

John Lumpkin's first home was a one-room log cabin on land carved out of the wilderness on Long Creek close to the territory of Creek and Cherokee Indians. William Bartram, one of the first American naturalists, had traveled through that area in the 1770s and found elk, bears, wolves, and wild cats, although, after finding what was called the "Great Buffalo Lick" in the southern part of the county, he reported that "The buffalo (Urus) once so numerous, is not this day to be seen in this part of the country."[5]

According to Wilson Lumpkin, his family initially "encountered all the difficulties and dangers of settling a wilderness, far removed from a dense population, and well cultivated fields, exposed too, to frequent depredations of hostile and savage Indian neighbors so far as to force them and their frontier neighbors to erect and live within the enclosed walls of a rough but strong built fort for several of the first years of their sojourn." In writing about Meriwether Lewis, who spent his youth in Oglethorpe County before setting out on his western expedition, E. Merton Coulter mentions that "on one occasion in the early 1790s, when there was great alarm among the Broad River settlers over an impending invasion by Cherokee Indians, a group of settlers fled for protection to a deep forest recess. In the midst of the night while they were gathered around a campfire and momentarily expecting an attack, Meriwether had the presence of mind to dash a bucket of water on the fire."[6]

A history of Oglethorpe County gives a somewhat different picture of the Lumpkins' early days as settlers: "The country was full of Indians, but they never molested this family, being awed by the bold bearing of Mr. Lumpkin." Wilson drew a more detailed portrait of his father, describing him as "blessed by nature with a fine commanding person, upwards of six feet high and perfectly erect in his carriage; naturally fluent in speech, polite, courteous, and exceedingly popular in his deportment and social intercourse. Rather excitable in his temperament, yet he had a command of his feelings to control his temper when his judgement deemed it proper and expedient to forbear." Wilson's description of his father's emotional nature bears a strong resemblance to later depictions of Joseph Henry Lumpkin's temperament, which he used to great advantage as a courtroom lawyer and judge.

John Lumpkin was clearly a leader in the local community, serving as foreman of the first grand jury ever convened in Oglethorpe County, judge of the inferior court, and member of the Georgia Constitutional Convention of 1798. He was chosen as a member of the Electoral College committed to Thomas Jefferson in the presidential election of 1800. Perhaps the most significant of Lumpkin's various public roles was his service in the Georgia legislature in 1796. The major issue facing him and other newly elected legislators was the heated backlash of the voters over the political corruption committed in the 1795 session, which had become known as the "Yazoo Land Fraud." As a member of the assembly, he participated in passing an act rescinding land grants of more than 30 million acres that had been made to four land companies through fraud and bribery. The general outrage was so strong that when the new law revoked the fraudulent sales, the Act of 1795 was publicly burned.

However, investors who had already purchased some of the Yazoo land started litigation that dragged on for fifteen more years and was ultimately decided
by the U.S. Supreme Court in 1810. The opinion in that case, *Fletcher v. Peck*,
which was written by Chief Justice John Marshall, held in favor of the Yazoo
claimants. It was one of the earliest decisions in which the U.S. Supreme Court
held that a state statute violated the federal Constitution and, in the view of
one leading legal historian, "aroused vivid and excited interest throughout the
country and vitally affected the course of political and economic history." This
was the first of several cases in which the U.S. Supreme Court ruled against the
interests of Georgia, causing increasing strains between the state and federal
governments and creating widespread animosity among Georgians toward any
central court, but especially the Marshall Court.[7]

The Lumpkin children benefited from contact with their father's friends and
colleagues from his various civic and political activities. As Wilson Lumpkin
recalled, "These different positions brought within reach of the family, a knowledge of many local public matters that were not accessible to many of the rising
generation of that day." Wilson's early exposure to politics and the connections he gained while his father was serving as clerk of the Superior Court of
Oglethorpe County were important factors in his winning election to the state
legislature in 1804, at the youthful age of twenty-one.[8]

In that year, Joseph Henry Lumpkin was only five years old. Unlike his older
brother, who grew up in a pioneer cabin, Joseph Henry grew up in a home
where, according to Wilson's account, there "were found more newspapers,
books and reading matter, than was common to families of that period in similar
circumstances." Just as a flair for a political life came naturally to Wilson, it
appears that Joseph Henry showed evidence of strong intellectual abilities at a
young age. In a memorial address given shortly after Lumpkin's death in 1867,
W. T. Brantly noted that "he developed so early such a thirst for learning, was so
constantly intent upon the acquisition of knowledge, that his father determined
to bestow upon him, if possible, the very best education which the country could
furnish."[9]

Wilson Lumpkin had attended a common county school, where one of his
teachers was his great uncle, Joseph Lumpkin, for whom his younger brother
may have been named. However, by the time Joseph Henry Lumpkin was ready
to progress in school, his father had achieved enough financial success to send

him to a new private school in Lexington. This was the nearby Meson Academy, which had been founded with funds left by Francis Meson, a wealthy local merchant who died without heirs in 1806. According to E. Merton Coulter, Meson had added to his success in the mercantile business by setting up one of the early cotton gins.[10] The academy was incorporated under an act of the legislature that also appointed five local citizens as trustees to oversee the academy. Among the original trustees were John Lumpkin and William H. Crawford, who was a U.S. senator (1807–1813) and later held cabinet posts in President James Monroe's administration as both Secretary of War and Secretary of the Treasury before running unsuccessfully for president in 1824.[11]

Coulter, an expert in the history of Georgia, writes, "Meson Academy was doubly fortunate. Unlike nearly all the 583 academies which at one time or another had existed in antebellum Georgia, Meson had sources of income arising from two endowments (until the state academy fund disappeared) and always an income from tuition charges." Thus, the trustees could prudently pay for a new schoolhouse for Meson Academy, which was a substantial brick building of two stories that cost four thousand dollars. According to Coulter, "This edifice was as handsome and commodious as any academy building in the state—among educational structures excelled only by Franklin College, completed in 1805, which was the sole building on the University of Georgia campus, twenty miles to the eastward in Athens."[12]

When Meson Academy opened in 1808, there was a charge of ten dollars per academic year for "Reading, writing, and vulgar Arithmetic" and double that amount for "Mathematics, Belles Lettres, Philosophy, natural and moral . . . and the dead languages." The first rector (head) of Meson Academy was the Rev. Francis Cummins, a native of Pennsylvania, who was well known in Georgia as both a Presbyterian preacher and teacher. He was succeeded as rector in 1813 by Ebenezer Newton, one of the early Presbyterian ministers in the state and a graduate of the University of Georgia. Newton remained at Meson until the spring of 1817 and thus had an important role in overseeing the education Joseph Henry Lumpkin received in his final years at the academy.[13]

As recalled by one of his childhood friends, Lumpkin had been from his birth the favorite of his acquaintances, for the high qualities of his head and heart— the model held up by mothers for the example of their sons. Scarcely any boy in the county was ever reprimanded for a wild frolic or piece of amusing mischief

who was not asked, "Why can't you be like Joe Lumpkin?" Although he was
very talented as a scholar, he had at least one challenger among the students
at Meson Academy for academic honors. That competitor was Miller Grieve,
brother of his future wife, Callender Grieve. An entry in the *Athens Gazette* of
August 3, 1814, lists the following names of students at Meson Academy who
had recently received honors:

> Latin: First—M. Grieve; second—J. Lumpkin
> Composition: First—M. Grieve; second—J. Lumpkin
> Elocution: First—J. Lumpkin; second—M. Grieve

The same list showed that in the examination for English grammar the first
prize went to Callender Grieve, but since she was four years younger than
Lumpkin, it is likely that neither he nor her older brother competed with her
for that honor.[14]

It is not surprising that Lumpkin was best at elocution since he was later
renowned for his oratorical skills, both as a lawyer and as a judge. In 1826, when
he was serving on the Meson Academy's board of trustees, an advertisement
appeared in a Savannah newspaper signed by him as secretary of the board that
gave details about the academy. Included was the following statement that most
likely was composed by him: "We were gratified also to see public declamation
revived in this School, convinced as we are, that in the pulpit, the senate, and
the forum, eloquence is the high road to success—Naked truth, supported by
the most solid arguments and subtle reasoning, will often prove unavailing and
unacceptable, unless embellished with the beauties and graces of rhetoric."[15]

While the secular education of the Lumpkin children was planned by their father, their religious instruction appears to have been guided by their mother. As
described by Wilson, Lucy Hopson Lumpkin "was a woman of great strength of
mind, deeply imbued with the Religion of the Bible, with which Book she was
so familiar, as to need no concordance, to find any passage of scripture, which
she desired. She was an accomplished reader, and spelt correctly almost every
word in the English language."[16]

The Lumpkins were probably members of the Methodist denomination
when they lived in Virginia. When they arrived in Georgia, however, there
was not yet any Methodist church in the area, so they joined the congregation of Salem Baptist Church. Wilson remained a lifelong Baptist, although he

changed his affiliation to another congregation in 1801. Joseph Henry became a Presbyterian as a young adult, some time after he had returned to Lexington from Princeton (which had strong Presbyterian ties) and had married Callender Grieve, who was born in Scotland and was very likely a Presbyterian herself.[17]

Until he left for college in 1816, Lumpkin lived with his family near the same place on Long Creek where his father and grandfather had erected their first log cabin. Wilson described the large tract of land in the rolling countryside as "fertile and excellent," but he noted that his grandfather, who was eager to encourage others to settle in the area, frequently sold off parcels of the land at relatively low prices. While George was especially partial to members of the Salem Baptist Church congregation, it is likely that in the early years any pioneer family whom he thought could help as a buffer against the threat of Indians might have been welcomed as neighbors. Thus, the original 1,250 acres probably had become a much smaller farm by the time Joseph Henry was born in 1799. However, the Lumpkin family did replenish some of their land holdings. In 1797 John Lumpkin advertised in an Augusta newspaper the sale of property in "Lexington or Oglethorpe Courthouse" (as the place was originally named) of "beautiful lots, quite convenient to the public square," indicating that John had begun to augment the family holdings in the countryside with property in town.[18]

By the early 1800s the village of Lexington contained not only a courthouse and jail but also a tavern and several stores, which attracted lawyers, merchants, and doctors who settled near the public square. However, Lexington still had more of a frontier than a civilized atmosphere, as indicated by an address made in 1801 by Judge Thomas Carnes to members of the grand jury. He complained that, despite improvements, "assaults, riots, disorder and confusion were still prevalent in the courtyard." By 1810 Lexington's population still consisted of only 109 whites and 113 slaves, and in all of Oglethorpe County there were few free blacks. However, one of the new residents around 1805 was a black physician by the name of Gowen who established an office in Lexington and, according to one account, "kept the fastest horses, and answered his calls to the country with a break-neck speed, which no white doctor would have risked. This pleased the country people . . . and he performed the most difficult surgical operations with wonderful nerve. . . . He soon had the leading practice of the county. . . . But he fell as suddenly as he had risen. He was detected in an intrigue with the wife of a foreign merchant. . . . Richard Bailey led the mob toward the office of Doctor Gowen. The colored Lothario leaped upon one of his fast horses, and escaped."[19]

When the Lumpkins moved to Georgia in 1784, they brought with them four slaves, two men and two women. In the 1800 census John Lumpkin was listed as owning eighteen slaves, making his one of the larger slaveholdings in Oglethorpe County at the time. According to an analysis of the 1800 census records, only 17 of the 521 slaveowners in the county had more than 20 slaves, the number generally used to define a planter or plantation. Between 1800 and 1820, the number of slaves in Oglethorpe County nearly doubled to 6,444 and outnumbered the white population. Although tobacco was initially the crop of choice, cotton production took off in the early 1800s, due to the invention of the cotton gin by Eli Whitney in 1793, and greatly increased the demand for slave labor. If John Lumpkin had been a full-time farmer, he might have continued to add more slaves, but his role as clerk of the superior court and his other professional and civic activities probably kept him from developing a large-scale plantation.[20]

An insight into Joseph Henry Lumpkin's own early interest in farming is provided in a letter he wrote to Callender Grieve shortly before their marriage in 1821. The letter mentions a discussion he had with Col. Randolf, a local plantation owner, about professional men in the community who, like his father, were "practical planters" subject to the "fraud and disposition of overseers." Randolf had asked if Joseph Henry knew anything of farming, to which he replied that, "practically I know very little, but that my father was called a skillful planter and from observations on his system of agriculture I had derived considerable knowledge of the art." He went on to tell Randolf of his view that "agriculture should be taught as a science in our colleges; assigning as reasons that it would serve as a vehicle of communication between professional men and farmers who now are kept aloof from each other merely because they are ignorant of each others employment."[21]

The letter shows that Lumpkin, even as a young man, was interested in exploring new approaches to economic improvement through communication of practical knowledge. Thirty years later, in a speech to the South-Carolina Institute, he made a similar point when he exhorted his audience to "make full trial of the mind of the State as well as the soil of the State. We want 'cultivated farmers as well as cultivated farms.' " Growing up in an agricultural community, he learned from his father and other planters about the economic realities of farming and slavery that he would later use to great advantage as both a lawyer and a judge.

The letter also indicates how early Lumpkin had developed strong intellectual interests, especially in the field of education. The scientific approach to agriculture he suggested to Col. Randolf in 1821 was echoed in the same South-Carolina Institute speech by a proposal that "the theory and practice of agriculture, must be introduced and thoroughly taught." Lumpkin's intellectual interests, first acquired through his family and Meson Academy in Lexington, were to flourish during his undergraduate years at the University of Georgia in nearby Athens and in the more cosmopolitan atmosphere of Princeton.[22]

CHAPTER TWO

Bright College Days

> If there be such a thing as a Presbyterian type of mind, Southern college boys were brought into close contact with it in the early nineteenth century.
>
> CHARLES SYDNOR, *Development of Southern Sectionalism, 1819–1848*

In 1816, when Joseph Henry Lumpkin entered the University of Georgia (then commonly known as Franklin College), it was still a young and struggling academic institution. Although it had been chartered by the legislature as a state university in 1785 (the first in the country), it did not open for classes until 1801. The legislature had dedicated a tract of 40,000 acres for the benefit of the university, but only 36 acres had been cleared for the original campus, on which a few wooden buildings had been erected. With the completion in 1803 of a three-story brick building, called Old College, plus a home for the president, the college yard began to take on a look of permanence.[1]

The influence of Yale could be found in almost every aspect of the new university, including the design of Old College, which had been patterned after the main building on the campus in New Haven. Abraham Baldwin, the founding president of the University of Georgia, was a Yale graduate who had also taught at Yale before moving to Georgia. In 1799 Baldwin resigned to become a U.S. senator, when the university was still in the planning stages, but he helped recruit another Yale graduate, Josiah Meigs, as president.

Meigs was appointed president at a salary of fifteen hundred dollars plus four hundred dollars to pay for the expenses of his move to Athens. Like Baldwin, he had also been a former tutor at Yale and was a mathematician with a strong educational interest in the sciences. By November 1803 he was able to report optimistically to the board, "The number of students has been between thirty and thirty-five. Twelve young gentlemen compose the senior class. They are pursuing with laudable ambition and singular industry a course of reading, study and academic exercises, and it is believed by the first of May next they will merit the first degree usually conferred in all regular collegiate establishments." Yet, by 1811 the fortunes of the university had reversed so far that all the underpaid faculty members had resigned, leaving Meigs alone to handle the teaching and administration. After protracted conflicts with some of the trustees, the outspoken Meigs was dismissed, causing a six-month suspension of operations before a new president was selected.[2]

The successor to Meigs, Rev. John Brown, was able to breathe enough vitality into the life of the college so that, at the commencement of 1814, the students not only presented the tragedy of *Cato* but also performed a closing farce entitled "No Song, No Supper." Yet Brown was still wrestling with some serious problems at the college when Lumpkin arrived as an undergraduate in 1816. Although Brown had succeeded in filling some holes in the faculty, he was far less successful in gaining financial support from the trustees and legislators. When a lack of funds in early 1816 required a reduction in both the salaries of faculty members and his own compensation, Brown decided to resign. His departure was followed shortly by the dismissal of the remaining members of the faculty. For the second time in less than five years the university was forced to close.[3]

While the suspension of studies so soon after enrollment was not an auspicious start to Lumpkin's higher education, it was only the first of several obstacles he would have to contend with in his undergraduate experience. The university reopened in early January of 1817 and functioned with two new faculty members and an interim president until June, when the Rev. Robert Finley arrived in Athens to take over as president. Finley was a prominent northern clergyman and a founder of the American Colonization Society, which sought to transport freed slaves to Africa. Perhaps he accepted his new position in Georgia with a similar missionary spirit. He had been convinced to leave his job as a Presbyterian minister in Basking Ridge, New Jersey, and had resigned also as a trustee of Princeton, where he had received his undergraduate degree. In accepting his resignation, the Princeton board of trustees honored Finley with a Doctor of Divinity degree.[4]

In a letter to a friend in New Jersey sent shortly after his arrival in Athens, Finley wrote: "The college is at the last gasp—forgotten in the public mind, or thought of only in despair of it—neglected and deserted—the buildings nearly in a state of ruins—and the Trustees doubtful whether it can ever be recovered.

This is a picture not overdrawn. You can readily conceive how all this has operated on my mind. I thank the Lord my spirits do not sink, nor is my heart discouraged."[5]

His optimism was effective in helping Finley establish good relations from the outset with the trustees and obtaining enough funds to pay salaries. He even found a positive side to the smaller student body, which had been reduced to twenty-eight from more than forty under Brown. The students were divided into the traditional four-class system, with freshmen and sophomores generally concentrating on Latin, Greek, and mathematics, while the curriculum for upperclassmen included logic, natural and moral philosophy, chemistry, and the law of nations.

Although there is no record of the specific courses Lumpkin took at the university, the established course of study for freshmen included Virgil, Cicero's *Orations*, the Greek Testament, arithmetic and bookkeeping, "interspersed with frequent essays in Elocution, both before their respective classes in the presence of their Tutor, and before the University collected." The sophomore class took courses on languages, Homer's *Iliad*, Horace, algebra, geometry, conic sections, as well as plane and spherical trigonometry. Frequent essays in composition plus public speaking during the year were also required.[6]

Given Lumpkin's love of the classics and skill at elocution, it is not surprising that he did well academically at the university. W. T. Brantly said in his memorial address, "I have heard on good authority, that in addition to sustaining the highest scholarship of his class, he read through, during the eighteen months of his connection with the University, all the important books of the Demosthenian Library, amounting at that time to nearly 300 volumes." It is likely that the library of the Demosthenian literary society, of which Lumpkin was a member, at that time contained more books than the university's own library. In either case, Lumpkin would probably have found many of the same books his brother, Wilson, said he read as a young man while living at home. These included works of Plutarch, Gibbon, Hume, and Adam Smith.[7]

Even though there was no senior class graduating in 1817 because of all the upheaval during the prior year, commencement ceremonies were still held on the last Wednesday in July, according to tradition. The occasion appeared to be a promising close to a difficult period, and President Finley gave an inspiring commencement sermon on the growth of science and the success of Christianity.

However, within two months, Rev. Finley died of an infection contracted during a trip around Georgia to raise money for the university. After his death, there was a period of more than two years until the Rev. Moses Waddel was chosen as the next president, but by then Lumpkin had already graduated from Princeton.

It is interesting to speculate how the choice of a northern college and specifically Princeton was made for both Joseph Henry Lumpkin and his younger brother, Thomas Jefferson, who entered the class of 1819 at Princeton together. If Rev. Finley had lived longer, his influence as a Princeton graduate and former trustee might have been assumed, but the connection between them lasted only a few months, and there is no indication Finley was a friend of the Lumpkin family. In that era, a choice of college was often guided, if not dictated, by religious affiliations, and Princeton's close ties to the Presbyterian Church might have explained the selection. Although it appears that the Lumpkin family members were Baptists at that point, Joseph Henry and his brother had both been at Meson Academy, whose first two rectors were both Presbyterian ministers.

It is also likely that the decision in favor of Princeton was influenced by the fact that it had long attracted a large share of its students from the South, many of whom subsequently had distinguished careers in government and the ministry. Certainly the most notable Princeton graduate at that time, southern or otherwise, was James Madison of Virginia, who only recently had completed his second term as president of the United States. Within Georgia, there were then a number of prominent Princeton graduates, including two future governors, George Troup and John Forsyth, and a future U.S. Supreme Court justice, James M. Wayne, as well as John MacPherson Berrien, who was then a well-known judge in Savannah and later became both a U.S. senator and attorney general in Andrew Jackson's cabinet.

Whatever was the impetus for going to Princeton, in the summer of 1818, Joseph Henry and Thomas Jefferson Lumpkin were on their way north. It probably took them most of a month to travel from Lexington to Princeton in 1818, based on Rev. Finley's account of his journey from New Jersey to Georgia the prior year. Most likely, they followed Finley's route in reverse, traveling by stage to Savannah and then via ship to New York, with a final stage to Princeton. They arrived at the College of New Jersey (as Princeton was then called) in September of 1818, and after taking placement examinations, they were both admitted to the junior class midway through the academic year.

The Lumpkin brothers found many other southerners among their fellow undergraduates during their eighteen months at Princeton. Of the dozen or so Georgians that were at the college with them, one (George W. Crawford) was to become governor of the state and two others (Walter T. Colquitt and Alfred Iverson) were future U.S. senators. Another classmate, Matthew McAllister, also had an active career in Georgia politics as mayor of Savannah and in the state legislature. As a senator, he played a key role in passing the legislation that finally created a supreme court for Georgia.

While McAllister withdrew from Princeton voluntarily before graduation, another member of the class, John Chestnut of South Carolina (nephew of Mary Boykin Chestnut), was dismissed for participating in the student "rebellion" of 1817. Chestnut was one of the many students who were expelled for actions that included imprisoning the tutors in their rooms, barring the doors of Nassau Hall, and making a bonfire with wood from the college outbuildings. It appears that the riot was triggered by the students' revolt against an increase in discipline and religiosity at the college under the leadership of the president, Ashbel Green, who was a strong Presbyterian. As Green described the situation himself, "The true causes of all these enormities are to be found nowhere else but in the fixed, irreconcilable and deadly hostility . . . to the whole system established in this college . . . of diligent study, of guarded moral conduct and of reasonable attention to religious duty. . . . The tornado which has struck us, though it was violent and in passing shook us rudely, yet has carried away in its sweep much of the concealed taint of moral pestilence and left us a purer atmosphere."[8]

Despite Green's own sanguine view of the atmosphere at Princeton when the Lumpkin brothers arrived in 1818, the college was still recovering from the turmoil of the previous year. In the aftermath of the rebellion and dismissals, the college vice president had resigned, requiring other changes in the faculty, which then consisted of only one professor and two tutors. Enough new students had been recruited by 1818, including the Lumpkins, to warrant hiring an additional professor to fill a new chair of experimental philosophy, chemistry, and natural history. However, in the view of T. J. Wertenbaker, an expert on the history of Princeton, scholarship and teaching reached their nadir during the time of President Green.[9]

Nevertheless, minutes of the faculty meetings during 1818 and 1819 show that Joseph Henry Lumpkin excelled academically, achieving first-grade standing in both junior and senior years. To qualify for a bachelor of arts degree at graduation, the senior class had to pass examinations in an extraordinary number of subjects, including belles lettres, moral philosophy, logic, English grammar, geography, the Greek and Latin languages, arithmetic, algebra, geometry, trigonometry, surveying, navigation, natural philosophy, chemistry, and the holy Scriptures.[10]

While Lumpkin must have devoted a good deal of time and effort to studying in order to achieve such academic success, it did not keep him from enjoying other aspects of college life at Princeton. Among the most important extracurricular activities for undergraduates of that era and throughout most of the nineteenth century were the two literary societies on campus: the American Whig Society and the Cliosophic Society, which were both founded at Princeton in the eighteenth century. They fulfilled an important social function for students and provided educational opportunities beyond the regular curriculum, especially as forums for public speaking and writing. Although students from the South most often became Whigs, both Lumpkin brothers joined the Cliosophic Society, which traced its origins to 1765 through a predecessor called the Well-Meaning Society. Clio claimed precedence by four years over its arch rival, the Whig Society, which had succeeded an earlier organization known as the Plain-Speaking Society.

Among the founders of the Cliosophic Society were some important Revolutionary War figures who later had illustrious careers. Three of them—Oliver Ellsworth, Luther Martin, and William Paterson—were all members of the Constitutional Convention. Paterson went on to become a U.S. senator and governor of New Jersey and later Associate Justice of the U.S. Supreme Court, while Ellsworth was a U.S. senator from Connecticut and Chief Justice of the U.S. Supreme Court. Martin was a noted trial attorney who defended Supreme Court Justice Samuel Chase in his impeachment trial and Aaron Burr in his treason trial. One other, Tapping Reeve, founded the first American law school in Litchfield, Connecticut.[11]

The examples set by these founders and other distinguished graduates must have made a strong impression on the undergraduate members of Clio, especially those, like Joseph Henry Lumpkin, who were considering careers in the law and public service. At the same time, the Whigs could point to James Madison as their founder in the never-ending competition between the two societies.

This rivalry, though generally amiable, did occasionally become heated and was taken most seriously in the annual competition for academic honors between members of the two societies. It was a perfect environment for Lumpkin to develop the skills he had begun to acquire in oratory, debate, and literary discourse as a member of the Demosthenian Society at the University of Georgia. It appears that he also assumed a leadership role in the Cliosophic Society soon after his arrival at Princeton. According to the society's minutes of July 29, 1818, "Brother J. Lumpkin gratified the Society with an address, it being the second evening of his office." Minutes of the meeting on August 6 record that "Oglethorpe," Brother J. Lumpkin, was in the chair, substituting for "Aristes," Brother Brewer. [12]

Apparently every member was required to assume a fictitious name by which he was known at all society proceedings. Lumpkin's pseudonym was obviously derived from his home county in Georgia, while Aristes was more in the early tradition of members adopting either Greek or Latin proper names or those of famous historic characters. As part of the secrecy maintained by both societies, members' fictitious names were never to be uttered outside their respective halls.

At almost every society meeting there was a debate on at least one topic, followed by a vote. The minutes for 1818 record debate topics ranging from lighthearted to serious, such as: "Is it better to be married or single?"; "Is it better for a college to be situated in a village or a large city?"; "Is religion founded on the fear of future punishment or the desire of future bliss?"; and "Would success of the revolutionists in South America be beneficial to our country?" The minutes for August 19 of that year show that the latter debate on South America was decided in favor of "Oglethorpe." By the meeting of September 2, Lumpkin had become the president of the Cliosophic Society, so the extracurricular life in his senior year must have been both active and fulfilling.

During the eighteen months Lumpkin attended Princeton, there were apparently no more major disciplinary problems. President Green wrote in his diary that "so far as the students are concerned in general, the order of the college was good during the session we now contemplate, although we dismissed a considerable number of students; and perhaps it owed its healthful state to that circumstance." There were, of course, a few minor incidents, including the burning of a privy, although the culprits could not be identified. Also, in 1819 the college adopted a rule limiting the amount of pocket money students could have, in an attempt to keep them from favoring the local taverns over the college refectory. [13]

According to President Green's diary, the summer session of the College in the year 1819 commenced on May 13. One of the high points of that last term of Lumpkin's senior year must have been the Fourth of July celebration. A sophomore described the event:

> We met in the Prayer Hall at eleven o'clock A.M. and marched in procession with our gowns on to the church, accompanied by a small band of Princeton Blues, about twenty-five in number. They were in the van. The freshmen followed, then the sophomores and so on, the faculty closing the rear. We stopped at the door and the order being then changed the faculty went in first, then the seniors, etc. The Doctor opened the ceremony . . . with a prayer. Then a hymn was sung and the Declaration of Independence was read by Mr. F. Schroder, a Cliosophian, a patriotic tune was then played. . . . The first oration was delivered by Mr. A. Venable, a Whig of Virginia, the second by Mr. J. Stuart, of South Carolina. Between and after each oration the band played some patriotic tune. [14]

Despite the heat of July and August, the college session in that era ran until the commencement ceremonies at the end of September. When the graduation honors were handed out, Joseph Henry Lumpkin received the second highest academic honor, and his brother was awarded a fourth-place honor. Brantly claimed in his memorial address, without giving his source, that Lumpkin was the first scholar in his Princeton class but "failed to receive the first honor only because the faculty were not willing to award that rank on one who connected himself with the College at such a late date." Even without earning the first honor, Lumpkin's experience at Princeton had been highly successful. He had not only achieved a record of academic excellence but also had established friendships and associations with many at the college, both southerners and northerners, whom he would encounter again in future years.

CHAPTER THREE

Making His Mark

For the family of a southern boy his return from college was a memorable event. They found that he had now grown into a young man whose bearing, clothing, and even accent had undergone a change, and who had lost something of the old provincialism, had become more cosmopolitan. Although still an ardent southerner, his sympathies were national rather than sectional.

THOMAS JEFFERSON WERTENBAKER, *Princeton 1746–1896*

Soon after his return to Lexington from Princeton in the fall of 1819, Lumpkin set out to become a lawyer. He might have chosen to study in the law department established at the College of William and Mary in 1779 or at the nation's first law school, founded at Litchfield, Connecticut, in 1774 by Tapping Reeve. The Litchfield Law School attracted many students from the South, including John C. Calhoun of South Carolina. If Lumpkin had been a northerner rather than a southerner, he might have chosen to attend the fledgling Harvard Law School, which had opened in 1817. Instead, like most young men of that era who aspired to be lawyers, he prepared for the bar examination through the apprenticeship system by studying law with a successful local attorney, Thomas W. Cobb. Unlike students at law school, who spent much of their time attending lectures, Lumpkin obtained his legal education primarily by observing the practice of law both in Cobb's office and in the courtroom. Acting as a clerk and scribe, he assisted in the drafting of deeds, wills, and other documents, sat in on client meetings, and attended court proceedings with his mentor, whose career included seats in the U.S. House and Senate as well as service as a superior court judge. Cobb was one of a number of distinguished attorneys practicing in what was then called the Western Circuit, presided over by Judge John M. Dooly. Lumpkin's apprenticeship also gave him an opportunity to observe the skills of other leading lawyers in Oglethorpe and surrounding counties. These included Stephen Upson, a graduate of the Litchfield Law School who was called "the most profound lawyer in the State," and Upson's former student, George Gilmer, a future governor.[1]

By 1819, there were a growing number of American law books in print, although some may not have been readily accessible to a law student in Lexington. However, it is likely that Lumpkin read Joseph Story's early textbooks, including his editions of works by Abbott, Chitty, and other English authorities. He would have also made use of the American edition of the work by the eighteenth-century jurist and legal scholar, Sir William Blackstone, known as "Tucker's Blackstone," which remained a principal guide to the common law for American lawyers. Twenty years later, when Lumpkin was tutoring some of the next generation of lawyers in his own law office, one of his students reported that, "Blackstone's *Commentaries* was the first book put into our hands to study, with the endorsement by Col. Lumpkin, a most enthusiastic admirer of this work, that it was the best book of all known to him for a beginner. In the same connection, he told us that Mr. Berrien, whom he designated as the most accomplished lawyer in the State, reviewed Blackstone every year, and carried it with him in his carriage around the circuit. He also told us that there was one chapter of the book, that on remainders, which Chancellor Kent expressed himself as having always read with admiration."[2]

In passing the bar examination after less than a year of preparation, Lumpkin showed not only aptitude for the study of law but an eagerness to begin his own law practice. There is no record of the questions he was asked by Judge Augustin S. Clayton at the October 1820 term of the Superior Court of Oglethorpe County. However, he probably fared no worse than members of the first class to receive a Harvard Law School degree, who were required on their final exam in 1820 to give a dissertation on "The Rules of Descent and Distribution of Real and Personal Property by the Civil Law, the Law of England and the Law of Massachusetts."[3]

Lumpkin's decision to begin his law practice in Lexington rather than pursue a legal career elsewhere may have been influenced by ties to members of his large family, but it is likely that his primary motivation was to be near his childhood sweetheart, Callender Cunningham Grieve. Born in Scotland in 1803, she was the daughter of Marion Miller Grieve and John Grieve, who was described as " 'a sturdy Scotchman,' . . . a man of great worth, and strong mind; a whig of the olden time." After leaving Scotland, the Grieve family had first settled in Savannah and then moved to Lexington around 1820.[4]

On February 27, 1821, only a few months after his admission to the bar, Joseph Henry and Callender were married in Savannah by the Rev. Mr. Cranston. On their return to Lexington, Callender set about establishing a household while her husband pursued his already prospering legal practice and formed a partnership with his brother-in-law, Miller Grieve. Like many young lawyers before and since, Lumpkin became active in various organizations to gain recognition and demonstrate his professional abilities. He was elected a member of the Oglethorpe County Agricultural Society and became active in the affairs of his alma mater, Meson Academy, where he was a member of the board of trustees. As secretary of the board he wrote a newspaper notice in 1826 that reported on the successful results of the semiannual examination, praised the "worthy preceptors who preside over this Seminary," and noted with pleasure "the facility with which the female pupils operated in Arithmetic, a branch too much neglected in female institutions." These and other civic efforts gave him visibility throughout the county and helped him gain the legal business needed to support his growing family, which by 1823 included two daughters, Marion and Lucy. Later in life he told one of his law students that becoming a successful man in middle Georgia was particularly difficult as there was "little commerce, few mail facilities and no periodical press."[5]

After attending to his professional and family responsibilities, Lumpkin still had enough energy to pursue some of his own interests. One of these activities took him back to the University of Georgia in Athens, where he helped nurture a new literary society called Phi Kappa. He had guided the organization of this society on Washington's birthday in 1820 to provide an alternative and competitor to the Demosthenian Society, which he joined during his brief enrollment at the university. From its founding in 1803, Demosthenian had been the only literary society on campus, but, according to E. Merton Coulter, "for some years before 1820 the society had grown somewhat lax and listless." However, since the university had been effectively dormant itself for most of two years, it is not very surprising that the Demosthenians went into hibernation as well. When Moses Waddel arrived as the new president in late 1819, he reportedly found "seven students playing 'hide and seek' in the rooms of the Old College building." However, thanks to Waddel's successful administration, within three years there were 120 students attending the university. With the increased enrollment and a renewed spirit on campus, the timing was right for Lumpkin to help a group of undergraduates launch Phi Kappa.[6]

At Princeton, Joseph Henry had seen the merits of having a healthy competition between two college organizations, especially in an era when there were few, if any, competitive sports and no other formal social clubs. In starting Phi Kappa, he may have been motivated by the example of the Cliosophic Society's founders, some of whom had been young graduates living in the Princeton area. He continued as a loyal adviser and benefactor for Phi Kappa throughout the rest of his life. Perhaps the occasion that gave him greatest pride and satisfaction was the dedication of a new hall for Phi Kappa on July 5, 1836, which, according to Coulter, "was memorable . . . on account of those who attended. John C. Calhoun was in the chair and ex-President Moses Waddel was first assistant. Among the other distinguished guests were Joseph Henry Lumpkin and Augustus Baldwin Longstreet, and among the members were the Cobb brothers, Howell and Thomas R. R., the former delivering an oration."[7]

Founding Phi Kappa was the first of many contributions that Lumpkin made for the benefit of the University of Georgia. It would be followed by his service as a trustee over many years, as a faculty member, and as founder of the law school. Throughout his adult life in Georgia, the university provided him with a source of intellectual stimulus and an outlet for his creative energies. It also put him in touch with influential people from all over the state of Georgia and beyond, which proved useful in his emerging political activities.

Since the citizens of Oglethorpe County had elected both his father and his brother, Wilson, to represent them in the state legislature, it was only natural that they would select the younger Lumpkin to perform the same service. Therefore, in 1824, at the age of twenty-five, he took his seat as a member of the House of Representatives in the capital of Milledgeville. He had been elected on the Democratic-Republican ticket, which was then headed by Governor George M. Troup. Before Lumpkin started his first term in the legislature, Governor Troup, as commander in chief of the state's militia, made him an aide-de-camp on his military staff with the rank of colonel, a title by which he was addressed until he went on the bench. Troup may have adopted him as a political protégé because the young man had the backing of the party patriarch, William H. Crawford, but it is interesting to note that Troup, Lumpkin, and another aide-de-camp of the governor, Seaborn Jones, were all graduates of Princeton. Whatever useful political connections Lumpkin may have enjoyed, he arrived at the legislature, according to one of his contemporaries, "with an exaggerated reputation for talent, especially for oratorical talent. . . . At the very opening of the session, Lumpkin took position with the first on the floor of the House of Representatives. His first speech was one of thrilling eloquence, and before its conclusion, had emptied the Senate chamber; many of its oldest and most talented members crowding about him and listening with delight."[8]

Troup, who had served as a Jeffersonian Democrat in both houses of Congress, had resigned his seat in the United States Senate to run in the 1819 gubernatorial race. Although backed by the politically powerful William H. Crawford, Troup lost the election in a bitterly fought campaign to John Clark. For a number of years thereafter, Georgia politics were dominated by the continuing battles between the Troup and Clark factions. The rivalry appears to have been based more on the social and economic differences between the competing constituencies than on any significant disagreements on local or national issues. Those in the Troup camp were more often planters and members of the aristocracy, while Clark's followers typically were small farmers and frontiersmen. There is some evidence that families with Virginia roots tended to vote with the Troup party, while those who traced their origins through North Carolina were attracted to the Clark faction. Yet, party affiliation was often based primarily on personal loyalties. Although the names of the principal political parties in Georgia changed over time, Joseph Henry Lumpkin's allegiances remained primarily with the Crawford–Troup–State Rights–Whig party while his brother, Wilson, remained a Clark–Union–Democratic party loyalist.[9]

In 1823 Troup was elected governor and was reelected in 1825. During his two brief terms as chief executive, he established himself as a staunch champion of states' rights in a long-running conflict with the federal government on a number of issues, but primarily over Creek Indian lands. Georgia's relations with the federal government were among the most critical issues facing the governor and the legislature during the regular fall sessions of 1824 and 1825 as well as a special session held in the spring of 1825. It was during the special session that Lumpkin, despite his junior standing in the House, was made chairman of a select committee with a difficult assignment. The committee's mandate was to investigate the governor's charges regarding attempts by "different branches of the general government to control the domestic affairs and to intermeddle with and to endanger the peace, the repose and union of the southern states."[10]

Troup charged that interference by Washington in Georgia's affairs was not limited to disposition of Indian lands but also included pressure from Congress and other states, such as Connecticut and Illinois, for the abolition of slavery. That led Lumpkin, in his capacity as chairman of the committee, to write his fellow Georgian, John Berrien, who was then in the United States Senate. Referring to the "intermeddlings of the United States government with our domestic concerns," Lumpkin inquired about the "extent of the doctrine maintained recently by the attorney general before the Supreme Court on the subject of slavery."

The case referred to by Lumpkin was *The Antelope*, in which the Supreme Court dealt with the question of whether the slave trade was illegal under international law. Attorney General William Wirt and Francis Scott Key had argued the case against Berrien and Charles Ingersoll, all noted lawyers. Lumpkin's inquiry to Berrien was directed at a report that Wirt, a Virginian, had maintained as a government position that slavery was contrary to the laws of God and nature. Wirt later denied that he had made such a statement, and the Supreme Court decided to follow existing precedents that did not regard the slave trade as piracy.[11]

The committee's report was submitted to the House by Lumpkin in June of 1825 during the special session, but by the opening of the regular session the following November, the relations between Milledgeville and Washington had deteriorated even further. When ordered by Washington not to survey land acquired by treaty from the Creeks, Troup wrote President John Quincy Adams, threatening to "send your Major General Grimes home to you in chains." Lumpkin introduced resolutions endorsing a celebrated declaration by Troup that "having exhausted the argument we will stand by our arms," but the resolutions were not adopted. The conflict between Georgia and the national government continued to dominate the 1825 session, but Georgia's eventual success in acquiring all of the Creek lands brought great praise to Troup as a champion of state sovereignty.[12]

Although his mentor, Troup, was reelected governor in 1825, and Lumpkin was assuming an increasingly important role in the House of Representatives, he began to tire of a political career by the end of the 1825 session. He did not find his work as a legislator at the state capital as satisfying as it had been to practice law closer to his family in Lexington. Also, he probably found the nonpolitical life to be generally uninteresting in Milledgeville, which was more a village than a city, with the exception of the memorable visit by General Lafayette on March 27, 1825. One account of the occasion reports that "a procession headed by Governor Troup met with the general's entourage on the east bank of the Oconee, and the two dignitaries rode into town in a barouche drawn by four bay horses. Citizens who lined the road all the way from the river to Government House proclaimed his welcome amid the firing of cannon and the peal of bells. Twenty-six veterans of the Revolution lined the walkway. . . . A reception was held for him at the Statehouse, followed by a barbecue, accompanied by lively tunes."[13]

Despite his success, both as a legislative leader and trusted adviser to Governor Troup, Lumpkin abandoned his budding political career after just two years. He may have felt the need to provide more income for his growing family, which by 1825 included his first son, Joseph Troup, named for his political mentor, who was followed a year later by his third daughter, Callie. Most likely, however, Lumpkin was driven by a desire to return full-time to the practice of law, which suited him far better than the bitter partisan battles between the political factions. Historian Ulrich Phillips notes, "After the close of the great gubernatorial contest in 1825 an increasing dissatisfaction was evident in the State regarding the personal character of the political factions into which the people were divided. There were continual complaints of this from intelligent voters, and demands were made that there be a change from 'men to measures' as a basis for political difference."[14]

CHAPTER FOUR

Riding the Circuit

⟫⟩◆⟨⟪

Of Lumpkin as he appeared at the bar, we have little but myths remaining;
part fact and more fiction.

DEAN E. RYMAN, *Joseph Henry Lumpkin, An Unintentional Autobiography*

By 1825, when he finished his second and last term in the legislature, Joseph
Henry Lumpkin already had six years of legal experience and enjoyed a reputation as a hard-working and skillful lawyer. He was beginning to capitalize on the
valuable connections and visibility gained through his political exposure, and
his law practice was expanding well beyond Lexington and Oglethorpe County.
His clients came from all the counties of the Northern Circuit and parts of the
Western and Ocmulgee Circuits as well. As W. T. Brantly recalled, "There was
not an important case tried in any part of his circuit in which he was not employed either for the prosecution or defence: whilst his services were frequently
brought into requisition in remote parts of the State."[1]

Georgia's Judiciary Act of 1789 had originally established two superior court
circuits, but from time to time additional circuits were created by the legislature
as the population grew and moved inland from the coast to all corners of the
state. By the 1830s there were ten judicial circuits in which a leading lawyer like
Lumpkin might be called on to represent a client. Thus, he needed to know
not only the strengths and weaknesses of many other lawyers who might some
day be on the other side of a case, but also the habits and prejudices of various
superior court judges.

The best way for any lawyer to gain such vital intelligence was to travel with
other members of the bar as they rode the circuit, following the superior court
judge and the local prosecutor (called "solicitor general") from county to county. Every superior court was required to hold at least two sessions a year in each
county within its circuit. In the early days, most of the lawyers rode the circuit

on horseback, because as one writer described the conditions faced by travelers in Oglethorpe County at the time, "their main link to the outside world was the winding, rutted, stump-clogged, and frequently impassable market road leading northeast from Augusta." However, as the roads improved, two-wheeled sulkies and, later, four-wheeled buggies became the preferred forms of transportation, at least for the more successful lawyers. Judge Garnett Andrews, a contemporary of Lumpkin, recalled the perils of such primitive forms of transportation: "During the sulky reign, some seven or eight were going to Lincoln court, when Judge Lumpkin [who was then still a lawyer]—our late Chief Justice—upset his, and there being six more before him, his horse running away drove them all (in point of time) to follow his example, when we had seven wrecked sulkies and as many frightened horses and lawyers. From this time we dated, from the wrecked riding, as the old people in Georgia did from the Yazoo fresh and the big May frost, and as we do, and will for a long time, the surrender."[2]

Like a company of Shakespearean actors, the traveling lawyers and judges dined together and stayed in inns or hotels where they often had to share rooms, and sometimes the rule of three lawyers to a bed had to be applied. Judges were usually afforded their own beds, if not separate rooms, out of respect for their office. At well-established county seats in the early days, the opening session of court could be quite a ceremonial event, with the local Sheriff carrying a mace as he escorted the judge from the tavern or inn to the courthouse. As Garnett Andrews recalled, "I knew one Sheriff—the first of a new county— highly appreciating his new dignity, when the judge first came to organize it, met him armed with his sword and decorated 'cap-à-pie,' including the cocked hat, with the gaudy uniform (but for its rust) of a Captain of Cavalry." However, in some of the newer counties, where there was not yet a courthouse, superior court sessions sometimes had to be held in the most suitable building available or even in the shade of a large oak tree.[3]

Although lawyers in other states faced similar challenges during the antebellum period, Georgia lawyers carried some significant additional burdens. Unlike twelve of the original thirteen states and every state admitted thereafter, Georgia had not yet created a state supreme court. As a result, there was no opportunity for a superior court decision to be appealed, either to resolve conflicts in decisions among two or more superior courts or to win reversal of errors made during a trial.

At the opening of the 1828 legislative session, Governor John Forsyth's message to the General Assembly echoed Troup's earlier criticism of the system. "Under the present arrangement of eight Superior Court Judges, each confined to the circuit for which he was elected, supreme in his authority, not bound by the decisions of his predecessors or contemporaries and not always his own," he complained forcefully, "there can be neither uniformity nor certainty in the laws. The confusion producing contradictory decisions every day increases; property is held and recovered in one part of the state and lost in another under the same circumstances; rights are asserted and maintained in one circuit and denied in another in analogous cases."[4]

Lumpkin and other Georgia lawyers of his time not only had to deal with inconsistent decisions among the superior courts but also had to practice without any digest of the state statutes or published rules of procedure. For a number of years, the only reported decisions they had were those of two judges from the Eastern Circuit, T. U. P. Charlton and R. M. Charlton, which were, however, often followed in other circuits.

The problems that prevailed in Georgia in the 1830s and 1840s had existed earlier in the northern states. The great Chancellor Kent of New York said that when he went on the bench in 1798 there were no published reports or state precedents, and all the time he was chancellor, not a single decision of his two predecessors was cited. As Perry Miller has observed, "A phenomenon of fundamental importance for both the social and intellectual history of America is the amazing rise, within three or four decades, of the legal profession from its chaotic condition of around 1790 to a position of political and intellectual domination."[5]

Finally, in 1836, G. M. Dudley published a volume of the decisions made from 1831 to 1833 by the superior court judges who had met in convention in an attempt to achieve greater uniformity. Prominently displayed at the front of the volume are testimonial letters from Lumpkin and Garnett Andrews, indicating how influential Dudley thought their views of his volume would be on their fellow lawyers. Andrews wrote that "the decisions show much more learning than I had anticipated" and praised the "skill of the Reporter and talent of the judges." With greater hyperbole, Lumpkin commented, "I have perused the manuscript volume of the decisions of the Judges in Convention. *It far surpasses my expectation.* As a copious depository of law learning it will not rank, of course, with similar productions in New York, Massachusetts, and some of the other States, highly distinguished for their legal science. I must insist, however, that it will compare advantageously with the Reports in the adjoining States of North and South Carolina, Tennessee and Alabama." It is doubtful that Lumpkin really believed that the Georgia superior court decisions equaled the supreme court opinions in the neighboring states. Most likely, he was exaggerating in order to help promote Dudley's work.[6]

Despite increasing demand by members of the bar, no other decisions were published until a law was passed in 1841 that resulted in publication of two volumes of "Georgia Decisions" containing all superior court decisions rendered in 1842 and 1843. Without the discipline that published precedents could bring to court proceedings, lawyers turned to oratory and sometimes theatrics to win cases. In this environment, Lumpkin's eloquence, combined with his reputation for intellect and integrity, made him one of the most successful lawyers in the state at an early age.

Describing the impression Lumpkin made as an advocate, his supreme court colleague Iverson Harris gave the following vivid picture:

> In early manhood he was distinguished by manly beauty. The contour of his face was highly intellectual, the forehead high, broad and fully exposed. He had dark gray eyes, restless and constantly varying in expression, and a quivering lip. . . . His voice was clear and melodious—a rich baritone—obedient to his will and modulated with consummate art, so that it continued to charm by its cadence so long as he spoke. . . . Add to these . . . his large and encyclopedic knowledge, gathered from libraries of law and literature, and we can begin to make some estimate of the resources with which his oratory was supplied. . . . With a vivid imagination quick to body forth the creations of the mind, his speeches at the bar abounded in imagery . . . drawn from the remembered bright and golden thoughts of Shakespeare and Milton, from the sacred poetry of Job and David, the wisdom of Solomon . . . in a word, from the whole Bible. . . . This style was peculiarly his own.[7]

In the first half of the nineteenth century, skilled orators were highly acclaimed not just in the South but throughout the country. John Quincy Adams, Harvard's first Boylston Professor of Rhetoric, told his students to pattern themselves on the ancient Greek and Roman orators because, in a republic, "eloquence is POWER." Some of the greatest orators of the time in various fields acquired the status of American heroes, such as the revivalist Charles Finney, political leaders like Henry Clay, and lawyers like Daniel Webster. In 1860 Lumpkin's son-in-law Thomas R. R. Cobb wrote that "even during his life, his eloquence is becoming traditionary. In every county, scores of witnesses will refer the inquirer to some noted cases where Col. Lumpkin made men's hearts throb quicker and their tears flow freer."[8]

Lumpkin was also noted for the intensity of his feelings, which were so strong when the life of a client was at stake that he had difficulty eating and sleeping. In one celebrated trial in Milbysville, Lumpkin defended a boy of fourteen accused of murdering another boy of the same age. Walter Colquitt, a Princeton contemporary, was prosecution counsel. At that time, juries determined matters of law as well as the facts in criminal cases. When Lumpkin made his summation for the jury, he paused briefly before making a closing statement that one eyewitness said was a masterpiece of its kind:

> Gentlemen of the jury—I am to be followed in this discussion by a man whom I have known from our boyhood. Walter Colquitt, even when a boy . . . was one who wanted a peer or a superior for his adversary. He was never one to contend with a weakling of any degree. . . . To-day to find himself unequally matched, the great, eloquent, powerful lawyer, with yonder stripling sitting silent, yet silently appealing for forgiveness of a vast act done without premeditation or malice, which from his heart he regrets, and he will regret more sorely than all the others. Walter Colquitt will find such a combat unfit for the prowess of the man that he is, and you will find that vain will be his efforts to maintain it.

According to another commentator, "the tears of the jury flowed freely in sympathy with the tears of the multitude who crowded the court room. . . . The history of criminal trials in Georgia records no other instance of feeling so profound and general as that which was awakened by the touching plea of the advocate on this occasion." Colquitt appears to have lost the case before he even had a chance to address the jury, and Lumpkin's client was acquitted.[9]

On another occasion, Lumpkin's passionate nature and dedication to the cause of his client were used against him by opposing counsel. This case, which was more about principle than money, was tried in Wilkes County between two local citizens, one of whom was a good friend of Lumpkin. The other litigant was represented by Alexander Stephens, then a young lawyer rising in the profession, who later became vice president of the Confederacy. As related by Richard Malcolm Johnston, a contemporary of Lumpkin, "Eyewitnesses expected a highly animated combat between the great advocate and the younger, who had been showing promise of the high career he was destined to make. They were strangely disappointed. When the case went to the jury, Stephens, in words and tones almost conversational, referred to the unfortunate controversy between two gentlemen of the county . . . and he could not but trust the balance, so nearly equal, would be found by them to weigh on the side of his client. Lumpkin, one of the most open of men, evinced disappointment. A greater part of his feeling subsided before an adversary who had parted from all his own." After winning the case, Stephens said, "I saw that Colonel Lumpkin was intensely excited, therefore I resolved to keep myself as calm as possible, although my feeling was as high as his; for if I had given full expression to it, it would have excited him still higher, and having the conclusion on me, he would have torn me to pieces and my case."[10]

Judge William Reese, who was a student in Lumpkin's law office in 1839 and 1840, recalled that his mentor's practice was very large and that he won a number of cases defending clients accused of murder. In one of the more famous of these trials, which took place in Milledgeville, he defended Col. William A. Harris, a former Georgia secretary of state and son of Iverson Harris, Lumpkin's future colleague on the supreme court. The younger Harris, who was charged with killing the son of General Sanford, was acquitted in a case that attracted statewide attention. Judge Harris, in his remarks at the memorial service for Lumpkin at the supreme court in 1867, referred obliquely to this case with deep feeling, saying, "After a lapse of nearly fifteen years since he withdrew from politics, he was called, in the discharge of his professional duty, to Milledgeville, the Legislature being in session, when an opportunity was furnished him for the exhibition of the wonderful powers of persuasion and pathos for which he was so renowned."

His persuasive powers were demonstrated all too well in one case, tried in Oglethorpe County, when the main witness for the state was disqualified from testifying on the grounds that he was a Universalist. According to Reese, "This objection was made by Col. Lumpkin, and as he was a man thoroughly religious, his objection was sustained by a powerful argument on the unfitness of the witness to testify in a case involving the life of a man. This case excited much attention all over the State, and led, no doubt, to the alteration of the law."[11]

Another case reported by Judge Reese demonstrated Lumpkin's ability to use both thorough preparation and intuition to win verdicts for his clients. He was counsel for a man in an action brought by a young woman claiming adultery as grounds for divorce. The wife was represented by Reese and his co-counsel, Robert Toombs, who later became a U.S. senator and then served as secretary of state in the Confederacy. As recalled by Reese, he and Toombs had introduced sufficient evidence of the husband's adultery that they assumed the case was won by the time the final witness, the plaintiff's father, took the stand. Lumpkin, however, was able to get the father to admit that the defendant and plaintiff had stayed together at his house after the suit had begun. The judge concluded such cohabitation amounted to "condonation" by the plaintiff and dismissed the case.

Lumpkin's expertise in criminal law led to his appointment as one of three commissioners, along with William Schley (a future governor) and John Cuthbert, to draft a revision of the Georgia Penal Code, which was enacted in 1833. However, like most successful lawyers of his time, Lumpkin was a general practitioner who not only tried cases in court but also prepared documents and gave advice to clients in his office. He handled a wide range of legal matters and transactions dealing with land, slaves, probate of wills and administration of estates, enforcement of notes, and partnership issues, as well as civil and criminal cases. He was involved in the growth of the railroad industry in Georgia from its earliest days, and when the Georgia Rail Road and Banking Company had a public offering of capital stock in 1836, Lumpkin was named as one of the representatives to accept subscriptions.[12]

According to a schedule of fees adopted by the Richmond County Bar Association in 1852, representative minimum legal charges were $5 for an oral opinion, $10 for mortgage foreclosure, $25 for drawing a will, $25 for a divorce action, and $50 for appearing in a felony case before a superior court. Richard M. Johnston observed that $3,000 to $4,000 was a large income for a lawyer in a circuit of eight or nine agricultural counties, holding two court sessions per year with each session averaging about five days. It was also Johnston's view that "no lawyer had ever been known to grow rich from the proceeds of his practice. A large fee was a rarity, because the wealthiest farmers generally chose to adjust serious differences by arbitration of common friends rather than resort to the law, whose uncertainties were well known to them, and whose frequent long delays they revolted from enduring."[13]

In 1852 Garnett Andrews analyzed the values of estates left by lawyers, doctors, and merchants who lived in one of the older and, presumably, wealthier counties in Georgia. Of the forty-five lawyers in his study, only two had left fortunes worth more than $100,000 (equivalent to nearly $2,000,000 in current value), and three others had estates valued between $20,000 and $50,000. It is likely that Lumpkin's wealth reached a peak during his prime years as a lawyer in the early 1840s. Despite his lower income as a supreme court judge and the economic impact of the Civil War, he still managed to leave an estate valued at $34,000 when he died in 1867, equal to roughly $375,000 in current dollars.[14]

Lumpkin's success as a lawyer provided a comfortable life for Callender and the thirteen children she bore between 1822 and 1842, ten of whom lived to adulthood. It also allowed him both the time and funds to support a growing number of benevolent, religious, and educational groups, which widened his horizons beyond the state of Georgia and began to establish his reputation both regionally and nationally.

CHAPTER FIVE

Evangelical Benevolence

> Benevolence, instead of malevolence, is beginning to be the grand master-
> spirit and motive-power of the world. All working for the good of all—this
> is society—all else is savagism.
>
> JOSEPH HENRY LUMPKIN, *An Address before the South-Carolina Institute*

Even though Joseph Henry Lumpkin's father was not a particularly religious man, his devout mother provided enough Christian influence within the family that two of his older brothers became Baptist ministers. The elder of these, Jack, was born in 1785 and ordained in 1812 by Jesse Mercer, one of the most influential of the early Baptist ministers in Georgia and the founder of a college bearing his name. Jack was pastor of a church at Antioch, Georgia, for twenty-five years and, according to one commentator, "no pastor was more beloved. His affectionate manner and feeling preaching endeared him very much to all his congregations." A history of Oglethorpe County notes that the other clerical brother, George, "was at first a Primitive Baptist and preached at the Skull Shoals Church, Greene County, for many years. His inclination to preach to the sinners of the community brought on a controversy . . . and when it was decided that Rev. Lumpkin was not exactly orthodox in their particular teachings, Rev. Lumpkin withdrew and, with about half of his congregation joined the Missionary Baptist Church."[1]

As a boy, Joseph Henry Lumpkin joined his family in attending the Shiloh Baptist Church near Lexington. There is no indication that he was very religious in his youth, but his upbringing prepared him to succeed in the moral and religious atmosphere that permeated Princeton under the influence of the president, Ashbel Green. After graduation, Lumpkin returned to Lexington during a period when evangelical Protestantism was becoming the predominant religious movement of the South. As defined by Donald Matthews, a hallmark of evangelicalism is its "elaboration of the Protestant perspective that the Christian life is essentially a personal relationship with God in Christ, established through the direct action of the Holy Spirit, an action which elicits in the believer a profoundly emotional conversion experience." Another important aspect of evangelicalism, according to Matthews, is its "focus on a continuous struggle with the self, continual engagement with the Bible, and persistent expectation of being further inspired by preaching."[2]

The growing success of evangelicalism was part of a broader religious revival, known as the Second Great Awakening, which occurred throughout the United States between 1800 and the Civil War. However, as documented by Christine Heyrman in her award-winning book *Southern Cross*, the evangelical movement still faced substantial southern opposition in the 1820s. Some, like Thomas Jefferson, objected to the evangelical emphasis on emotion rather than reason, while others were not prepared to give up their worldly pleasures.[3]

In view of Lumpkin's family influences and his emotional nature, it is not surprising that he was a candidate for an evangelical conversion experience. The moment came for him at a Methodist camp meeting in Oglethorpe County held in the early 1820s, not long after he had married and begun practicing law. Camp meetings were among the most distinctive features of southern religious life in the first half of the nineteenth century, providing occasions for baptisms, weddings, and general socializing, as well as individual conversions. They were frequently interdenominational, but the Methodists seemed to excel in handling both the logistical and ceremonial aspects of these gatherings.

At a typical camp meeting in Georgia at the time, cabins were erected around the sides of a square with a hall down the center. There were sleeping apartments for the campers who had traveled a distance; along the sides of the hall and in front were benches and a few chairs. The cabin dwellers brought provisions for themselves and others, entertaining as many as fifty or more at a meal. Toward the center of the square stood a tabernacle for worship services, which was lighted by small tin lamps without chimneys, while around the tabernacle and over the grounds were low scaffolds holding pine knots that were lit for illumination.

Lumpkin's experience might well have been like that of one convert who reported, "There was the largest encampment I ever saw . . . estimated at 10,000. . . . Preaching was had at two stands regularly; great power attended the word and there was wonderful outpouring of the Spirit and scores of souls were converted. I recollect one evening in particular, while the sweet songs were sounding from hundreds of voices, while converts were shouting all around, it seemed almost as if heaven were coming down to earth. All creation seemed to brighten, and even the tops of the tall pines to wave 'glory to God.' "[4]

While it is possible to picture Lumpkin responding emotionally to the dramatic atmosphere of a camp meeting, it is likely that his conversion on that occasion was largely due to the eloquent preaching of Lovick Pierce. One of the great Methodist ministers of the period, Pierce had established a reputation by the 1820s as the foremost preacher in the state. A contemporary of Lumpkin, W. H. Sparks, described Pierce as a "young, spare man, with sallow complexion, and black eyes and hair. I remember the gleam of his eye, and the deep, startling tones of his voice—his earnest and fervent manner." After undergoing his own evangelical conversion in 1803, Pierce joined the Methodist ministry, but, following his marriage to a wealthy woman, he decided to pursue a career in medicine. He graduated from the University of Pennsylvania Medical College in 1816 and established a successful medical practice in Greensboro, Georgia, where Lumpkin frequently attended court sessions. During the years he was practicing medicine, Pierce continued to preach at a church in Greensboro and at camp meetings, before returning to the regular ministry in 1823.[5]

Although Lumpkin was fourteen years younger than Pierce, it is likely that he found in Pierce a kindred spirit in both intellect and breadth of interests as well as someone who shared his appreciation of the power and art of rhetoric. Even though the caliber of preaching at the Shiloh Baptist Church did not match Pierce's eloquence, Lumpkin apparently remained a Baptist after his evangelical conversion, as there was no Methodist church in Lexington until 1828. However, he was still able to maintain his association with Pierce for a number of years, since Pierce's preaching circuit included Lexington, Athens, and other nearby communities. In 1825, when Lumpkin was in the legislature, he showed his esteem for Pierce by using some of his political patronage to have Pierce (as well as his wife, Callender) included among "the ladies and gentlemen appointed Trustees for a Female Seminary to be established in this state."[6]

The popularity of camp meetings and conversions, such as the one Lumpkin experienced, were not uniquely a Georgian or a regional phenomenon. In 1801 more than twenty thousand people attended a camp meeting at Cane

Ridge, Kentucky, which is credited with triggering the religious revival movement throughout all regions of the young republic that lasted more than thirty years. In a number of areas, such as the so-called "burned-over" district of western New York, the revivalist fires of the Second Great Awakening flared up on several occasions during the period 1800–1830.

The scope of the Second Awakening has been attributed by some writers to widespread anxiety over the rapid social and economic changes in the years following the War of 1812. Others have seen the revival movement as a necessary antidote to the waning of revolutionary idealism, symbolized by the deaths of both Thomas Jefferson and John Adams on July 4, 1826. Whatever might have been their psychological underpinnings, revivals and camp meetings pragmatically formed the center of communal life and supplied much-needed fellowship for many individuals and families, especially in the southern and western frontier areas. Except when the circuit court was in session, revival meetings also provided most of the local drama and entertainment that were available in many parts of the country during the first few decades of the nineteenth century.[7]

The spark of evangelical Christianity that was ignited by Lovick Pierce was not caused by any feeling of anxiety or isolation within Lumpkin, for he was already well embarked on a successful career in the law and surrounded by his family and friends. Instead, it is likely that he, like many other intelligent and ambitious individuals of the period, was led to his conversion by an innate optimism about what he could achieve through evangelical religion for himself, his family, and his community. One scholar has noted that, "In philosophical terms it meant that if immediate conversion is available by an act of the human will, then, through God's miraculous grace, all things are possible: human nature is open to total renovation in the twinkling of an eye and so, then, is the nature of society. . . . It was from this assumption, pervasive in the nation after 1830, that perfectionism and millennial optimism grew to such importance."[8]

Not long after his conversion by Lovick Pierce, Lumpkin met Thomas Goulding, a Presbyterian minister who arrived in Lexington in 1824 and became head of the female department of Meson Academy where Lumpkin was a trustee. Goulding was raised in Liberty County, Georgia, as a member of the Congregational Church, but after attending school in New England and preparing for a legal career he decided to become a Presbyterian minister. He thus had much in common with Lumpkin, who became a member of a small group in Lexington that studied the Old Testament with Goulding. Whether it was due to Goulding's influence or otherwise, Lumpkin's diary indicates how deep his evangelical conviction had become by 1827. In an entry made on Sunday, July 22, 1827, he wrote, "Do I rejoice with joy unspeakable at the thought that my sins were nailed to the cross on Calvary and my pardon purchased there! Do I indeed love the Lord for what he has done for me!" Two weeks later he noted that he "heard Rev. Goulding's sermon this afternoon." Then in August of 1828 Lumpkin joined the newly established Bethsalem Presbyterian Church in Lexington, following the lead of Goulding, its first minister. [9]

During the same year, Goulding became the founder of a fledgling Presbyterian seminary and, as its sole professor of theology, began teaching a group of five students at his home in Lexington. Two years later, he moved his family and the seminary to South Carolina, where it subsequently became known as Columbia Theological Seminary (now located in Decatur, Georgia). Later in his life, Lumpkin wrote of Goulding, "His intellect was much above the ordinary standard. . . . He was a thorough Calvinist of the Genevan School; nor could any considerations of policy induce him to relax, in public or private, one jot or tittle of his creed. The doctrine of justification by faith he regarded as an epitome of the Christian system—as embodying its life and power; and this, in its connections, undoubtedly formed the favorite theme of his ministrations." [10]

Lumpkin became a ruling elder of the new Bethsalem church in Lexington and took an active role in the governance of the Presbyterian Church through the Hopewell Presbytery. He was able to combine his religious and educational interests by serving for twelve years as superintendent of the Union Sunday School in Lexington. On one occasion, he substituted in the pulpit with great success when a visiting preacher failed to arrive. An individual who was a member of the congregation on that occasion admitted to Lumpkin twenty years later that he had been a professional gambler and that, "Your words entered my heart. . . . I set about the reformation of my life. . . . I have been a Christian for many years. I now thank you as the instrument of my conversion." [11]

If Lumpkin had not been so successful as a lawyer, he might well have become a notable preacher, arguing to a congregation as if it were a jury, as Charles Grandison Finney said he often did. Finney, who started out as a lawyer, was one of the driving forces of the Second Awakening among Presbyterian ministers in the North, before he switched his allegiance to the Congregational Church

because of differences on matters of both substance and form with other prominent evangelicals like Lyman Beecher. Although the friction created by Finney's
passionate revival methods was of concern mainly to Presbyterian leaders in the
North, his theological arguments would have been closely followed by southern church leaders and intellectuals like Lumpkin. Perry Miller wrote of Finney,
"Not only could he slay thousands in the frenzy of a revival, but in 1835 could
articulate his *Lectures on Revivals of Religion*, indisputably the most powerful
theoretical statement of the significance of the titanic enterprise. . . . Finney's
book stands—though many of his fellow-revivalists disagreed with him, though
many attacked his methods—as the key exposition of the movement, and so a
major a work in the history of the mind in America."[12]

While there is no evidence that Lumpkin and Finney ever met, they knew a
number of the same people, including the Rev. Benjamin Wisner, minister of
Boston's Old South Church, who had arranged a truce between Finney and his
antagonist, Lyman Beecher, which led to Finney preaching in Boston in 1831
and 1832. However, by the time Lumpkin met with Wisner in Boston during
the summer of 1833, Finney had moved to New York. Nonetheless, they most
likely would have agreed on many subjects, including the best uses of oratory
to reach some individuals through the mind and others through the heart.[13]

Lumpkin, as a so-called "Old School" Presbyterian, would have disagreed
with Finney on some doctrinal issues, but he would have embraced Finney's
perfectionist view of salvation, which held that those who are converted and
reborn become totally unselfish or altruistic, because "all sin consists in selfish-
ness; and all holiness or virtue in disinterested benevolence." This view, which
has been called "romantic perfectionism," replaced the Calvinist assumptions
of a predestined elect and the depravity of man with a belief in the perfectibility
of all who were converted. It was this belief that generated an important moti-
vating force for Lumpkin as he began in the late 1820s to invest more of his own
evangelical energies in various benevolent and reform movements.[14]

The first benevolent cause to capture his interest was the temperance reform
movement, which was founded under the banner of the American Society for
the Promotion of Temperance at a meeting in Boston on February 13, 1826. One
of the founders and guiding lights of the American Temperance Society was the
Rev. Justin Edwards, a Massachusetts minister who later became a good friend

of Lumpkin. With Edwards leading the way, the Society's initial strategy was "to induce *those who are temperate to continue so*," and thus it did not originally require any pledge of abstinence. However, under the strong influence of Lyman Beecher and other leaders of the movement, the strategy was soon changed to one of total abstinence in the belief that requiring a pledge would aid in recruiting members. [15]

Helped by the surge of revival meetings, where the evils of intemperance were a favorite target of preachers, there was an extraordinary growth in the number of state and local temperance societies across the country in the next few years. By the end of 1829, more than one thousand societies had been formed comprising one hundred thousand members, including the Georgia State Temperance Society, which was formed in April 1828. However, a census done by the national organization in 1831 showed that New England, with less than one-sixth of the nation's population, accounted for more than one-third of the temperance pledges, while the southern states, representing over 40 percent of the population, had less than 10 percent of the pledges. [16]

In the words of Thomas R. R. Cobb, writing for the *Temperance Crusader* in 1860, Lumpkin "was the father of Temperance in Georgia. Becoming convinced that the drunkard could be reclaimed and the young man protected only by the example of all their neighbors, he emptied his well-filled cellar into the barn-yard, and then took the field preaching Temperance." In 1829 Lumpkin was elected president of a new Oglethorpe County Temperance Society and succeeded in persuading the students at the University of Georgia to form their own society. While not yet thirty years old, Lumpkin was already in the vanguard of a growing number of southern evangelicals who believed that intemperance not only undermined the family and church but was also a principal cause of the poverty and crime that threatened social order. [17]

Although demon rum was not as much a problem in rural Georgia as it was in the urban centers of the north, Lumpkin and his fellow temperance advocates had an alcoholic nemesis of local origin to contend with. As a former law student and Lexington neighbor of Lumpkin, George Paschal, recalled,

> Before the commencement of the temperance reformation by Col. Lumpkin, it
> may be literally said, that, in that section of the country, we were "born into

brandy." The whole county abounded in large orchards of delicious peaches. Upon almost every farm there was a distillery of more or less capacity. Brandy was manufactured in every neighborhood and kept in every house. It was drank at births by the suffering mother, the midwife, and the gossips who attended. The lips of the infant were moistened with a weak beverage. It was drank for joy and sorrow, in adversity and prosperity, at house-raisings, corn-huskings, harvestings; at balls, quiltings, dinners and suppers; at funerals and administrators' sales. It was a medicine, in cold weather and hot; in the fever and the ague; for the colic, headache, consumption, dyspepsia, and gout. It was upon every sideboard, and visitors were asked to drink on arrival, during stay, and on their departures. The ladies sipped it with honey; the men drank it in their coffee, and called it "laced coffee."[18]

To some extent, Lumpkin was able to combine his circuit-riding travels as a lawyer with his speeches on behalf of temperance reform in various locations in Georgia. However, during one hiatus in the legal calendar, he visited South Carolina and made twenty speeches in as many days. His friend, Justice John Belton O'Neall of South Carolina, who accompanied him and heard every speech, is reported to have said that "though he made so many addresses on the same subject, each appeal was different, and thus recommended by all the freshness of novelty as well as by the eloquence of the advocate."[19]

In November 1832 the Georgia State Temperance Society held its annual meeting in Milledgeville, coinciding with the opening of the legislature in order to achieve the best attendance. At that meeting, Judge Augustus B. Longstreet became president of the State Society, and Lumpkin was elected one of three vice presidents. He was also appointed to deliver one of the addresses at the next annual meeting and selected as one of two delegates to the national meeting of the American Temperance Society. Although he was unable to attend the national meeting, he and Longstreet were the chief speakers at the next annual meeting of the State Society in November 1833.[20]

Lumpkin and Longstreet had much in common besides the long service that each of them devoted to the cause of temperance reform. Longstreet is probably best known as the author of *Georgia Scenes*, a collection of sketches about life in middle Georgia, published in 1835. Born in 1790, he graduated from Yale and attended the Litchfield Law School before being admitted to the Georgia bar in 1815. He practiced law in Greensboro and, after serving one term in the state assembly, was elected judge of the superior court of the Ocmulgee District in 1822. Although he was nine years older than Lumpkin, their interests and careers, especially in the earlier stages, were remarkably similar. Even after Longstreet entered the Methodist ministry in 1838 and became president of Emory College a year later, he and Lumpkin continued to have very similar religious and educational interests. [21]

The first National Temperance Convention met at Independence Hall in Philadelphia on May 24, 1833. Reuben H. Walworth, who followed James Kent as Chancellor of New York, was president and, among the sixteen vice presidents in attendance, the only two from states south of Maryland were William McDowell of South Carolina and Joseph Henry Lumpkin of Georgia. On a positive note, it was reported at the meeting that over sixty thousand societies, with more than one million members had been organized; more than two thousand distilleries had been stopped; more than five thousand retailers had quit the traffic; ardent spirit had been banished from the army and nearly from the navy; and more than five thousand drunkards had been reformed. However, concerns were also expressed openly at the convention that the American Temperance Society had become tainted with New England abolitionism, which led to relocating the headquarters of the national organization from Boston to Philadelphia. [22]

Participating in this Philadelphia meeting as an officer of the national society gave Lumpkin his first opportunity to meet and deal in person with some of the most influential northern leaders of the temperance movement. Following the Philadelphia meeting, he traveled to New England, apparently on business connected with the educational interests of the Presbyterian Church in Georgia. While in Boston he had a chance encounter with two representatives of the Theological School of the Synod of South Carolina and Georgia, located in Columbia, South Carolina, which his friend, Rev. Thomas Goulding, had founded. As a result of that encounter, he was invited to attend a fundraising dinner for the seminary hosted by the Rev. Benjamin Wisner, minister of the Old South Church in Boston.

Wisner and John Tappan, another of the organizers of the dinner, were among the founders of the American Temperance Society and most likely had attended the Philadelphia meeting with Lumpkin. Because of his connections with so many of the participants, it is not surprising that Lumpkin was asked to give one of the addresses that evening. It is surprising, however, that he chose that occasion to talk, among other points, about his support of emancipation. He may not have realized that his speech would be covered in detail by a Boston newspaper, let alone that the article from the *Boston Courier* would be reprinted verbatim in two Georgia newspapers. [23]

Given the politically charged atmosphere in Georgia at the time, the speech became a highly controversial topic, subjecting Lumpkin to a great deal of criticism. There was already a growing suspicion about the temperance movement in the South because of perceived and actual connections between the abolitionists and the temperance press in the North. The first temperance paper in the country was the *National Philanthropist*, founded in 1826, which in 1829 merged with the *Investigator*, a paper edited by William Lloyd Garrison. In 1831 Garrison's new paper, the *Liberator*, became the main voice of abolitionism and began publishing vitriolic attacks on the South, together with demands for immediate freedom for the slave population without compensation to the owners. Garrison had become so hated and feared in the South by 1832 that, pursuant to a resolution of the Georgia legislature, the then governor, Wilson Lumpkin, offered a reward of five thousand dollars for the arrest of Garrison so that he might be brought to trial under the laws of Georgia. [24]

The temperance cause in Georgia and elsewhere in the South declined significantly throughout the 1830s, not only because of the abolitionist connections but also because more compelling political issues, such as the Nullification debate, captured popular emotions. Temperance activity was reduced outside the South as well, due to financial losses suffered by prominent backers of the American Temperance Union in the panic of 1837 as well as controversies over the inclusion of wine and beer in the temperance pledge. [25]

Throughout this difficult period, however, Lumpkin maintained his official position in the Georgia State Society, which severed all connections with the national organization in 1835 because of the slavery issues. If there was anyone in the state of Georgia who was even more committed to the temperance cause in the late 1830s than Lumpkin, it was Josiah Flournoy, a staunch Methodist and successful planter from Eatonton. In 1839 Flournoy led a petition movement aimed at persuading the legislature to outlaw "tippling houses." Some critics expressed concern that Flournoy's tactics were too aggressive while others, like the *Columbus Enquirer*, charged that circulating the petition had harmed the temperance cause. Supporters of the unsuccessful State Rights candidate for governor blamed his defeat on his support of the "Flournoy movement."

Despite all this controversy, Lumpkin nonetheless became one of Flournoy's principal supporters, even co-signing with him an advertisement for the petition campaign that ran in a number of newspapers throughout the state. The campaign not only failed to achieve any legislative changes but also resulted in Flournoy having his buggy broken and his mule shaved and painted, along with other forms of harassment. Despite Lumpkin's participation in the ill-fated Flournoy movement, he managed to avoid the abuse that was heaped on his friend. Nonetheless, it showed again that Lumpkin was willing to risk public criticism to promote social reforms he supported. [26]

The cause of temperance thereafter grew so weak in Georgia that in 1840, when the Phi Kappa Literary Society debated the question "Are the temperance societies beneficial?" the negative side won easily. That outcome probably reflected the general view in the South that the temperance movement was then under the control of the antislavery forces. However, Lumpkin continued to enjoy such a solid reputation among the Georgia temperance advocates that at the annual convention in November of 1844 he was chosen president *in absentia*, succeeding Augustus Longstreet. It was a particularly difficult time to rebuild popular interest in the temperance movement because of the heated political climate during the presidential campaign of that year, including controversy over the annexation of Texas. Even Lumpkin, who was seldom involved in party politics at the national level, decided to attend the Whig National Convention at Baltimore in May of 1844 to support his friend, Senator Theodore Frelinghuysen of New Jersey, as a candidate for vice president. [27]

After Henry Clay was nominated as the candidate for president, the convention became deadlocked over the choice of a running mate until Frelinghuysen was finally selected. According to one report, "Colonel Lumpkin, of Georgia, who had gone to the convention solely as a friend of Mr. Frelinghuysen, of New Jersey, watched the happy moment when he arose and put his friend in nomination, commencing his remarks upon his Christian name, Theodore—which in Greek means 'gift of God'—and such was the happy gift of his name, Theodore, and the Christian character of Mr. Frelinghuysen, that the nomination was carried by Colonel Lumpkin triumphantly through the convention." [28]

Lumpkin remained head of the temperance movement in Georgia while he

was traveling in Europe during 1845 and even during 1846 when he was preoc-
cupied with his new responsibilities on the supreme court. In 1847 he headed a
delegation of Georgians to the South Carolina state convention, reciprocating
attendance by his friend, Justice John O'Neall, and other South Carolinians at
the Georgia convention. The cause of temperance had recovered sufficiently by
1848 that when the State Temperance Convention met in Atlanta in July, with
Lumpkin as president, there was "such an assemblage of temperance delegates
and visitors as had never before been seen in Georgia." At the next year's convention in Macon, it appears that the movement was still making good progress
in Georgia, despite rumors that the national organization was meddling again
with the slavery issue.

A high point of the convention was the decision to hold a special session if and
when the famous Irish temperance leader, Father Theobold Matthew, visited
Georgia in the course of his travels around America. However, after issuing
an invitation to the priest, Lumpkin received a newspaper article reporting on a
meeting in Boston between Father Matthew, William Lloyd Garrison, and other
leading abolitionists.

In a letter to Father Matthew asking for an explanation of his actions, Lumpkin emphasized that on his answer would "depend your capacity for usefulness
at the South." The initial response from Father Matthew was deemed unsatis-
factory and the invitation was therefore withdrawn. In the midst of the following
storm of controversy, which even reached the floor of the U.S. Senate, Georgia's
Senator Berrien wrote Lumpkin a letter of support criticizing Father Matthew
for "an officious intermeddling with the domestic institutions of a people, of
which he knew little—in behalf of a portion of their population of whose actual condition, he knew less." However, a subsequent letter to Lumpkin from
the priest appears to have provided sufficient reassurance of his neutrality on
the slavery issue to resolve the conflict and allow him to visit Georgia in January 1850.[29]

Not long after, Lumpkin and his fellow temperance leaders had to wrestle
with even more difficult problems. At the state temperance convention in 1852
there was active debate about whether to seek legislation to curb the liquor traffic, following the example set by Maine the prior year. No action was taken
at that meeting, but in 1853 there was renewed effort to achieve legislative action through a more moderate plan called the "Atlanta Proposal." Although the

initiative had the backing of many of the state's temperance leaders, they could not persuade Lumpkin to join in the legislative effort.

Then in June 1854, pleading continued ill health, Lumpkin resigned as president of the state temperance society. In a lengthy letter, which was published in the *Southern Banner*, he advised his fellow temperance crusaders against seeking legislation, such as the Maine Liquor Law, "which will authorize the searching for, or seizure, confiscation and destruction of private property." It is clear that his participation in the ill-fated Flournoy movement fifteen years before had taught him that "one thing is certain, whatever may be the relative advantages of moral suasion and legal coercion, no law to abolish the traffic can ever be passed, or if passed, permanently sustained, unless the public conscience and judgement are properly instructed. Eschew all connection with politics and parties. Next to the union of Church and State, I know of no alliance more unholy."

One commentator has speculated that Lumpkin opposed any legislation providing that alcoholic products could be legally seized because it might lead to similar laws affecting other types of property and might ultimately threaten the institution of slavery. However, a more likely reason for his opposition was that he had been following the ripple effect of Maine's Liquor Law, as similar legislation was enacted in twelve other northern states between 1852 and 1855. When the Massachusetts court struck down the search and seizure provisions of the commonwealth's law in 1854 (followed by the New York court in 1856), Lumpkin's concerns were vindicated.[30]

Although his claim of poor health as the reason for his resignation is supported by letters to family members, Lumpkin still managed to maintain a grueling schedule while traveling around the state for Supreme Court sessions. Perhaps he was concerned that his leadership role in the state temperance society might someday conflict with his Supreme Court duties. Whatever may have been the incidental reasons, it is clear that after more than twenty-five years of campaigning and battling for temperance, Lumpkin was ready to devote his energies to other important causes.

Twenty-one years had passed since he had stated in Boston that he sided with the most ardent abolitionist in seeking a way to achieve emancipation. He had changed many of his views about slavery, states' rights, and the Union over the intervening years, as he grew ever more concerned about the South's ability to achieve its own economic and cultural destiny. The strength of Lumpkin's feelings about these issues is shown in his letter to Father Matthew in 1850, warning him that "justice to our families, our firesides, everything dear to us, forbids that we should call *any man* brother who unites with our enemies in waging an unprovoked and relentless warfare upon our hearths and homes, our peace and prosperity."[31]

CHAPTER SIX

Sounding the Trumpet

⟫◈⟪

> In 1833 Col. Joseph Henry Lumpkin made a speech in New England, in
> which he avowed that he and others in the South, for a long time, had de-
> sired the emancipation of the negroes. . . . A few years earlier Col. Lumpkin
> might have advanced the sentiments with impunity; a few years later, to have
> said the same thing would have driven him from the country.
>
> GEORGE W. PASCHAL, *Ninety-four Years, Agnes Paschal*

Lumpkin named his first son, Joseph Troup Lumpkin, in honor of Governor
Troup, who had been his political mentor during his legislative years. When
his third son (sixth child) was born in 1829, he was named William Wilberforce
Lumpkin, after one of the major figures in the English evangelical reform movement. William Wilberforce (1759–1833), an Anglican cleric, was the architect of
legislation in the British Parliament that outlawed the slave trade in 1807. He
was also the head of a group of evangelical philanthropists and reformers called
"The Clapham Sect," which organized and sponsored numerous benevolent
societies to attack vice on the home front and fund missionary work abroad.

At the same time, a growing number of benevolent societies in America were
pursuing goals similar to those of the Clapham Sect. The eight largest of these
societies, known as the "Benevolent Empire" or "Great Eight," were headed by
a relatively small and cohesive group of clergy and laymen operating from bases
mainly in Boston, New York, and Philadelphia. Although Wilberforce did not
visit the United States, his example and influence were widely felt among American evangelical reformers, primarily through his book *A Practical View*, which
had twenty-five American printings. One New York newspaper at the time called
William Wilberforce "a name with which there is probably associated more of
love and veneration than ever fell to the lot of any single individual throughout
the civilized world."[1]

For Lumpkin, Wilberforce was the epitome of an intelligent and forceful evangelical leader whose views on the relationship of religion to government and to society in general may well have influenced Lumpkin's decision to abandon a career in politics and to pursue an active role in both church affairs and benevolent organizations. In *A Practical View*, Wilberforce called on the English upper classes to "consider as devolved on them the important duty of serving, it may be of saving their country, not by busy interference in politics . . . but rather by that sure and radical benefit of restoring the influence of religion."[2]

As much as Lumpkin must have admired Wilberforce for his overall achievements in social reform, he probably would not have named his third son after the "Great Emancipator" if he had not become committed to emancipation himself by the time of his son's birth in 1829. Yet the only public statement he is known to have made in favor of emancipation was during his speech at Boston in 1833, which also happened to be the year that Wilberforce died and Britain abolished slavery. A Boston newspaper article commenting on the speech reported,

> Colonel Lumpkin, who spoke with much enthusiasm, stated that . . . there were strong feelings at the South against the North, and he and others had striven to disabuse the public mind. The Union had been in danger and this meeting formed a strange contrast to the notes of defiance, which had recently been sounded in his own State and the State of South Carolina. He spoke of slavery with much feeling and philanthropy, and remarked that, strange as it might seem for him, coming from a slave State, he would call upon his Maker to witness that the most violent abolitionist at the North could not more seriously desire the dissolution of the ties between the master and the slave, than himself. Several circumstances were now concurring to hasten that result; a change had taken place even within a year, in the sentiments of the planters; he truly believed that the interests of the owners and the slaves were alike identified in emancipation, and the time was rapidly coming on when the principle would be abandoned, and the only difference of opinion would be, how can the thing be done in the best manner?[3]

There are several intriguing aspects to Lumpkin's statements in support of emancipation on that occasion. First is the question of whether he expected the speech to be reported in such detail by any Boston newspaper or, more importantly, to receive so much publicity in Georgia. Given the prominence of the hosts of the meeting and the interest in the subject of emancipation, however, he might well have anticipated the result. It is also strange that he chose to identify himself so closely on the emancipation issue with the "most violent abolitionist at the North." He must have known that his brother, Wilson, then governor of Georgia, had signed a legislative resolution not long before that put a five thousand dollar price on the head of William Lloyd Garrison or anyone else caught publishing abolitionist statements in Georgia.

In view of the political climate at the time, it is surprising that criticism of Lumpkin's Boston remarks in the Georgia newspapers was not more negative. An article in the *Southern Banner* on July 13, 1833, stated,

> We were not a little astonished on reading the following sketch of an address delivered by Joseph Henry Lumpkin, Esq., at a meeting lately held in Boston. . . . It is well that Col. Lumpkin is looked upon by the agitators of the South, as belonging to the foremost rank of those who profess to hold in their hands exclusively the honor, happiness and prosperity of the Southern States—we mean the Nullifiers. If the sentiments on slavery advanced by him at the Boston meeting had been, in the same place and on the same occasion, pronounced by one from the South equally averse to the South Carolina nullification, we hesitate not to say that the cry of treason and traitor would ere this have been proclaimed."[4]

The Milledgeville *Federal Union* of July 18, 1833, commented on Lumpkin's remarks in an even more balanced tone, noting first that "if similar sentiments, in such an assembly, and at such a place had been expressed by a member of the Union party of Georgia, what bitter anathemas would have thundered . . . by all the Nullification presses in the State. . . . But Col. Lumpkin is a prominent member of the Nullification party of Georgia. . . . Will they believe him . . . or will they denounce him as a deserter, a traitor, an enemy to the South? In our view, as a witness he stands on very strong ground."[5]

Not long after the Boston Speech, Lumpkin was in Northampton, Massachusetts, where, according to the *Northampton Courier* of July 10, 1833, he made a plea "for assistance to aid in christianizing the blacks and elevating their moral condition, and by extending the hand of Christian fellowship and love, to bind adhesively the several parts of the Union more firmly together." The *Courier* then editorialized: "His declaration that slaveholders were eager and solicitous to have their blacks enlightened by Christianity was wholly new to us, conflicting as it does with several legislative acts of the southern states expressly interdicting it." The newspaper also contrasted Lumpkin's statements with those of Senator

Robert Hayne of South Carolina, who "in the great debate in 1830 [with Daniel Webster] reprobated in the severest terms the efforts of 'benevolent associations' and 'missionaries' from the North among the blacks of the South."[6]

As indicated by comments in the Georgia newspapers, the subject of nullification was a great deal more contentious in Georgia in the early 1830s than the issues of emancipation and abolitionism. It seems surprising that Lumpkin was viewed by the press as still having a leading political role as late as 1833, more than seven years after he completed his service in the legislature as a member of the Troup party. However, Ulrich Phillips, an eminent historian of antebellum Georgia, has noted that, until roughly 1833, "the parties in Georgia had a certain intangibility resulting from the obscurity of their manipulations. Each was controlled by a ring which transacted business in caucuses and kept no minutes."

What the newspaper accounts of Lumpkin's speech called the Nullification party was actually the newly formed State Rights party of Georgia, which had an equally new opponent in the Union party. In the view of the *Niles Register*, "These parties, now called *union* and *state rights* were heretofore arrayed under the name of *Clark* and *Troup* parties—but what they differed about we never fully understood; and the present arrangement, we think, have [*sic*] a more intimate relation to the doctrines concerning *nullification* than to the political parties, proper, which generally divide the people of the United States."[7]

To make matters more confusing, two factions within the State Rights party held different positions on Nullification. Lumpkin was part of the moderate faction, headed by John Berrien, which opposed the "tariff of abominations" but did not endorse the extreme course of nullification that Calhoun and his South Carolina cohorts were championing. In his younger and more partisan days Lumpkin may have, as the *Milledgeville Federal Union* claimed, "maintained that the States containing slaves ought to dissolve the Federal Union, and to form a Southern Confederacy." However, the paper went on to note that "his remarks at Boston were made in opposition to these prejudices, which he had fostered, and on which he had acted, for many years. This also is a strong badge of truth. His testimony would be believed by an impartial jury; and it is entitled to full credit with his friends in Georgia, by whom he has been listened to with deference."[8]

By siding with the moderate arm of the new State Rights party and opposing nullification, Lumpkin managed to suffer relatively little damage to his reputation, despite his stand on emancipation in 1833. Like a cat, he landed on his feet, and in January of 1834 a newspaper article even included Lumpkin's name on a list of names recommended as alternatives to those nominated by the State Rights party as candidates for Congress. The author of the article, who was identified only as a member of the old Troup party, claimed that the doctrines of the new State Rights party "are identically those of Nullification" and then observed that "nine-tenths of the Troup Party are Troup men *yet. . . . They cannot, and never will become Calhoun men.*"[9]

While Lumpkin chose not to resume the life of a politician, his brother, Wilson, continued his successful political career, running in 1833 as the Union party candidate for governor and gaining reelection by a substantial margin. If Wilson's reelection marked the "death-blow to nullification," as Coulter contends, it was in large part because Wilson was able to convince influential members of the opposing party, such as his brother, to agree on a unified Georgia position. Coulter also argues that the failure of nullification in Georgia "bespeaks her strong attachment to the Union," but it appears that for some Georgians, including Joseph Henry Lumpkin, attachment to the Union depended primarily on finding solutions to the issues of slavery that threatened it.[10]

Lumpkin probably anticipated and, perhaps, even cultivated the publicity that his Boston speech received in order to promote an agenda for emancipation that would be acceptable to both the North and the South. For example, a letter he wrote to the *Augusta Chronicle* about his speech at Boston became the subject of an article in the *Boston Patriot*, which in turn was reprinted in the *Niles Register* in October of 1833. In the letter he praised a speech made by Caleb Cushing, a Boston lawyer and politician who opposed slavery but rebuked the abolitionists for endangering the Union by antagonizing the South. Sounding equally statesmanlike, Lumpkin concluded the letter with the view that "the North is entitled to discuss, in their newspapers, their periodicals, and in any other mode, except politically, the abstract question of slavery, if it seems good to them to do so . . . provided it be done with a view to assist, and not to injure—to convince and not to irritate. Beyond this they have no right nor do I believe they desire or design to interfere."[11]

Although it appears from his Boston speech that Lumpkin was then ready to promote emancipation in Georgia, he was not prepared to indicate how he thought emancipation could be achieved. He said only vaguely, "Several circumstances were now concurring to hasten that result" and then added, with equal obscurity, that "change had taken place even within a year, in the sentiments of the planters" and that it was necessary only to resolve a difference of opinion as to "how can the thing be done in the best manner."

Some insights into Lumpkin's thinking at that time are provided by his opinion in *Cleland v. Waters* (1854), where he recalled that the Georgia legislature in 1824 (of which he was then a member) criticized a resolution it had received from the state of Ohio on the subject of abolition of slavery. However, he noted that the legislature had reserved "the right, with her southern sisters, of moving this question when an enlarged system of benevolent and philanthropic exertions . . . shall render it practicable." He then asked rhetorically, "Is it not apparent, that up to this period, the true character of the institution of slavery had not been fully understood and appreciated at the South; and that she looked to emancipation, in some undefined mode, in the uncertain future, as the only cure for the supposed evil."[12]

Although there was some support in Georgia and elsewhere in the South during the 1820s for the goal of gradual emancipation, by 1833 two events had convinced many that the highest priority should be the removal of free Negroes through colonization. First, in the fall of 1829 a pamphlet was discovered in the possession of some blacks in Savannah, written by a freeborn black, David Walker, which asserted that slaves could attain freedom by destroying their masters. Within a few months, additional copies of the pamphlet were found elsewhere in Georgia and in other slave states, causing widespread concerns about possible slave revolts. As fears grew, promotion of colonization appears to have diminished. Then, in 1831, these fears were realized when Nat Turner's rebellion in Virginia resulted in the deaths of more than eighty whites. It is possible, therefore, that when Lumpkin talked in 1833 of changes in planter sentiments, he was referring to a brief renewal of interest among Georgians and other southerners, following the Nat Turner scare, in the efforts of the American Colonization Society to send freed slaves to Africa.[13]

The American Colonization Society had been formed at Washington in December of 1816, largely through the efforts of the Rev. Robert Finley, who was then a Presbyterian minister in New Jersey but shortly thereafter became president of the University of Georgia in Athens. Finley's brother-in-law, Elias

Boudinot Caldwell, who was clerk of the U.S. Supreme Court, and Francis Scott Key, a successful Georgetown lawyer (most famous as the author of "The Star-Spangled Banner"), assisted Finley in arranging the first meeting on December 16, 1816. Bushrod Washington, nephew of George Washington and a justice of the U.S. Supreme Court, presided at that meeting. Among the speakers on that occasion was Henry Clay, then Speaker of the House of Representatives, who also presided at a second large meeting held five days later. Although Finley's goal was to extinguish slavery eventually through colonization, Clay warned at the outset that the colonization society needed to avoid the issue of emancipation if it was to be successful in the South and West.[14]

Because of Finley's leading role in the American Colonization Society, Lumpkin may have first learned of the colonization movement while he was still a student at the University of Georgia, perhaps even before Finley arrived in June of 1817 to start his brief term as president. In any case, Lumpkin was sure to have been aware that the most distinguished citizen of his hometown of Lexington, William H. Crawford, was one of the original vice presidents of the society. In 1819, when Crawford was secretary of the treasury, President James Monroe stopped in Lexington to visit Crawford on his way from Augusta to Athens during a political trip through the southern states. They then attended a round of receptions and banquets in Athens, and it is reported that, among the various toasts, one was made by Monroe to the American Colonization Society, whose goals he was known to endorse, praising it as "planned by the wisest heads and the purest hearts. May it eventuate in the happiness of millions." Another toast denounced the slave trade as "the scourge of Africa; the disgrace of humanity. May it cease forever, and may the voice of peace, Christianity, and of civilization, be heard on the savage shore."[15]

Despite the enthusiasm for colonization that was displayed on that occasion, it appears that during the 1820s there was less public support for colonization in Georgia than in several other southern states. In 1825, when Lumpkin was in the legislature, Governor Troup denounced a proposal made in the United States Senate to establish a special fund for the emancipation and colonization of slaves. Two years later Troup's successor, John Forsyth, signed a resolution protesting the appropriation by Congress of funds for the benefit of the society, whose "real objective was to remove the whole colored population of the Union to another land to the economic detriment of the southern states." It also criticized the "unthinking zealots, who formed themselves into abolition societies" and were attempting to make the blacks in the South "discontented with their present situation."[16]

The earliest indication of Lumpkin's involvement with the colonization movement appears in a letter, quoted in the *Niles Register*, describing his participation in a meeting of the Massachusetts Colonization Society on July 4, 1833, which "was attended by the lieutenant governor and most of the influential and distinguished men of the place." There is no record of Lumpkin's active involvement with the American Colonization Society prior to 1847, although the society's records show him as a donor and his contributions, totaling two hundred dollars, were among the highest of those made by Georgians. Then in 1847, a year after he became a member of the Georgia Supreme Court, Lumpkin agreed to become a vice president of the society. In his acceptance letter of March 18, 1847, he wrote,

> It is an honor of which one may well be proud—to have their names enrolled in any enterprise with those of Jefferson, Madison, Marshall, Monroe, Carroll, Crawford and Clay, and many other bright worthies who were and are, the firm and efficient friends of African Colonization. I love and have long loved this noble cause. It is the only efficient scheme which philanthropy has yet devised for ameliorating the condition of the negro in this country and for diffusing the blessings of civilization and Christianity through the lands of his fathers.[17]

The colonization movement was just then beginning to recover from a decade of problems resulting from the loss of federal support during the Jackson administration as well as increasing opposition from abolitionists. Even the Presbyterian schism in 1837 between the Old School and New School groups had undermined a solid front in favor of colonization. In publicly endorsing the American Colonization Society in 1847, Lumpkin was joining distinguished company from both the North and the South and no doubt had assured himself that the society would not be a forum for abolitionist attacks on slavery. Henry Clay remained president of the society until 1849, and among the other vice presidents in the late 1840s were such notable individuals as General Winfield Scott and Lumpkin's good friend Theodore Frelinghuysen.

By the early 1850s the annual meetings of the American Colonization Society in Washington attracted prominent members of all three branches of the federal government, including Daniel Webster, Stephen A. Douglas, U.S. Supreme Court Justice and Georgia native James M. Wayne, and President Millard Fillmore. In *Cleland v. Waters* (1854) Lumpkin explained that "the policy of transporting our free blacks to Liberia, received at its commencement in 1816, the sanction and approbation of our greatest and best men. . . . And Mr. Justice Wayne of the Supreme Court bench and others of our most distinguished citizens, continue to give it their countenance and support."[18]

In the 1850s even Abraham Lincoln believed it represented the best solution to the twin problems of slavery and racial prejudice against freed slaves. In his 1852 eulogy to Henry Clay, Lincoln said, "If, as the friends of colonization hope, the present and coming generations of our countrymen shall by any means, succeed in freeing our land from the dangerous presence of slavery; and, at the same time, in restoring captive people to the long-lost father-land, with bright prospects for the future; and this too, so gradually, that neither *races nor individuals* shall have suffered by the change, it will indeed be a glorious consummation." Lincoln continued to support colonization as late as 1857, saying in a speech at Springfield, "Let us be brought to believe it is morally right, and at the same time, favorable to, or, at least, not against our interest to transfer the African to his native clime, and we shall find a way to do it, however great the task may be."[19]

In contrast to Lincoln, Lumpkin grew increasingly skeptical during the 1850s about the benefits of colonization to either blacks or whites. In *Bryan v. Walton* (1853), he wrote,

> Whether the scheme of African colonization be feasible or not the ablest and most discriminating minds have doubted. There yet stands on our Statute Book, a resolution of the representatives of the people in favor of this colonial enterprise, as presenting to the philanthropist, the citizen and the statesman, the only means, not only of benefitting the nominally free who are scattered over the land, but everywhere treated as an inferior race; but as affording an outlet to the humane feelings of the benevolent, as well as a drain for that relative increase of the slave over the white population of this country, and which in some sixty years, has swelled to between 350 and 400 thousand.[20]

In an opinion written four years later *(American Colonization Society v. Gartrell)*, Lumpkin finally rejected the concept of colonization in ruling against the society, which sought to transport slaves of a Georgia decedent to Africa. Although most of his opinion was highly legalistic, he concluded on a personal note:

> I was once, in common with the great body of my fellow citizens of the South, the friend and patron of this enterprise. I now regard it as a failure, if not something worse; as I do every effort that has been made, for the abolition of slavery, at home or abroad. Liberia was formed of emancipated slaves, many of them partially trained and prepared for the change, and sent thousands of miles from all contact with the superior race. . . . And at the end of half a century what do we see? A few thousand thriftless, lazy semi-savages, dying of famine, because they will not work.[21]

When read in the context of his overall slavery opinions, the *American Colonization* case provides important insights into Lumpkin's patriarchal and racist views about slavery, both as an evangelical Christian and, by 1857, as a southern nationalist. In rejecting any hope that colonization could achieve the goals he had outlined in *Bryan v. Walton*, he was influenced by the reports of famine and disease suffered by freed slaves in Liberia. However, he was by then also convinced that whites were ordained by God to assume the burden of improving the lot of slaves within the South, as "under the superior race and no where else, do they attain to the highest degree of civilization."

He had expressed similar paternalistic sentiments as far back as his speech at Northampton in 1833, when he asked his northern hosts "for assistance to aid in christianizing the blacks." The Massachusetts newspaper account, as reported in a Georgia newspaper, noted that Lumpkin's view "was wholly new to us, conflicting as it does with several legislative acts of the southern states expressly interdicting it." After the Nat Turner rebellion, Georgia had even made it an offense to let slaves have paper and writing utensils, but as Eugene Genovese explains, "Throughout the South, churches and individuals quietly defied the proscription, and the bolder spirits campaigned against it. Some masters saw practical advantages to plantation life by having literate slaves; some masters, as Christians, had troubled consciences, whatever their fears."[22]

Although the motivations cited by Genovese may have been common, not every slaveholder was prompted by mere practicality or conscience when he decided to educate his slaves. One individual who most likely was motivated by both practicality and conscience was the Rev. Doctor Charles Colcock Jones. In the 1830s and 1840s Jones served both as a Presbyterian minister in the Savannah area and as professor of theology at the Theological Seminary in Columbia. During that period, he wrote two widely used books that were designed for "the oral instruction of colored persons." Through the Presbyterian Church and other associations, Lumpkin and Jones shared many interests and were also friends for many years as confirmed by Jones's wife, Mary, in a letter written in 1858 to their son Charles Jr. Commenting on the Lumpkin family, she said, "They are amongst our most worthy Christian people. The judge and your father have long been friends, and we shall be happy to entertain them." Jones added, "I have a very high esteem of the judge and his excellent lady."[23]

The Jones family was among the larger slaveholders in Georgia, owning more than one hundred slaves in 1850 on their three plantations near Savannah, whereas Lumpkin was shown on the 1848 rolls as owning thirteen slaves. According to Anna Parkes, who was one of Lumpkin's slaves (although only a small child when the Civil War ended), "Ole Marster and Ole Miss, dey took keer of us. Dey sho' was good white folkses, but den dey had to be . . . kaze Ole Marster, he was Jedge Lumpkin, and de Jedge wus bound to make evvybody do right, and he gwine do right his own self 'fore he try to make udder folkses behave. . . . He 'splained dat us wuz not to be 'shamed of our race.' He said us warn't no 'niggers'; he said us wuz 'Negroes,' and he 'spected his Negroes to be de best Negroes in the whole land."[24]

One of the other slaves mentioned in Anna Parkes's narrative is Bill Finch, who was called "William" at "de big house" and who acted as tailor for the household, especially for the eight Lumpkin sons. Finch was purchased in 1848 and remained with the family until 1866, even serving with one of the Lumpkin sons in the Confederate army. During his years with the Lumpkins he was taught to read and write and also underwent a religious conversion, almost certainly under the influence of Lumpkin. After leaving the Lumpkins, Finch moved to Atlanta and became one of the organizers of the Republican party during the Reconstruction period, serving as a city councilman in 1871. Like Lumpkin, Finch was active in his church, and he became a champion of education and literacy as essential to advancement for blacks.[25]

The picture of Lumpkin as a benign, even enlightened, slaveholder revealed by the narrative of Anna Parkes and the biographical sketch of William Finch is consistent with the attitude he expressed in *Dudley v. Mallery* (1848). In that opinion, he refused to sanction the separation of a slave and her owner, saying, "Those who are acquainted with this institution know that the master and slave form one family, or social compact, being usually reared together on the same lot or plantation, and feeling toward each other the kindest sympathies of our nature." However, he made it clear that the fundamental reason for such sentiments was because "the very nature and security of the South consists in the loyalty of our Negro population to their owners."[26]

By 1850 he had hardened his views about the institution of slavery, both in terms of slaveowners' security and their obligations to their slaves. In his speech at the South-Carolina Institute in 1850, he said, "But for the demon-spirit of abolition, who can say what folly the South might not have committed with respect to her black population. Under the influence of a mistaken philanthropy, we were inclined to go much too fast and too far upon this momentous subject." He then indicated that the change in his views was due to the "settled conviction" that "slavery had its origin in . . . Divine wisdom" and that "the universal opinion of the South now is, that the spectacle of three hundred thousand barbarians, emerging under the mild and humane treatment of their owners, into four millions of civilized Christians, is not only without parallel in the history of the African race, but of the whole world." Along with many other southern evangelicals, Lumpkin had found a divine sanction for slavery to counter the abolitionist attacks on his morality.[27]

CHAPTER SEVEN

Aristocracy of Talent

⋙⋅◆⋅⋘

Let the race and the battle be to the "swift and strong."
Haywood v. Mayor (1853)

Whether he was winning academic honors in his youth, achieving success as a lawyer, or serving with distinction on the supreme court, at each stage of his life Lumpkin managed to combine a keen intellect with abundant energy. Armed with those talents, he sought and achieved a prominent position in what Jefferson's generation called the "aristocracy of talent." As an evangelical Presbyterian, he believed in the perfectibility of everyone, even blacks. However, as both a southerner and a Whig, he believed that the future prosperity of the region would be achieved more through a system of meritocracy than through the egalitarian ideals of the Jacksonian Democrats. As he wrote in a tribute to the first supreme court reporter, James M. Kelly, "He has added another to the countless number of examples, in this free and happy country, to show that *merit* is the sure road to fame and fortune." To achieve the goal of a meritocracy, Lumpkin devoted much of his energy throughout his life to the improvement of education in Georgia at all levels. [1]

During his two terms in the state legislature, he served on the committee responsible for public education and free schools. Perhaps because of that experience, he was one of four men in Georgia to receive a letter in 1830 from Governor Gilmer saying that he had been requested by the legislature to "correspond with distinguished and intelligent gentlemen of our country upon the best practical plan of extending the benefits of education to the children of the poor, at the public expense." Gilmer asked in his letter, "If you are of the opinion that the education of the people should be conducted at the public expense, ought not the children of all classes receive an equal benefit?"[2] Lumpkin, who was aware that only twenty thousand dollars was being made available by the legislature for the education of the poor, responded to Gilmer:

> The present provision says—scatter it throughout the state—in other words upon the wings of the wind. Like water spilt on the ground it can never be gathered again in any beneficial results in improving mentally the poor of the country. . . . Education like water must descend . . . . Then this twenty thousand dollars afford [sic] the means [at the university] for one or more of our most promising poor from each county to be graduated. . . . There will be no necessity of binding those beneficiaries of the public munificence to teach. . . . Disperse then throughout the state annually from fifty to one hundred graduates. . . . Soon every foreigner will be dislodged from our Academies & every town & neighborhood within our limits supplied with a classical Instructor. Then & not till then will our state be remunerated for bestowing its patronage on elementary instruction.[3]

While this was a creative suggestion, it was not egalitarian enough to be politically saleable at that time or for many years to come. Nonetheless, Lumpkin continued to promote ways of improving the state's educational system by having graduates of Georgia colleges assume teaching positions. In 1851 a convention was held in Marietta to discuss plans for forming a public school system. The convention, which was attended by 150 delegates representing sixty counties, was chaired by Eugenius A. Nisbet, an associate of Lumpkin on the supreme court. As one commentator noted, "The presence of Joseph Lumpkin of Athens, the first chief justice of the supreme court of the state, added dignity to the occasion." One proposal that came out of the convention recommended that a school fund of five thousand dollars per year be given for four years to each of the principal Georgia colleges, Franklin, Oglethorpe, Emory, and Mercer. The fund would support the education of young men who would sign an agreement to teach for five years in the common schools of Georgia. Like Lumpkin's earlier suggestion, this proposal was rejected.[4]

Writing in the *Southern School Journal* in 1853, Lumpkin emphasized the material advantages the state would realize from having educated citizens. They would "make full trial of the mind of the State as well as the soil of the State. We want 'cultivated farmers' as well as cultivated farms." Reflecting his concern about the growing conflicts between the South and the North, he went on to stress that an educated citizenship would be especially necessary when it came time to vote on such momentous issues as whether to choose "peace or war."[5]

During the 1850s Lumpkin was joined in his efforts to improve Georgia's schools by his son-in-law Thomas R. R. Cobb. Echoing Lumpkin's proposal of 1830, Cobb recommended in 1858 that the state's colleges and university provide free education as well as board and clothing to selected students from each county. In return, these students would teach in their native counties for a period equal to the time spent in college so "in a few years every neighborhood in Georgia will be furnished with *competent, home-taught* Teachers." Then in November of 1858, both Cobb and Lumpkin addressed the legislature in support of a proposed law establishing free public education for children between the ages of eight and eighteen. When the act was passed the following month, it called for combining the poor-school fund with an annual appropriation of one hundred thousand dollars from the income of the state-owned Western and Atlantic Railroad and sharing the total amount among the counties according to specified rules and conditions.[6]

While Lumpkin had to wait nearly thirty years to see free primary and secondary education established in Georgia, he was able to derive a great deal of satisfaction throughout his adult life from his involvement with higher education in the state. This was especially true of his relations with the University of Georgia, which shortly after his return from Princeton had started to recover under the leadership of the Rev. Moses Waddel. The Waddel presidency began auspiciously in 1819 when President Monroe visited Athens and, at a dinner in his honor, responded to Waddel's welcoming remarks with a toast wishing "success to the University of Georgia." It is likely that Lumpkin, who founded Phi Kappa the following year, was among those who attended the festivities that evening at the university, which was illuminated by almost a thousand lights while the students entertained Monroe and the other dignitaries.[7]

Lumpkin maintained an active role as an advisor to Phi Kappa over many years and was invited on a number of occasions to be the principal speaker or honored guest at meetings of the society. A letter inviting him to participate in the annual meeting, slated for August of 1838, noted that "the two other chairs will be filled by the Hon. Robt. Y. Hayne & Mr. James L. Pettigru." The former, a distinguished South Carolina politician, was noted for his debate with Daniel Webster in the U.S. Senate on constitutional issues, and the latter, a leading

Charleston lawyer at that time, later achieved notoriety as a die-hard Unionist in the state that was the crucible of the Confederacy.[8]

Given his own love of reading and research, Lumpkin undoubtedly took an active interest in seeing that Phi Kappa's library kept up with the one at the rival Demosthenian Society. One account of the early years of these literary societies notes, "While oratory was their primary purpose, the development of their libraries claimed much of their enthusiasm and interest. The first floor of each hall contained a well-stocked library which equalled [*sic*], and in some fields surpassed the college library." In 1825 the two societies managed to collaborate in supporting a bill seeking funds from the legislature for their libraries rather than the college's. They argued that access to their libraries was easier for students and the "laudable rivalry which exists between them" would assure the best application of any funding.[9]

Despite this unusual show of cooperation and Lumpkin's position in the legislature, it appears they were unsuccessful in obtaining any financial support from the state. Both societies were able, however, to continue adding to their collections through gifts from alumni, friends, and honorary members. Although there is no longer any record of the early years of the Phi Kappa collection, there is a "Catalogue of the Demosthenian Society Library," which shows acquisitions from 1803 to 1828. Among the volumes listed, together with the year or period of acquisition, are: *Sheridan's Lectures* (1803–1808), *Cook's Voyages* (1808–1815), *Vicar of Wakefield* (1820), *Last of the Mohicans* and *Salmagundi* (1821), and *Byrons's Works* (1823). The libraries also had subscriptions to the leading American and British journals, including *Southern Review*, *Southern Literary Messenger*, *North American Review*, *London Quarterly Review*, *Edinburgh Review*, *Blackwood's Edinburgh Magazine*, *Metropolitan Magazine*, and *Knickerbocker Magazine*.[10]

When Lumpkin was living in Lexington and later in Athens, the libraries of the college and the literary societies provided invaluable sources of research for the increasing number of speeches and other writing he undertook in the 1830s and 1840s. When he wasn't speaking on temperance, religious, or educational issues, he was delivering courtroom arguments to judges and juries. He was fond of using biblical and classical allusions to illustrate his points and often drew on his extensive knowledge of history, science, political economy, and belles lettres.

A good example of his wide-ranging interests and skill in assimilating information is found in an address he gave on July 1, 1836, before the Phi Delta and Ciceronian Societies at the Mercer Institute (which later became Mercer University). He told his primarily student audience at this Baptist institution that he had considered directing his remarks "to the charms of Oratory . . . [or] to Books,—that inexhaustible source of pleasure." Instead, he chose to speak on the subject of natural history from an evangelical point of view by surveying "the wondrous volume which the Creator has spread out before us." He then proceeded to present an impressive array of facts ranging from the circumference of the earth (25,000 miles) and the size of Jupiter (900 times larger than the earth) to the number of eggs in a typical codfish (9,384,000). He cited the writings of Derham and Paley on natural theology but had particular praise for the "master-spirit of the age, Lord Brougham, who has employed his pen in almost every branch of the arts and sciences." It is understandable that Lumpkin admired Lord Brougham (1778–1868), whom he called an "eminent statesman, jurist and scholar," since Brougham was a leading British reformer, like Wilberforce, and as a member of the House of Commons had fought for abolition of slavery, law reform, and public education.

The scope of the research Lumpkin must have done in preparing the address is indicated by several obscure facts: "The rein-deer is found in the coldest parts of Lapland," he maintained, "because his chief food, which is the liverwort, grows there in abundance." Moreover, he told the students, "Some of the most pernicious insects afford us valuable medicine; as the cantharides" (which is also known as cantharis or "spanish fly"). Overall, the speech shows Lumpkin's boundless curiosity about the world around him and his appetite for knowledge of all sorts, from the abstract ("How wonderful, that the bee should always fashion her cell uniform, and in the form of a hexagon") to the practical (fire "generates steam, the mighty agent in all modern enterprizes").[11]

Once the Baptists had established Mercer and the Methodists had chartered Emory College, the Presbyterians followed suit and established their own Oglethorpe University. On March 31, 1837, the cornerstone of the new university's main building was laid by the masons, and Lumpkin delivered the address. An account of the occasion reported, "The procession . . . halted at the appointed place, when, after the prayer, the stone was placed in position by the order, according to their rites, among other things pouring oil and wine upon it, and concluding with an ode, in which there was more of the praises of Masonry, than the worth of learning and scholastic training." The author also noted that because of rain, the location for Lumpkin's address had to be moved to one of the churches in Milledgeville. [12]

On this occasion, Lumpkin managed to cover several of his favorite topics, including temperance reform and improvement of academies and common schools. However, his principal message was the need to multiply significantly the graduates of local colleges, noting that "in Georgia, most of our Seminaries are under the superintendence of foreigners and Northern men . . . [who] constitute a large proportion of our Lawyers, Physicians, Merchants, Mechanics and Ministers." Then, with echoes of his talk in Boston and subsequent letter to the newspaper four years before, he warned, "And who is so blind as not to see, that severe conflicts await us, resulting from our local interests. We want men thoroughly disciplined, to vindicate our peculiar institutions in our State, and Federal Councils, and ecclesiastical judicatories; men, who, should a separation be forced upon us in Church or State, by our misguided assailants, which we deprecate as the greatest of all evils, would be able to appeal successfully to the judgment of mankind, as well as the searcher of hearts, to show we are blameless." [13]

Having sounded an alarm, Lumpkin did not miss the opportunity to make an appeal for funds from his audience on behalf of the Oglethorpe trustees. He called on "all true believers" to "contribute of their substance to assist us in turning the healing and fertilizing streams of science and religion through many a parched territory." Taking an ecumenical approach, he predicted that "Methodists, Baptists, Independents, and Episcopalians will delight to meet with us on this neutral ground." It was a clever way to reach a wider base of prospective donors and introduce a less sectarian atmosphere, which could benefit future enrollment at the university.

Influenced by his association with benevolent northern merchants like the Tappan brothers, Lumpkin exhorted business owners in his own state to become "the prominent instruments in the hands of Providence, for the civil, literary, and religious regeneration of this wide creation." Like a good lawyer, he buttressed his case for philanthropy with detailed evidence to prove how rich the men of commerce in Georgia had become. "As regards our pecuniary ability," he argued, "look to the four principal towns in the State—Columbus,

Macon, and Augusta receive yearly three hundred thousand bales of cotton, which at the market would sell for 15,000,000 of dollars. The sale of merchandize would fully equal that sum, making their aggregate commercial business 30 millions of dollars. Savannah, our principal seaport, exports 250,000 bales of cotton, estimated at 13,750,000 dollars; 24,000 casks of rice, worth 450,000 dollars; lumber and other articles are computed at 750,000 dollars, making an aggregate of near 15,000,000 of dollars, exported of products of the State, in one year from one seaport."

Although the status of Georgia's commerce was not a primary subject of Lumpkin's Oglethorpe address, it shows his growing interest in the potential benefits the state could gain by diversifying the predominantly agricultural economy into commerce and manufacturing. In that same year (1836), a charter was obtained for the first railroad in Georgia, which was to run from Macon to Savannah. Lumpkin became an early investor in the securities of several regional railroads, believing they would provide another important means of improving the region's ability to progress and achieve self-sufficiency.

He shared this belief with his brother, Wilson, who, as governor, had proposed in 1835 to the Georgia legislature that a rail line be built to connect the Ohio Valley with the Georgia coast. Despite the widespread economic problems surrounding the panic of 1837, the Georgia Railroad and Banking Company was still able to complete a link between Augusta and Athens in 1841, while the Central of Georgia Railroad and Banking Company finished the connection between Macon and Savannah in 1843. At that time, Wilson Lumpkin, who had retired from the U.S. Senate, was overseeing construction of the state-owned Western and Atlantic Railroad, whose main line was connected to Chattanooga in 1851.

By then, much of Wilson Lumpkin's 1835 proposal had been realized: more miles of railroad tracks had been built in Georgia than in any other southern state (and many of the northern ones). Political leaders like John C. Calhoun, however, were promoting an even grander railroad network in the region as the sectional conflicts intensified. Calhoun predicted, "Such is the formation of the country between the Mississippi valley and the south Atlantic coast, from the course of the Tennessee, Cumberland, and Alabama rivers, and the termination of the various chains of the Allegheny Mountains, that all the railroads which have been projected or, commenced . . . must necessarily unite at a point in

Dekalb County, in the State of Georgia, called Atlanta . . . so as to constitute one entire system of roads, having a mutual interest in the other, instead of isolated rival roads."[14]

That meeting point in Dekalb County was initially called Terminus, but in 1843 the town was incorporated by the legislature with the name of Marthasville. It appears the organizers and promoters of this new community wanted to name it for Wilson Lumpkin in recognition of his leadership as governor as well as his efforts on behalf of the railroads. He declined the honor, however, as both a county and town had already been named for him, so his daughter Martha was selected instead as the namesake. A few years later, the town fathers decided that the growing size and commercial importance of the town warranted a more cosmopolitan name, and in 1846 it was officially renamed Atlanta. There are several accounts of how the name was selected, including the legend that it was based on a nickname, "Atalanta," that Martha had been given by her father. However, that theory is not consistent with a letter Wilson Lumpkin wrote Martha in 1853, in which he told her, "And you may always remember that one of the most distinguished towns in Georgia was located by your father, and by its original and first proprietor named in honor of yourself 'Marthasville.' The name being stolen from you will never change the facts appertaining to the case."[15]

Although Georgia was a leader in establishing railroads, the state's economy continued to suffer from its dependence on agriculture until factories began to operate in the late 1840s. Passage of a law allowing incorporation and providing some tax exemptions for manufacturing companies provided an important stimulus for industrial development in the state. Yet there were still many obstacles in the path of those who promoted the benefits of industrializing Georgia. Prospective manufacturers had to contend with more than the usual issues of obtaining necessary labor and capital. As one noted historian summarized the problem, "The rural opposition to manufacturers was not mere inertia, but a more or less rational protest against the development of an industrial society. This was the traditional Jeffersonian opposition to urban industrialism and all its works."[16]

Despite such resistance, a number of influential leaders, including Lumpkin, continued to promote a vision of industrial prosperity for Georgia and the rest of the southern states. On November 19, 1850, Lumpkin delivered an address in Charleston before the South-Carolina Institute. This association, which had been organized the year before by a group of Charleston manufacturers "for the promotion of arts, mechanics, and other industry and ingenuity" already had enrolled over four hundred members and had constructed a large hall for its annual fairs. In the early years of the institute, the only speaker, besides Lumpkin, who was chosen from a state other than South Carolina was Edmund Ruffin of Virginia, a national leader in soil chemistry and scientific farming. Lumpkin's skills as an orator were well known in South Carolina from his temperance activities, but his selection by the institute as the speaker at its second annual fair was most likely based on his reputation for progressive social and economic views.[17]

The purpose of his address, he told the audience, was to "engender a general and universal spirit of improvement, and to bring its influences to bear, not only on the peculiar interests of agriculture, but on all the great and vital interests of the State." Citing England's success in combining industry with agriculture, he painted an idyllic picture of the benefits brought by "a manufacturing establishment of any sort in fostering the various branches of trade and business, in producing comfort, refinement and intelligence, and in stimulating the growth and populousness of the surrounding country." Addressing concerns that factories would become "hot-beds of crime," he said, "I am by no means ready to concede that our poor, degraded, half-fed, half-clothed, and ignorant population . . . will be injured by giving them employment. . . . After all, the most powerful motives to good conduct, is [*sic*] to give suitable encouragement to labor, and to bestow proper rewards upon meritorious industry."

In his conclusion, Lumpkin set forth an agenda for change that advocated legislation to encourage the chartering of manufacturing corporations, criticized the waste of farmers who wore out the land, and promoted the expansion of railroads and telegraph wires to continue improving the region's systems of communication. However, he was most eloquent in arguing his favorite case for educating "our whole population . . . to give them a head to plan and a hand to execute in the new field of enterprize in which 8,000,000 of the South are about to embark." Despite the value he placed on the advantages of classical learning, he insisted that "in this age of utility and reform, when invention of a new machine is of more importance than the discovery of the planet Neptune by Le Verrier, if our youth are to be trained in such a manner as shall fit them for the practical duties of life, our plastic institutions must in this respect, as in all others, adapt themselves to every improvement."

More than a year after Lumpkin spoke at the South-Carolina Institute, his address was published in *De Bow's Review* under the title "Industrial Regeneration of the South." Publication of his remarks in this influential journal, whose motto was "Commerce Is King," undoubtedly enhanced Lumpkin's reputation as a social and economic reformer throughout the South as well as among the many northern readers of *De Bow's* with whom he still had much in common. As Timothy Huebner has cogently argued, "Lumpkin, while certainly not typical of southerners—or even southern evangelicals—in his attitudes toward social improvement, nevertheless brings to light an often neglected side of southern society, a side not unlike that of the North." [18]

Joseph Henry Lumpkin, about age fifty.
Courtesy of the Hargrett Rare Book and Manuscript Library,
University of Georgia.

The Lumpkin home, Lexington, Georgia.
Photo by Wingate Downs.

The Lumpkin home, Athens, Georgia.
Courtesy of the Hargrett Rare Book and Manuscript Library,
University of Georgia.

Thomas R. R. Cobb in Confederate uniform.
Courtesy of the Hargrett Rare Book and Manuscript Library,
University of Georgia.

Joseph Henry Lumpkin, from a Lumpkin Law School
diploma dated June 11, 1861.

Courtesy of the University of Georgia School of Law.

CHAPTER EIGHT

Paterfamilias

Families are the original of all societies and contain the foundation
and primitive elements of all other social institutions.

Vance v. Crawford (1848)

Throughout his married life, Lumpkin was frequently away from home and family, while living in Milledgeville as a young legislator, riding the superior court circuit with his fellow lawyers, making speeches as far away as Boston and Philadelphia on behalf of temperance or other benevolent causes, and presiding over supreme court sessions in cities around the state. During these absences, he always missed the comfort of sleeping in his own bed and dining at his own table, but most of all he desired the company and affection of his wife and children. From the few letters between Lumpkin and his wife that have been found, it is clear that they had a warm and caring marriage. Writing from Savannah in the late 1840s, Lumpkin told his wife of more than twenty-five years,

> Dearest—I was made very happy this morning by the receipt of your letter. The wife of my youth has lost none of her power to charm her husband. The fragrance of her girlhood is now the rich ripe fruit of Autumn. And who would not prefer the fruit to the flower? The very sight of your writing agitates me. Would that all my sons and sons-in-law could realize in the morning of marriage the unchangeable reward of living a life of intimacy and devotion to her who has sacrificed all for them! Although in the city you and you alone are my companion in the streets and thoroughfares. And when alone in my chamber and on my bed at night "how sweet to mingle all my waking thoughts and sleeping dreams with you."

In another undated letter to his daughter Callie (sent from Macon, which did not become a supreme court site until 1855), he wrote: "O, I long to see you all so much—especially my patient self-sacrificing wife. Callie I almost worship your mother."

The author of an article in 1851 described Lumpkin as follows: "Eminently domestic in his habits, he has sought peace in the bosom of his family. What the honors of intellect and station—the applause of the world, and the esteem of good men even, do not always yield, contentment, he has found in a happy home." In an 1860 article for a temperance newspaper, his son-in-law Thomas R. R. Cobb wrote, "But the loveliness of Judge Lumpkin's character appears to best advantage in the social and domestic circle. . . . Affectionate to devotion, indulgent to a fault, loving home with all the ardor of his warm nature and making home the most desirable spot on earth to each one of his large family."[1]

In 1827, not long after completing his second term in the legislature, Joseph Henry and Callender moved into a plain-style home near the center of Lexington that had been built at the end of the eighteenth century. According to the local real-estate records, the Lumpkins acquired the two-story house, which had two rooms on each floor, plus 184 acres of land for $763.95. As they already had five children, Marion, Lucy, Joseph, Callie, and Thomas (who died in 1829), they added a federal-style wing to the home shortly after the purchase in order to gain more room. This addition had two spacious rooms on the first floor and three rooms on the second, all of which opened onto a central hall containing the staircase. A description of the home long after the Lumpkins lived in it noted that "traces of former grandeur are revealed in paneled dadoes, mantelpieces of the delicate Adam design, and a frieze of oak leaves above the picture moldings. . . . The front entrance has a segmented elliptical fanlight over the door and sidelights, both with frosted designs in the glass. The pilaster-like door framing is given a reeded effect with rounded applied dowels, also found in Governor Gilmer's house."[2]

According to a history of Oglethorpe County, "By the 1820s, Lexington was a thriving town with an elegant courthouse, 38 dwellings, 15 stores, numerous shops and hotels, male and female academies, a public library, and churches. . . . Lexington was home to some of the most noted lawyers and politicians in Georgia including William Harris Crawford, George Rockingham Gilmer, Wilson Lumpkin, Joseph Henry Lumpkin, Stephen Upson, Thomas Willis Cobb, John Henry Lumpkin, and Samuel Lumpkin." Not only could Joseph Henry Lumpkin enjoy the society of stimulating friends as well as many Lumpkin family members living nearby, but his home was also within walking distance of his office, the courthouse, and the Presbyterian church, his three most frequent destinations in town. Those of his children who attended Meson Academy could sleep late, as the school building was just across the street from the Lumpkin home.[3]

After the death of their son Thomas, Callender bore eight more children (all sons) between 1829 and 1842. They all survived to adulthood except Chalmers, who was born next after William Wilberforce and was probably named after the Rev. Thomas Chalmers, a noted evangelical Presbyterian leader in Scotland, whom Lumpkin admired. It is hard to imagine how the Lumpkin home could comfortably hold eleven children and two adults plus various servants working around the house. However, their home grew even more crowded when the older Lumpkin children began to invite their friends and prospective spouses to visit.

The first to marry was Lucy, who wed William L. C. Gerdine, a local planter from Oglethorpe County. Then, in January of 1844, the eldest child, Marion, was married at the family home in Lexington to Thomas R. R. Cobb, a promising young attorney from a distinguished Georgia family. His older brother, Howell, who was then a congressman in Washington and later a senator and governor, was unable to attend the wedding. Marion's eighteen-year-old sister, Callie, wrote him to describe the occasion, saying, "Pardon me Sir—but I have been selected as the most suitable member of the family to communicate to you— the late 'doings' at Lovers Lodge . . . the new baptismal name by which we have christened our sweet home . . . on account of the recent nuptials." Then, with a humorous allusion to the partisan differences between Joseph Henry (a Whig) and Howell (a Democrat), she went on, "Although the weather was very inclement we had quite a gathering. A great number were invited from the neighboring villages & father who is the only *real* democrat I ever knew would have on this as at Lucy's wedding every family in the place included. It is a part of his religion to make no distinction between the rich & the poor."[4]

Following a week of post-wedding parties and visits with relatives, the newlyweds settled into a house in Athens, which, along with much of the furniture, was a wedding gift from Lumpkin. Cobb had written Marion prior to their wedding, "As to the furnishing of the house, assure your Father he shall have full scope to gratify his own taste, for I will leave it entirely to him." Marion did not have to be separated from her parents and siblings for long, however, as Lumpkin purchased a home in Athens in 1843, and after it was remodeled, the Lumpkin family moved there from Lexington around 1846.[5]

The remodeling, which nearly doubled the size of the home, added two rooms on each of the two floors. On the south side of the house, facing Prince Avenue, a two-story portico and side porches were constructed in the Greek revival style with ten large Doric columns, a small balcony over the entrance, and entablatures over the windows and doors. Inside, two large parlors flanked the central hall, leading to a stair hall and dining room beyond. There were also two smaller rooms, which served as Lumpkin's office and library and could be entered from the parlors as well as from the portico and side porches. The dignified but simple style of the Lumpkin home helped influence the construction of a number of other classical revival houses along Prince Avenue during the 1840s, making it one of the prime residential areas in town.[6]

Athens was then a thriving community, whose population grew from about three thousand in the early 1840s to over five thousand by 1850. It had been recently connected to Augusta via a branch railroad line running from Union Point, forty miles away. One description of the town in that era said that because of its "healthful climate, and being the seat of the highest educational institution in the state, it had attracted a class of citizens for the most part educated and refined according to antebellum standards. Here lived the Cobbs, Lumpkins, Hulls, Rutherfords, and Hillyers. The social life was 'brilliant,' and a certain degree of genuine culture existed among [the] people." Elizabeth Greer, who enjoyed coming into Athens from her Clarke County plantation, described the atmosphere of the town in a letter to her cousin in 1847, saying that Athens was "rather ahead of any place in the union now in pride, vanity, and dress," adding that "the people seems [sic] busy all the time, and walk about lively; we have two splendid hotels there now. Some say they are the best hotels in the state, as regards comfort." The undergraduates at the University of Georgia undoubtedly added to the energetic atmosphere of the town, as well as to the supply of young bachelors. One alumnus, who entered the college in 1844, recalled that he "was 'persona grata' at the houses of most of the best families in Athens and was always invited to all the parties given by the young ladies," including one that he said was given by "Miss Callie Lumpkin."[7]

Lumpkin probably decided to move to Athens at that time because he wanted a more dynamic and cultured environment for himself and his family than Lexington could offer. Also, his appointment as professor of law at the university and his plan to send all of his sons there made it convenient for them to live only a short distance from the campus. Although the university had prospered for nearly fifteen years under president Alonzo Church, by 1844 it was beginning to suffer from a lack of state funds, despite the efforts of influential supporters like Lumpkin.

However, the same legislators who refused to authorize funding for the university would never think of missing the commencement events. The commencement week in August not only provided an opportune time for politicians to debate issues and gain visibility, but it was also one of the main social seasons of the year for Athens residents and visitors from around the state. During commencement week in 1853, Lumpkin hosted a dinner at his home, which he described in a letter to his daughter Callie: "A more brilliant party of gentlemen— I never saw assembled. We could only seat twenty-two guests and the difficulty was in making the selection.—Judge Berrien and two U.S. Senators— Dawson and Toombs . . . Ex-Governor Schley—James Hamilton Cooper . . . who manages personally eleven hundred negroes—Col. Ward of Savannah—the orator of the societies—Dr. Wingfield—Adam Alexander etc.—were part of the company—No lady dined—Mr. Cobb occupied your Ma's seat. It all went off well. The feast was scrumptious. The ice cream item cost ten dollars."[8]

In the view of Coulter, "The University commencement in the ante-bellum days was itself an institution in the state. It had its attractions for the educators, the politicians and statesmen, for the business men, the farmers and the planters, for the poor whites and the slaves, for the fine ladies and gallant gentlemen, for the giddy girls and the foppish dandies. It was an educational, political, and social force of no little significance."[9]

Frequently, members of the Lumpkin family and others left Athens after the end of the commencement festivities for a vacation at Madison Springs, a resort community located about twenty miles northeast of Athens. The owners of the resort advertised it as both a source of health-giving waters and as a more convenient alternative to such fashionable northern resorts as Saratoga Springs in New York state. Lumpkin and others of his generation visited Madison Springs primarily because they considered the mineral waters to be very therapeutic for their ailments. The resort's advertisements claimed that the waters from the local springs would benefit those suffering from stomach disorders, rheumatism, ague, consumption, dropsy, dyspepsia, and many other afflictions. However, its hotel and cabins appealed to a wide range of tastes, and in 1845 the owner announced that he was making room for as many as three hundred guests. It became so crowded on occasion that comfortable accommodations were hard to find, and Lumpkin's son James once wrote his sister Callie that he had to choose one night whether to sleep "in a small church with about thirty or else to make a bed of the billiard table—with baggy cushions etc. I choosed [*sic*] the latter—and managed to sleep very well—from two o'clock until six."[10]

However, any discomforts that the younger generation had to suffer were more than compensated by their enjoyment of the fancy dress ball, which occurred at Madison Springs shortly after the annual college commencement. According to one commentary, "Sometimes the ball would begin after tea time and continue on for some hours with . . . cotillions, waltzes, polkas, scottishes, Virginia reels, promenades, and any others that anyone might know. Music was generally afforded by some Charleston band—for instance the Battery Band. Then the grand banquet with champagne corks popping, after which the dance was resumed and did not stop until 2 A.M. or later. Apparently, the costume part of the ball did not begin until after the banquet; then, as soon as possible, in came the costumed participants (not all those dancing elected to wear costumes) with or without masks."[11]

In August of 1854, after adjournment of the supreme court session in Columbus, Lumpkin joined various members of his family at Madison Springs. He wrote Callie in Alabama that "the fancy ball came off on Tuesday night. There were at the Springs about 300 persons—most of whom attended. Many of the gentlemen were in splendid costumes. . . . Being honored with an invitation from the Managers—of course I attended—although I was too unwell to sit up for the supper. Your Ma saw the show though." James, giving Callie his own account of the ball, wrote, "Will had the most amusing dress & sustained his character well—it was that of a Yankee Country-man. Ed went in his uniform. Miller went as a Mexican—with one of the most amusing faces I ever saw—I personified Sir Walter Raleigh. . . . After supper, at which there was an abundance of champaigne [*sic*] the crowd were very happy. . . . Numerous courtships and engagements took place up there."[12]

News of courtships, engagements, and marriages was almost always included in Lumpkin's letters to his daughter Callie. Before she married Porter King and moved to Alabama (in 1852), Lumpkin teased her about her own experience with courtship. In a letter dated January 18, 1849, when she was probably visiting her sister Lucy in Mississippi, he wrote, "Callie—what think you of the young gentlemen of the West? How nearly has any of the beaux . . . approximated to the standard of manly beauty?" He then proceeded to give a detailed description of each of the ideal manly features of someone "5 ft. 10 inches high . . . forehead high . . . his hair inclining to curl . . . his shin rather slender," who appears to bear a close resemblance to himself. He then asked her, "Have you met with such a man and with manners corresponding with his external appearance—bold but modest—ardent and intellectual? If you have and your heart should be a little touched I should not be [surprised]."

The Christmas season was another favorite time for Lumpkin family gatherings and festivities. When Thomas Cobb spent the Christmas of 1842 with them in Lexington, his fiancée, Marion, was moved to write his sister-in-law: "I have heard many complain of having spent a very 'dull Christmas,' but could they have . . . caught a glimpse of 'our little world' I think that 'dull care' would have been driven away." In 1852 Thomas and Marion moved into a house on Prince Avenue in Athens, which was next door to the Lumpkin home, and thereafter the holiday celebrations spanned both households. [13]

In a letter written to Callie on Christmas afternoon in 1853, Lumpkin reported, "Yesterday and last night we had a most beautiful fall of snow. What a splendid scene when the sun arose on it so bright this morning." On December 26 three years later, he wrote her that "Mr. Cobb [he almost never referred to Cobb in letters by his first name] was busy for two days before hand in preparing a Christmas Tree, and on Wednesday night we went over to see it. All the grandchildren including little Annie and Lizzy were present. And it was a very pretty sight." He went on to describe "the novel spectacle of skating" on Carr's pond, which was obviously a highlight of that holiday season.

Clement Moore's poem "A Visit from St. Nicholas" (better known as "The Night before Christmas"), written in 1822, had introduced both northerners and southerners to the pleasures of Santa Claus and Christmas stockings. Thus, on Christmas mornings, the ritual of opening presents from Santa Claus was enjoyed by Lumpkin and Cobb children of all ages as well as by the slave children in the cabins out behind their houses. According to the narrative of a former slave whose family belonged to Thomas Cobb, "Christmas was sompin' else. Us sho

had a good time den. Dey gave us chilluns china dolls and dey sont great sacks
of apples, oranges, candy, cake and evything good out to de quarters. At night
endurin' Christmas us had parties, and dere was allus some Nigger ready to pick
the banjo. Marse Thomas allus give de slaves a little toddy too, but when dey
was havin' deir fun if dey got too loud he would sho' call 'em down. I was allus
glad to see Christmas come. On New Year's Day, da General had big dinners
and invited all de high-falutin' rich folks." [14]

Most of the food served to the many family members in the Lumpkin household—and to their frequent guests—came from their own farmyard, fields, and
orchards, which were spread over twenty-five acres behind their home. The
day after Christmas in 1848, Lumpkin wrote Callie that "today we are making
arrangements to kill twenty-eight hogs; so you can see what fun you have missed.
Will has built me a fine cow house, put up my cabbage for the winter, laid in a
bountiful supply of wood and altogether done himself great credit." Their milk
came from a Devon cow, and they raised chickens, ducks, geese, turkeys, and
pigs, using their smokehouse to cure ham and bacon, along with some of the
game they caught from time to time. [15]

Even when Lumpkin was away from home on supreme court business, nothing could fortify or lift him out of a dark mood better than a good meal. When
the court was sitting in Columbus in January of 1852, he wrote Callie on the 28th
of that month, just after he and the other judges had returned from a two-hour
midday dinner at the home of a Mrs. Howard. With great pleasure he reported,
"It was a fine affair—ham, beef, pig, turkey roast and boiled ducks, oysters,
ices, jelly, ice cream, syllabub, oranges, apples and etc." There was no meal,
however, that he enjoyed more than one that included fresh fish, such as the
perch and trout from the local Oconee River, but his favorite treat of all was to
dine on shad and oysters when he was in Savannah for supreme court sessions.
In an undated letter to Callender from Savannah, he described a particularly
sumptuous dinner at the home of Judge Charlton:

In the center of the table was a tall candelabra with seven candles at each end of
a branch candlestick with . . . three beautiful flower pots with the richest roses,
camellias and other natural flowers—two large silver tankards at opposite corners
with ice-water and smaller silver vessels with ice, broke up—nothing on the table
but turtle soup. This dispatched, a boiled turkey was set before Mrs. Charlton

with oyster sauce and boiled mutton at the other end, with cauliflowers, etc., etc. This over, a roast turkey before Mrs. Charlton—roast venison before the Judge— ham in the middle, pheasant birds, etc. Then a large pillar of ice-sherbet was set before Madam—a similar one of ice-cream before the Judge. In the center of the table, a large bowl of trifle, etc. surrounded by jelly glasses . . . dishes of . . . Charlotte, etc.

Lumpkin's letters to Callie often included details about the planting and harvesting of vegetables and fruits, including potatoes, peas, grapes, strawberries, peaches, and apples. In one undated letter he told Callie, "You never saw such a quantity of strawberries. Your Ma is sending off bushels to the market." However, he also worried about the damage that pests like the armyworm did to his garden and corn patch and was as keen an observer of the local weather as any full-time farmer. In a letter of September 25, 1856, he told Callie, "Last night and the night before we had frosts that have killed the pea vines, tomatoes, etc.—a thing unheard of before in Georgia. In 1834 we had a frost the first Monday in October—but the 23rd of September—nobody ever heard of such a thing. Even the cotton is killed in the low land."

One pleasure that Joseph Henry and Callender could enjoy together was cultivation of the flower gardens around their home, which contained roses, dahlias, lilies, and many other varieties that were picked for the floral decorations that Callender placed around the house. In a letter she wrote to Callie's husband, Porter King, in April of 1852, Callender asked him to "tell Callie that both of her Antwerp lilies are jutting up vigorously—and one of her Augusta roses has bloomed. . . . I never saw anything richer. Our front yard is litterally [*sic*] covered with roses." Lumpkin was equally enthusiastic on April 17, 1856, when he wrote, "I wish, dear Callie, you could see the Wisteria in bloom on the green house this morning." There was a great deal of interest in gardens among residents of antebellum Athens, probably inspired by the botanical garden at the University of Georgia that had been started in 1833 and continued to provide enjoyment until it was sold by the trustees in September of 1856 for $1,200, apparently to raise needed funds.[16]

Because its location was far from the seacoast, Athens was able to escape the periodic outbreaks of cholera and yellow fever that afflicted port cities like Savannah and Charleston. However, among the Lumpkins, like most large and extended Georgian families of the antebellum period, there were frequent illnesses and occasional deaths to endure. Lumpkin's daughter Lucy died in her early thirties leaving her husband, William Gerdine, to raise their nine children. A number of Lumpkin grandchildren died at early ages from various causes, including Callie's second child and two young sons of Thomas and Marion Cobb. Then, in 1857, the Cobbs lost their eldest daughter, Lucy, through scarlet fever, which also claimed the life of the youngest son of Joseph Troup Lumpkin in 1859.

Given the prevalence of illness all around them, it is remarkable that Callender and Joseph Henry did not have more serious ailments themselves. In a letter to Callie in June of 1854, James described their mother, Callender, as looking "fat and healthy," but eighteen months later Joseph Henry wrote Callie, "Your Ma suffers a great deal. She lost every tooth but a few under ones in front and the consequence is that she cannot chew at all." Lumpkin suffered from recurring headaches as well as chest and throat problems, but, as he wrote his son-in-law Porter King, "I find my health fluctuates with the weather." His ailments were also intensified by his rigorous supreme court schedule that required him to travel long distances and be away from the comforts of home and the care of his family for extended periods. [17]

In a particularly melancholy mood, he wrote Callie from Decatur in August of 1854, where the court heard fifty-seven cases involving nearly seventy lawyers, saying, "I sometimes feel, dear Callie, as if my troubles are more than I can bear and long for the deliverance of death." Ten days later, however, he told her that his health had improved enough to "get through with the business of the court." His work ethic was sufficiently strong that he told Callie in October of 1853, "I have been sick for ten days, although I have attended court at Gainesville in the meantime." Similarly, in June of 1854, he wrote her, "I had improved in my health very much but relapsed that night and continued sick until Saturday morning when I left for Augusta. An hour or two before starting, I had made up my mind to remain at home, but when the time came, never having missed a court, I resolved to go."

It was these successive episodes of illness in 1854 that convinced Lumpkin to resign as head of the Georgia temperance movement in order to conserve his energies for his family and supreme court duties. He had apparently learned a lesson from an earlier experience when, in 1845, the stress of his legal career and constant speech-making on behalf of his benevolent causes had caused a serious

breakdown in his health. Fortunately, all of his hard work had brought him sufficient financial success that he could then afford to take enough time off in order
to restore his health. He and Callender may also have decided that it was a good
time to plan a trip while they were in the process of moving from Lexington
and their Athens home was being remodeled. Therefore, in the spring of 1845,
Joseph Henry and Callender departed for Europe with their only unmarried
daughter, Callie, who was then nineteen years old.

Although the British had begun to discover the pleasures of "grand tours"
and leisure travel on the continent by 1845, there were not many in the United
States at that time who were traveling to Europe, especially from as far away
as Georgia. For Lumpkin there were numerous historical places to visit and
many cultural experiences to savor. As an admirer of Washington Irving, he
had probably read and been influenced by Irving's accounts of his European
travels:

> Having been born and brought up in a new country, yet educated from infancy in
> the literature of an old one, my mind was early filled with historical and poetical
> associations, connected with manners and customs of Europe, but which could
> rarely be applied to those of my own country. To a mind thus peculiarly prepared,
> the most ordinary objects and scenes, on arriving in Europe, are full of strange
> matter and interesting novelty. England is a classic ground to an American, as
> Italy is to an Englishman; and London teems with as much historical association
> as mighty Rome.[18]

Unfortunately, no diary of the trip or even letters to the family back in Georgia
have been preserved, but the few known details of their travels indicate that they
chose an itinerary followed by most transatlantic travelers of the period. Like
Charles Dickens, who sailed from Liverpool to Boston in 1842, the Lumpkins
could well have taken one of the earliest steamships. However, they would have
embarked for England from New York, after sailing there from Savannah, and
could well have gone ashore at Dover and then traveled to London via Canter-
bury Cathedral.

Edinburgh was one of their principal destinations, not only because Callender was born in Scotland, but because of Lumpkin's interest in the Scottish
influence within the Presbyterian Church in America. He carried a letter of
introduction to the Rev. Thomas Chalmers, a prominent Scottish theologian,

written on his behalf by the Rev. Samuel Miller of Princeton Theological Seminary, which said, "The bearer, Joseph H. Lumpkin, Esquire, an eminent lawyer
of the State of Georgia, & a Ruling Elder of the Presbyterian Church, visits
Scotland for the benefit of his health. He will probably spend some weeks in
Edinburgh & is accompanied by his wife, who is a native of Scotland, and a Lady
who is greatly esteemed by all who know her & also by a Daughter, a young lady
of whom I hear excellent things." Another letter of introduction to Chalmers was
written for Lumpkin by Dr. Thomas Smyth of Charleston: "He visits Europe
and is especially desirous of making a personal acquaintanceship with one in
whose writings he has taken a great delight." It appears that Chalmers's support
was being sought at the time by both advocates and opponents of slavery in
the United States, as Smyth added in his letter that "Mr. Lumpkin will hand
you a copy of a discussion which will give you a correct unbiased view of the
opinions on the subject of slavery which are entertained both in the North and
South of this country." Although it appears that Lumpkin did not meet with
Chalmers during his time in Scotland, he was sufficiently impressed by his visit
to Holyrood Palace, "the ancient residence of Scottish royalty," to refer to it in
his address to the South-Carolina Institute five years later.

In the same speech, he compared South Carolina to Tuscany and rhapso-
dized about "the valley of the Arno, from Pisa to Florence. Its corn, and grapes,
and figs, and olives, and mulberries—its luxuriant vallies and romantic hills,
covered with plantations of pines, make it one continued scene of perfect en-
chantment." There are occasional references about the trip in his later letters
to Callie, such as the following: "It seems to me but yesterday since we were
wandering our way along the coast of the Mediterranean and then through the
hills . . . to the Eternal City." Lumpkin even included a veiled reference to the
trip in an opinion, *Johnson v. State* (1853), in which he wrote, "Man is capable
of any folly or wickedness. . . . For the demonstration of its truthfulness, visit
the secret chamber of the Royal Museum at Naples."[19]

However, the most detailed account of the trip appeared in an article about
Lumpkin published in 1851, which seems almost to be quoting him. It reported
that his travels took him to "England, Scotland, and the principal states of
Southern Europe. He saw for himself, Italy—the land of venerable renown—her
melancholy and magnificent monuments, her mouldering ruins, the abjectness
of her people, and her moral desolations. He felt the inspiration of her clime, and

returned, no doubt, a wiser and better, certainly a more healthful man. He was asked what places in Italy interested him most. He replied, the Three Taverns, where St. Paul met the Roman Christians, and the tomb of Virgil. The answer was characteristic, illustrating his devotion as a Christian, and his enthusiasm as a classic."[20]

Shortly after Lumpkin returned to Athens from his European trip in late 1845, he found that the Georgia legislature had finally voted to create a supreme court and had elected him as one of the three initial judges of this new high court. As he prepared to assume his judicial duties, he would need all of the health and energy that, fortunately, had been restored by his travels abroad.

CHAPTER NINE

Establishing the Court

Eleven judges, each supreme in his authority and capable of being appealed
from himself only to himself, cannot be presumed to decide with uniformity.
Without uniformity, law itself is a chance and has been called a miserable
servitude.

GOVERNOR GEORGE W. CRAWFORD

addressing the General Assembly, November 1845

If there was any doubt that Georgia's supreme court faced a daunting challenge
from its inception, Lumpkin set the record straight in 1849. As part of a memorial
to James M. Kelly, the first supreme court reporter, he wrote,

It is well known that when the court bill was passed in 1845, a large majority of the
people were decidedly hostile to it. To secure its enactment, by accommodating
its provisions to the wishes of all, it contained inherent defects, well calculated
to insure its miscarriage. To obtain the service of suitable men, under the circumstances, to fill the offices, to steer the ship through a crowded sea of contrary
winds, was a task of no ordinary difficulty. Who was willing to risk what little
reputation he might have acquired by a lifetime of toil, to be crushed, perhaps
forever, beneath the superincumbent ruins of a fallen fabric?[1]

Opposition to a supreme court had been a powerful political force in Georgia
from the earliest days of its statehood. The state constitution of 1798 not only did
not establish a supreme court but also prohibited appellate review or correction
of errors by any court other than the superior court in the county where the case
was originally tried. When there were still only three superior court circuits, the
legislature provided in the Judiciary Act of 1799 for the Superior Court judges
to meet annually at the state capital "to determine upon such points as may be
reserved for argument and which may require uniform decision."[2]

Only two years later, however, the legislature abolished the authority of the superior court judges to act in conference as a court of review, indicating how early the opposition to any centralized judicial authority had developed. In searching for reasons for Georgia's longstanding rejection of a supreme court, some legal historians have cited periods of friction between the judicial and the legislative and executive branches of government or the unwillingness of judges and lawyers in the lower courts to lose local power. Others have cited various expressions of concern by politicians and others about the expense and delay inherent in reviews by an appellate court, which would result in favoring wealthy over poor litigants. Yet any of these reasons could have applied as well to each of the other twelve original colonies, all of which had created high courts long before Georgia finally acted. Even Florida, which was not admitted as a state until 1845, managed to establish its supreme court before Georgia did, although both courts held their first sessions in January of 1846.

A convincing reason for the unusual opposition in Georgia to a state supreme court, however, can be found in the history of losses suffered by the state in the Supreme Court of the United States. This bitter experience began in 1793 with a decision in the case of *Chisholm v. Georgia*, which sustained the right of a citizen of one state to bring suit against another state in the U.S. Supreme Court for breach of contract. According to an eminent historian of the Supreme Court, Charles Warren, "The decision fell upon the country with a profound shock. Both the Bar and the public in general appeared entirely unprepared for the doctrine upheld by the Court; and their surprise was warranted, when they recalled the fact that the vesting of any such jurisdiction over sovereign States had been expressly disclaimed and even resented by the great defenders of the Constitution, during the days of the contest over its adoption."

In Georgia, outrage over the adverse outcome in the *Chisholm* case became so great that the state House of Representatives passed a bill providing that any person who attempted to carry out the decision of the United States Supreme Court would be declared "guilty of felony and shall suffer death, without benefit of clergy, by being hanged." Although this expression of defiance against the Supreme Court was never enacted, the conflict produced throughout the country by the *Chisholm* decision did result in adoption of the Eleventh Amendment to the federal Constitution, which prohibits litigation against a state by a citizen of another state.[3]

The antagonism in Georgia to the U.S. Supreme Court was strong during John Jay's term as the first chief justice, but it reached an even greater intensity when John Marshall was chief justice, beginning with the decision in *Fletcher v. Peck*. This case, decided in 1810, involved the infamous Yazoo land sales, which had been authorized by an act of the Georgia legislature in 1795 but were soon found to have involved widespread fraud and political corruption. The 1795 law was revoked in the next session of the legislature, whose many new members included John Lumpkin, Joseph Henry's father. However, Chief Justice Marshall, delivering the opinion of the Supreme Court in *Fletcher v. Peck*, held that the repeal law passed by the Georgia legislature in 1796 was unconstitutional because it conflicted with contractual rights of individuals who were ignorant of the fraudulent circumstances. This decision triggered great resentment throughout Georgia.

Then, in the early 1830s, when Marshall was still chief justice, the Supreme Court ruled against the interests of Georgia again in a series of Cherokee Indian cases. In the first of these, involving the conviction of a Cherokee named Corn Tassel for murder under Georgia law, Governor Gilmer blatantly ignored a writ of error issued by the U.S. Supreme Court, and the execution of Tassel was carried out. The following year, it was Wilson Lumpkin's turn as governor to defy the court's attempt to enforce an order. Marshall held in that case, *Worcester v. Georgia*, that a Georgia statute, under which two missionaries to the Cherokees were convicted and imprisoned, was unconstitutional on the ground that the federal government had exclusive jurisdiction over the Cherokees. Shortly after the case was decided, U.S. Supreme Court Justice Joseph Story wrote to a friend that, "We have just decided the Cherokee case, and reversed the decisions of the State of Georgia, and declared laws unconstitutional. The decision produced a very strong sensation in both houses; Georgia is full of anger and violence. . . . Probably she will resist the execution of our judgment, and if she does I do not believe the President will interfere. . . . The Court has done its duty. Let the Nation do theirs."[4]

A widely held view among historians is that Andrew Jackson, aiming to keep Georgia from joining the South Carolina Nullification camp in 1832, refused to enforce the judgment of Marshall in *Worcester v. Georgia*. According to a report attributed to Horace Greeley, Jackson is supposed to have stated, "Well John Marshall has made his decision: now let him enforce it." Not long after the decision was rendered, Worcester and his fellow missionary were released, which effectively settled the conflict between Georgia and the Supreme Court. Nonetheless, the Cherokee cases had given the Georgia opponents of a state supreme court all the ammunition they needed to prevail for another decade, despite the adoption in 1835 of an amendment to the state constitution that provided for an appellate court.[5]

Beginning with George M. Troup in 1824, almost every Georgia governor included an appeal for a supreme court in his annual message to the general assembly. In his message to the assembly in 1839, Governor Gilmer said: "The necessity for establishing a Supreme Appellate jurisdiction . . . has frequently been brought to the attention of the legislature, in previous communications. The continued, indeed, increasing wealth and population of the State and the enlarged value and diversity of the interests, which must of consequence be adjudicated by our courts, make my justification for again recommending to the legislature, the organization of a Supreme Court for the correction of errors."

Although the economic argument advanced by Gilmer was not sufficiently convincing in 1839, six years later it may well have helped tip the scales in favor of the bill to create the court, despite the continuing opposition of many legislators. One member of the House, a representative named Kenan who had served as a superior court judge, opposed the bill, saying, "Sir, I shall vote against it and by the Eternal God, when the people of Georgia find the bill operating upon them, they will have a yoke upon their necks more galling and more slavish than that worn by my oxen." Nonetheless, the bill was finally passed in a close vote and signed into law by Governor Crawford on December 10, 1845. It appears that partisan politics did not play a key role in the final vote on the court bill, as the Democrats controlled the Senate while the Whigs held the majority in the House. Moreover, both Governor Crawford, who was a Whig, and Matthew McAllister, his Democratic opponent in the 1845 gubernatorial election, had long been strong supporters of the supreme court. Coincidentally, both Crawford and McAllister had been contemporaries of Lumpkin at Princeton, but there is no evidence that their college affiliation had any bearing on Lumpkin's selection as one of the three original supreme court judges who were elected on December 16, 1845, in a joint session of the Senate and House of Representatives.[6]

Lumpkin, who was elected for a term of six years, was the oldest of the three judges at age forty-six and brought to the court nearly twenty-five years of experience as a practicing lawyer and legal scholar. Hiram Warner of Greenville, elected for a term of four years, had been born in Massachusetts in 1802 and moved to Georgia as a teacher in 1820. He was admitted to the bar in 1824 and, with experience as superior court judge in the Coweta Circuit from 1833 to 1840, he was able to add valuable judicial perspective to the new court. The third member of the court, Eugenius Aristides Nisbet, who was born in 1803, had served in the U.S. House of Representatives and was then a successful lawyer in Macon. Following Warner's death in 1881, the then chief justice James Jackson wrote, "Lumpkin, Warner, Nisbet, the last of these Roman triumvirs is gone. Illustrious triumvirate, founder of the jurisprudence of Georgia, farewell! Pioneers of great work, they have done it well, strongly and deeply the foundations are laid. The arch on which the structure of our written law rests, reposes on three noble columns, each unique and dissimilar, yet blending in harmonious unity. Corinthian, Gothic, Doric, what a strong and beautiful composite they made."[7]

Because of his seniority, Lumpkin was recognized from the outset as the presiding judge, yet it took twenty more years for the position of chief justice to be officially established under Georgia law. The position of presiding judge, however, would not have gone to Lumpkin if another Princeton alumnus, John MacPherson Berrien, who was the first choice for the court, had not declined the honor. Berrien, who was then age sixty, had been attorney general in the first Jackson cabinet and in 1841 had returned for a second time to the United States Senate, where he enjoyed a position of power and influence in the Whig party. In a letter to a friend in Georgia, Berrien explained,

> I would willingly have contributed my mite to the successful introduction to the people of our Court for the Correction of Errors, if its organization had been such as to have given me hope that I could do so. That I thought impossible. Independently of the sacrifice of individual comfort in attendance upon an itinerant court for eleven months in the year, the fact that it was required, in many instances, to be held in remote places, where the judges could not have access to a tolerable law library and would probably be aided only by the local bar, was decisive against my acceptance of the office.[8]

There were many defects in the legislative design of the supreme court, as indicated by Berrien in his letter and later acknowledged by Lumpkin. The greatest burden facing the judges was a requirement that they hold sessions at least annually in nine different cities within the state's five judicial districts. As a historian of the court, Bond Almand, observed,

> What a task this court had before it. It had no central headquarters. It did not have the necessary tools for an appellate court—a library. The most important requirement was physical endurance: ability to travel to nine different points in Georgia from Cassville to Savannah and from Milledgeville to Americus in one year and decide all cases argued. What a task this was when most of the travel was by stagecoach. Law libraries inaccessible, and all writing in long hand. To the lawyer who loved home and friends, the position of judge of the Supreme Court of Georgia was not alluring, nor did the salary of $2,500.00 seem attractive. With the hardships incident to the position and the unpopularity of the court, Lumpkin, Warner and Nisbet were true public servants in accepting such a thankless task.

To make matters worse, Lumpkin, in his administrative role, had to convince Governor Crawford and the legislature that each judge's initial salary of $2,500 covered the one-year period from the date of his commission on December 24, 1845, and should not be prorated to October 31, the end of the "political year."[9]

The first session of the supreme court was held in Talbotton on January 26, 1846. Although the minutes of the proceedings note that Lumpkin did not attend the session, "owing to the indisposition of his family," no cases were argued during the two-day session, which was devoted to the admission of lawyers to practice in the supreme court. All three judges were in attendance for each of the other sessions in the court's first year, including Macon in February, Cassville in March, Milledgeville in May, Hawkinsville in June, Americus in July, Decatur in August, Gainesville in September, Milledgeville again in November, and Savannah in January of 1847, the final session.

With the exception of the months of April, October, and December, the members of the court were required to be on a continuous circuit, covering well over one thousand miles each year. Most of the travel in the early years was by stagecoach rather than by rail, and the judges had to pay all of the costs, including food and lodging, out of their salaries. In 1852 Augusta was substituted for Hawkinsville and Columbus for Talbotton; then in 1855 the number of cities was finally reduced to five: Athens, Atlanta, Macon, Milledgeville, and Savannah. Although Lumpkin appears to have accepted the burdens of this onerous travel schedule stoically, in an undated letter written from Columbus he told Callie, "I have been here a week. We have three weeks work and then three weeks more in Macon. My fear is that I shall not be able to visit my family in the interval. I shall try hard to reach Athens this day two weeks and spend Sabbath at least with you all—six hundred miles travel is nothing to twenty-four hours of such enjoyment."

In addition to imposing travel demands on the court, the statute creating the court included two other provisions that proved to be very problematic for the judges. First, they were directed to review "any error in any decision, sentence, judgment or decree" in every case brought before them. Unlike appellate courts in some other states, where reviews were limited to points of law, the Georgia court had to examine all errors alleged in each Bill of Exceptions. Another provision required that each case had to be decided during the term it was submitted. In the view of Bond Almand, that requirement "meant if the Court heard a case that was argued on the second Monday in January in Savannah, it would have to decide that case before the fourth Monday in January, which was the beginning of another term in another place." Without any law clerks or stenographers to assist them, the judges had to take their own notes during the oral arguments in order to prepare their opinions. They were only able to meet the statutory time limit by giving their decisions orally and then writing out their opinions later for publication in the *Georgia Reports*. Some critics have blamed this practice for causing the judges to deliver a number of opinions without sufficient deliberation. Aware of this concern, Lumpkin commented in an early case, "Much sympathy has been expressed for the Court . . . for the 'constitutional haste' with which it is compelled to decide cases. *Personally* its members are entitled to this sympathy; for our peculiar organization imposes on us an amount of labor bodily and mental, without parallel in any other appellate tribunal in the world. But if it be designed by this to weaken the force of the decisions themselves *as law*, then however kindly intended we must respectfully decline the apology thus *volunteered* on our behalf." [10]

In its first year, the court reversed superior court decisions in forty-four of the seventy-two cases it reviewed. Most of the appeals were in civil cases dealing with such issues as negligence, contracts, real estate, and wills and with questions of procedure. Of the seven criminal appeals heard by the court, four involved murder convictions, and new trials were granted in each of these cases.

Cities on Georgia's Supreme Court Circuit
1846–1867

The court circuit covered well over one thousand miles each year.

1846-1852	1852-1855	1855-1867
Americus	Americus	Athens
Cassville	Augusta	Atlanta
Decatur	Cassville	Macon
Gainesville	Columbus	Milledgeville
Hawkinsville	Decatur	Savannah
Macon	Gainesville	
Milledgeville	Macon	
Savannah	Milledgeville	
Talbotton	Savannah	

Lumpkin's opinion in one of the cases heard by the court in 1846 has received considerable attention in recent years from constitutional law scholars writing about gun control issues. In that case, *Nunn v. State*, a man named Hawkins Nunn was charged with "having and keeping about his person, and elsewhere, a pistol" in violation of a Georgia statute, which was aimed at protecting "the citizens of this State against the unwarrantable and too prevalent use of deadly weapons." In his opinion, Lumpkin discussed in depth the constitutional right to bear arms incorporated in the Second Amendment, and acknowledged that he was "aware that it has been decided, that this, like other amendments adopted at the same time, is a restriction upon the government of the United States, and does not extend to the individual States." Nonetheless, he found that the language of the Second Amendment "was broad enough to embrace both Federal and State governments." He then went on to conclude, in a passage that has been cited by gun control opponents, that, "The right of the whole people, old and young, men, women and boys, and not militia only, to keep and bear *arms* of every description, not *such* merely as are used by the militia, shall not be *infringed*."[11]

Lumpkin and his judicial associates managed to accomplish a great deal during the court's first year, but they still faced some formidable opponents. In an undated letter to his wife, which appears to have been written in August of 1846, Lumpkin complained: "I have felt deeply depressed in spirit since reading the anonymous attack upon the Court and me especially in the newspapers. And yet I know it proceeds from that malignant creature Merriweather—countenanced and encouraged by the clique above Augusta—who were opposed to my election. Col. Irwin of Marietta and others assure me that in the estimation of the Bar—here and elsewhere—it is deemed a vile and base slander and that it will do me good instead of injury. And yet it pains me." It must, therefore, have been particularly gratifying to Lumpkin when Governor Crawford, in his annual message to the General Assembly in 1847, said, "The Supreme Court, whose establishment was so long of questionable utility, in the opinion of several legislatures, has realized to the fullest extent the expectations of its most steadfast advocates."[12]

In the same year, the legislature acknowledged the court's value by asking the judges to make a report "stating any existing defect in the laws of Georgia, and suggesting a remedy for the same and to give their opinion on the expediency and practicability of . . . condensing and simplifying the laws." Although he had little extra time and received no additional compensation, Lumpkin apparently undertook the assignment without the participation of his fellow judges. He must have been encouraged in his efforts by a letter he received in December of 1847 from his brother Wilson, which enclosed two articles on the subject of law reform: "I am now done with everything like leadership. . . . But if I was of your age, had your qualifications and position—I would put down the miserable petty-fogging abuses of our judiciary system." When Lumpkin delivered the report to the legislature in December of 1849, he was the sole signatory, and he emphasized at the outset that he was submitting it "for *himself*." It is likely that the lack of involvement by his colleagues in the report was not a sign of any disagreement among them. Given the demands of their court duties, it probably seemed more efficient for only one of them to research and deliver the report. Lumpkin may have volunteered for the assignment because he thought it was his responsibility as presiding justice and because he could draw on his experience as one of the three authors of the 1833 Georgia Penal Code. [13]

The law reforms that Lumpkin recommended to the Georgia legislature reached a much wider audience when his report was published in two national law journals during 1850. Charles Haar, editor of *The Golden Age of American Law*, included the report among the most significant legal documents of the antebellum period, noting that "Judge Lumpkin presented what might be called the lawyer's traditional attitude toward reform: 'Let well enough alone,' as he put it, and change only where unavoidable." In Lumpkin's own estimation, however, his most radical proposal was to "break down the wall of separation between Law and Equity, and to blend into one, the two jurisdictions" and thus "let *one* law-suit settle any matter in controversy between the parties." He noted that a similar fusion of law and equity had been included in the 1848 Code of Civil Procedure in New York which, "important as it is, stops short of accomplishing all that was practicable in this department of the law."

Jurisdictional rivalry between the courts of common law and equity had been exported to the original English colonies in America and was well entrenched in most states during the antebellum period. Under the separate systems, for example, when a contract was broken, a court of equity would often compel the defendant specifically to perform the contract; however, a court of law could only give money damages for a breach of contract. In promoting the fusion of the two separate systems, Lumpkin was siding with David Dudley Field, the noted author of the New York code. Following the example of the New York code, many states passed acts in the latter half of the nineteenth century aimed at abolishing the distinctions between actions at law and suits at equity. In other states, including Georgia, the two systems were eventually merged or administered by the same courts, although this did not occur in the federal courts until the adoption of the Federal Rules of Civil Procedure in 1938.[14]

In summarizing his proposals for the legislators, Lumpkin submitted "for their consideration the following plan of condensing and simplifying the laws so as to place them within the reach and comprehension of the citizens of the state generally; and thereby securing the more certain and speedy attainment of the ends of justice. . . . A single volume of convenient size, would contain the entire revised code. . . . It is right therefore that every man should be enabled to read and understand the law—for himself—and for this purpose it should be divested of all technicality and intricacy, as far as it is possible." With his proposals for codification, Lumpkin joined an important group of reformers within the American legal profession, which included not only Field in New York but also U.S. Supreme Court Justice Joseph Story and Timothy Walker, editor of the influential *Western Law Journal*.[15]

It took the Georgia legislature more than a decade to adopt Lumpkin's proposal for codification. In the interim, however, his son-in-law Thomas R. R. Cobb kept working toward this objective, which was one of the many goals and beliefs he shared with Lumpkin. In his biography of Cobb, William B. McCash wrote of the close relationship between Cobb and Lumpkin that, "From the outset of his courtship of Marion Lumpkin, Cobb felt a deep admiration for her father and was treated like a son in return. His ultimate acceptance of the Presbyterian faith, his beginning interest in temperance reform, his continuing determination to stay clear of debt, and his early ambivalence about party politics were all attributable, in some measure, to the influence of Judge Lumpkin." Not only were the two men next-door neighbors in Athens, but after Lumpkin arranged Cobb's appointment as supreme court reporter, in January of 1849, they spent long hours together on the court's circuit.

Among the many references to Cobb that appear in Lumpkin's letters to Callie there is only one indication of any conflict ever occurring between the two men. In an undated letter written probably around 1856, Lumpkin complained to Callie about Cobb's insufficient support of his brother-in-law William Wilberforce Lumpkin in some unspecified pursuit, saying,

> I feel that I have many [claims] upon Mr. Cobb. While he was poor, I could pass by his selfishness. But the time has come in his affairs when he ought to reciprocate towards my sons—the many acts of kindness which he has received at my hands. And I am resolved to make him feel the sincerity of my resentment. . . . The just complaint against Mr. Cobb is his utter indifference towards Will—in a matter that concerned his feelings so deeply. I never divided with Mr. Gerdine [another son-in-law] my fees. I never made him reporter of the Supreme Court. In short, I never assisted him to a position where he could command fame and fortune. For all Mr. Cobb's kindness to my child [Marion] I am grateful. I wish I could say the same for his conduct toward my sons. Don't think me still angry—I am not and the matter is arranged.

Like Lumpkin, Cobb had extraordinary energy, and, in addition to his duties as court reporter, he was able to maintain a law practice while still undertaking numerous other projects. One of these projects was the publication of *A General Digest Index to Georgia Reports*, a compilation of laws prepared jointly with his brother-in-law William Wilberforce Lumpkin (during a period of more harmonious relations between the two brothers-in-law). However, an even more significant achievement was Cobb's publication of *A Digest of the Statute Laws of the State of Georgia*. According to McCash, "Thomas Cobb's new *Digest* had achieved the lopping, winnowing, and engrafting process that Lumpkin had in mind. It was not strictly speaking a code, but, in the opinion of a former associate justice of the Georgia Supreme Court, 'it was a code in embryo.' "[16]

While the efforts of Lumpkin and Cobb to promote law reform and codification continued throughout the 1850s, the prestige and influence of the supreme court was steadily increasing. In the January 15, 1850, issue of the *Savannah Daily Morning News*, it was reported that "a regular term of the Supreme Court commenced yesterday in this city; present their honors Judges Lumpkin, Warner and Nisbet. The citizens of Georgia have cause to congratulate themselves upon the establishment of this tribunal so much needed, and in the ability and dignity of the gentlemen whom they have selected to preside over it."[17]

CHAPTER TEN

First among Equals

≡►◆◄≡

> There is in each of us a stream of tendency, whether you choose to call it
> philosophy or not, which gives coherence to thought and action. Judges
> cannot escape that current any more than other mortals.
>
> BENJAMIN CARDOZO, *The Nature of the Judicial Process*

By 1850 Lumpkin's reputation as an influential appellate judge and advocate of
legal and economic reforms had begun to be recognized in the North as well as
throughout the southern states. This was due, at least in part, to the publication
of his report to the Georgia legislature on law reform and his speech to the
South-Carolina Institute in some influential national journals. One indication
of this increased recognition was his receipt of an honorary doctorate of laws
from his alma mater, Princeton, in June of 1851. He was also one of a select
number of judges and lawyers from around the country who were invited in 1851
to join the Story Association at the Harvard Law School. The membership of
that association, which had been formed in 1850 to honor Judge Story for his
contributions to Harvard Law School, consisted of "the former and immediate
members of the . . . Law School, and of such gentlemen of distinction in the
legal profession as they may from time to time elect into their ranks."

The association held its first meeting in Boston, and although it appears that
Lumpkin was unable to attend, the distinguished guests included Judge James
Kent of New York, president of the association, Chief Justice Lemuel Shaw of
Massachusetts, Chief Justice George Eustis of Louisiana, and Rufus Choate, a
former Massachusetts senator and noted lawyer. Boston was then a center of
opposition to the recently enacted Fugitive Slave Law of 1850, which expanded
the power of owners to recover slaves from northern states. Charles Warren, describing the event in his *History of the Harvard Law School*, says, "The meeting
was a brilliant success. . . . But the anti-slavery men of the day were in such a

supersensitive condition that they could brook no reference that might be construed as even remotely adverse to their cause, and they resented the attacks they professed to find in the speeches. . . . After this, the Story Association seems to have dropped out of existence. . . . Its life had become somewhat ineffectual, for it never recovered from its baptism of politics."[1]

In 1853 Lumpkin was elected a vice president of the American Bible Society, headquartered in New York City. The same year the society also included a letter from Lumpkin in a publication entitled "Testimony of Distinguished Laymen to the Value of the Sacred Scriptures." Despite his increasingly negative views toward the North over slavery, Lumpkin expressed a remarkably optimistic attitude in his letter, testifying to the influence of the Bible "for the general temperance, industry, and contentment of the teeming millions of this happy and highly favored country." However, a year later, he had a less sanguine reaction when Yale, not to be outdone by Princeton and Harvard, attempted to honor him as well. In a letter to Callie from Decatur on August 18, 1854, he wrote,

> Callie I received to-day by the way of home a most astonishing communication—the official notice that I had been elected to deliver the next anniversary address before Yale College. I was told that this appointment was announced in the papers. I did not believe it, for not long ago I wrote three sheets of letter paper to the Professor of Languages of Yale—abusing New England generally and New Haven in particular and stating among other things, that if I had as many sons as old Priam I would prefer them to be raised in ignorance of the alphabet, rather than send them to that institution.

Not surprisingly, there is no record in the Yale archives of Lumpkin's selection as speaker for any anniversary in that period, nor of any correspondence on the subject between him and any Yale representative.[2]

In 1851 Lumpkin was reelected by the General Assembly to a second six-year term on the supreme court, while the terms of Judges Eugenius Nisbet and Hiram Warner continued to 1853 and 1854, respectively. In July of 1853, however, Judge Warner resigned to run for Congress, and although unsuccessful that year, he was elected in 1855. Ebenezer A. Starnes was appointed on an interim basis to fill the vacancy created by Warner's resignation and was then elected to the court when the legislature met in November of 1853. Starnes, a native of Augusta, was a highly regarded superior court judge in the Middle Circuit at the time of his election to the supreme court and had served previously as solicitor general of the same circuit. In his unpublished diary, Judge Nisbet described Judge Starnes as follows: "His voice is bad, and he hems and haws and drawls outrageously. But his judgments show clear discrimination and strength." After serving the final two years of Hiram Warner's six-year term, Starnes failed to be reelected to the court and returned in 1855 to Augusta, where he built a successful law practice.

On October 13, 1853, Lumpkin wrote Callie about the recent election results and reported that, even though there had been a close race for governor between Herschel Johnson and Charles Jenkins, "the Democrats will have a majority of 27 in joint ballot in the Legislature. That is, 9 in the Senate and 18 in the House—which gives to that Party—the United States Senator—in the place of Mr. Dawson and two Judges of the Supreme Court. . . . I apprehend that my Brother Nisbet cannot compete successfully against such odds." His apprehension was well founded, as Judge Nisbet failed to be reelected, despite his fine record during eight years on the court. He was replaced by Henry Lewis Benning, who was then thirty-nine years old. Benning had graduated first in his class from Franklin College, where his classmates included fellow Democrats Howell Cobb and Herschel Johnson, the newly elected governor. By the time of his election to the court, Benning was already an ardent secessionist, and when disunion and war finally came, he served with distinction as a Confederate general.[3]

Despite the changes in the court's makeup, Lumpkin appears to have enjoyed as good relations with his new associates as with his original colleagues. In a letter to Callie from Decatur on August 15, 1853, shortly after the departure of Judge Warner, he noted, "We got in harmoniously with our new Brother Starnes." Then on March 5, 1854, he wrote her from Macon, "My official and personal relations with my new colleagues are of the most pleasant kind. They treat me with more like the respect & consideration of juniors—than equals. Judge Benning . . . is an able man—elevated & honorable in his principles." This collegial spirit prevailed despite the fact that Benning and Starnes wrote a number of dissenting opinions, whereas the three original judges had endeavored to resolve their conflicting views in order to reach unanimous opinions. It was not until 1856 that Lumpkin finally dissented in a case, stating in *Gray v. Gray*:

I am compelled, very reluctantly, after a service of eleven years upon this bench to dissent, *for the first time*, from the judgment of a majority of the Court. Of such paramount importance have I considered the *unanimity* of opinion, with a view to *uniformity* and *permanence* in its decisions, the great end for which this tribunal was established that I have not hesitated to sacrifice the pride of professional opinion, and . . . even now, I might have yielded my own convictions, strong as they are, to those of my brethren, but for the magnitude of the questions involved. [4]

The harmonious relationship he enjoyed with his two younger associates on the bench, as well as with Thomas Cobb, helped Lumpkin endure all the hard work and personal sacrifices that were increasingly demanded by his supreme court duties. His descriptions in letters to Callie of the court session at Decatur, during a period of five weeks in August and September of 1854, show how grueling the work schedule could be. He had just returned to Athens from the session at Americus, when he wrote Callie on August 10 that he was "greatly broken down in body and mind as I always am at the adjournment of that Court." Just over a week later, he was in Decatur; in a letter dated August 18 he noted, "We have a crowded docket here, 57 cases—the largest since the organization of the Court. There are or have been in attendance between 60 and 70 lawyers, an unprecedented number, constituting one-sixth of the profession in the State." Among this army of lawyers were some of the most prominent men in Georgia, including his two former associates on the court, Nesbit and Warner, as well as a former governor, Charles McDonald, who would join the court the following year. In what appears to have been almost a contest of Whigs versus Democrats, Lumpkin told Callie that "Judge Nesbit and Mr. Dougherty were pitted in one of the celebrated Bank cases against Judge Warner, Gov. McDonald and Mr. Toombs, and I must say that the former two carried off the forensic palm most triumphantly." The bank cases Lumpkin referred to eventually produced twenty-six supreme court decisions dealing with the rights of creditors and depositors against the shareholders and directors of the Planter's and Mechanic's Bank of Columbus, following its dissolution.

By August 29 his mood had grown so melancholy that he complained, "This is the Tuesday of the 3rd week of the court and we have just entered this morning on 'disposing' no. 27, a Bank case, leaving 30 still to hear—we may get through in this and the two ensuing weeks I fear we may not—I came here dear Callie sick— my soul exceedingly sorrowful almost unto death—indeed I felt that I would be glad to be relieved by death from all my afflictions. But my health has improved to get through my business with a good degree of comfort." He then went on to describe the court's exhausting schedule: "We hear arguments from 1/2 past 8 o'clock till dark and sometimes by candlelight—as we did last night and then meet after tea and consult till 12. Last night we were up till a quarter after 12 and I had to draw my watch upon my Brethren—at 12 Saturday night to prevent a violation of the Sabbath."

This work schedule was so debilitating that he confessed to Callie, in the same letter, "I would gladly lay aside the harness—they begin to press heavily upon me. You will be surprised to see how rapidly I am turning old. . . . But I must wait till I see my younger children provided for." Part of the problem was the heat they had to endure both at the courthouse and in their bedrooms. On September 3 he reported, "It continues very hot here—I can't bear my coat or waistcoat. . . . Last night I slept in my little room under a sheet with three windows up—without blinds to them. We are arguing the 37th case, leaving 20 on the docket, which will take us far into the fifth week. We sit up every night until 12."

Finally, on September 18, he was back home in Athens. To Callie he wrote, "I was very sick Saturday night and yesterday, but crawled down to the office this morning and have just finished a difficult opinion of 30 pages— Pretty good day's work for an invalid." His home in Athens must have seemed an especially safe haven at that point, not just from the rigors of his life on the court circuit but also from the natural calamities that other parts of the state were then suffering, especially in Augusta and Savannah. In his letter of September 18, he told Callie, "You can't imagine how much we are excited about the yellow-fever, which has broken out in Augusta. . . . The report is that 6,000 had left Augusta. Every physician had sent their families off. The intelligence from Savannah is deplorable—notwithstanding the handful left there—upwards of 50 dying daily. The mortality is greatly aggravated by the stench from the fish and dead carcasses washed up by the storm in the city. . . . I suppose such a scene of destruction never has presented. Every tin roofed house in the city—but one—was uncovered by the gale of the 7th and 8th. Every tree in the City prostrated . . ." Although he would have to leave home again in less than two weeks for the court's session at Gainesville, he could expect that the extreme heat would have broken by then, and it would be months before the court would be sitting again in either Savannah or Augusta.

In 1855 Judge Starnes was replaced on the supreme court by Charles J. McDonald, a Democrat, who had served two terms as governor (1839–1843). McDonald had lost the 1851 gubernatorial election race to Howell Cobb, in which he strongly defended the right of secession, and had also been an unsuccessful candidate for the U.S. Senate in 1853. In a letter to Callie dated November 23, 1855, Lumpkin wrote, "Governor McDonald has been elected to the Supreme Bench—such was the repugnance of the Legislature to elevate 'young America' to the station that Mr. Jenkins would have been chosen by a Democratic Legislature had not Governor McDonald's name been put in nomination. This proceeding is equally creditable to the Legislature and complimentary to the Court. Thank God the day is yet distant where age is a disqualification for the Senate of the National and State Legislatures and the highest Judicial tribunals."

Lumpkin welcomed the addition of the sixty-two year old McDonald to the court, even though the younger candidate for the seat, Charles Jenkins, was a fellow Whig, whom Lumpkin had supported in the gubernatorial election two years earlier. In a letter written to Callie on October 13, 1853, he talked about his political philosophy: "I voted for Jenkins for Governor. . . . I am a *Trimmer*— no intelligent conscientious man can be anything else in politics. Before reading McCauley's life of Lord Halifax, I was ashamed of the title. I now glory in the name. Other things being equal, I have always voted the Whig ticket and always expect to do so. I am determined never to change my party relations. But if the Democratic candidate is the better man or my personal friend, I unhesitatingly vote for him, in preference to his Whig opponent."

Lumpkin's skill in trimming his sails to take account of the political winds earned him a reputation for independence, which was an important factor in his reelection to the court without opposition on three occasions, regardless of which party was in control of the legislature. His philosophy carried over into national politics as well. Commenting to Callie on the presidential election of 1852, he reported in a letter of August 6 that Howell Cobb was trying to coalesce the Union and Southern Rights supporters in Georgia behind the Democratic candidate, Franklin Pierce, and that there was little support for the Whig nominee, Winfield Scott. After describing the maneuvering by politicians like Toombs and Stephens, he concluded, "But enough of such nonsense. Let the dead bury their dead."

His apparent support for the Democratic over the Whig candidate in that

election may have influenced the decision by President Pierce to select Lumpkin as one of the original judges of the court of claims in Washington when it
was established in 1855. The law creating the court authorized the appoint-
ment of three judges to adjudicate claims against the government of the United
States and to serve during "good behavior," reflecting, as one legal historian
has observed, "the dignity with which Congress intended to clothe this court."
When Lumpkin declined the appointment, Pierce chose John J. Gilchrist of
New Hampshire, Isaac N. Blackford of Indiana, and George P. Scarburgh of
Virginia, all of whom were highly qualified for the new court. Gilchrist and
Blackford had served on the supreme courts of New Hampshire and Indiana,
respectively, while Scarburgh had been a trial court judge in Virginia and a pro-
fessor at the College of William and Mary.[5]

There were many reasons why Lumpkin may have decided not to accept
the appointment on the court of claims. Even if he had been younger (he was
then fifty-six) and in better health, a move to Washington would have been very
disruptive to his family. He was concerned about the welfare not only of his
two youngest children, Robert and Frank, who were still young adolescents,
but also about some of his older children and their families, who depended on
him for both emotional and financial support. An even more important factor,
however, was his commitment to protecting and enhancing the stature of the
Georgia Supreme Court. As recently as 1854, an effort had been made in the
General Assembly to have the people of Georgia vote on abolishing the court,
but the resolution had been voted down. Also, with the departure of Starnes in
1855, the court would have been severely weakened if Lumpkin had resigned,
leaving Benning as the only experienced member of the court at a time when
the number of appeals was steadily growing. In the initial year of 1846 the court
had reviewed 93 cases, but the number of appeals had more than doubled to
231 by 1855.

Staying in Athens also meant that he could continue serving on the board of
trustees at the University of Georgia, which he had joined in 1854. After serving
briefly as a professor of law in the early 1840s and declining another position
on the faculty as professor of rhetoric and oratory in 1846, his involvement with
the college had been limited by his court duties. His contact with the university
during those years had been mainly through the experiences of his sons, seven of
whom ultimately became undergraduates. As a trustee, he was now in a position

to have an influence on higher education in the state as well as to participate in guiding an institution he valued highly. The periodic board meetings also gave him an opportunity to escape from the pressures of the court while enjoying the company of his peers.

On July 28, 1855, the Trustees' Committee on Law and Discipline, chaired by Lumpkin, proposed that the board obtain from the legislature "a large and liberal appropriation for the endowment of the college—upon a scale adequate to the views of its future." This resolution was considered at the next meeting of the board on November 6, 1855, which was attended by a large number of trustees, including the current governor, Herschel Johnson, and three former governors—Wilson Lumpkin, George Gilmer, and Howell Cobb. Wilson Lumpkin was made the head of a campaign to seek an endowment for the college from the legislature. Joseph Henry showed initial optimism about the prospects in a letter to Callie on March 2, 1856, reporting that "the House of Representatives have passed the Bill for the endowment of our College—$35,000 annually for 1856 and 1857 and $24,000 yearly thereafter. Should it go through the Senate—it will be a proud day for Georgia." Unfortunately, the bill was defeated in the Senate, and the trustees, pressed for funds, had to sell college property. At the August meeting of the trustees that year, Joseph Henry moved that "the Prudential Committee be authorized to sell the Botanical Garden and that the proceeds be used to enclose, with iron railings & suitable gateways & to ornamenting with trees, etc. the college grounds."[6]

Later that same year, the trustees faced an even more difficult challenge, as indicated by Lumpkin's letter to Callie on December 12, 1856: "We have just passed through a most exciting scene—the reorganization of the college Faculty. Twenty-two Trustees were in attendance and I will say that I never saw such an assemblage of men for the same size. Five ex-governors beside the present chief magistrate and all the rest would have compared favorably with these." He went on to describe the votes on faculty positions in detail, including the fact that President Alonzo Church was reelected by a majority of only twelve to ten. Despite improvements in faculty relations and enrollment over the next few years, some on the board pressed for a wider reorganization of the college. Finally, in 1859, a broad plan of reorganization was adopted by the trustees, which then included Thomas Cobb, who had joined the board the prior year.

The plan provided for incorporation of independent schools of agriculture, civil engineering, and law into a new university system to be headed by a chancellor, whose duties included promoting higher education and fundraising around the state, presiding over faculty meetings, and teaching English and belles lettres in the college. When President Church decided to retire rather than assume this position, the trustees unanimously selected Lumpkin to be the first chancellor at a meeting on July 30, 1860, but once again he declined to leave the Supreme Court, which then needed his leadership more than ever.[7]

CHAPTER ELEVEN

The Front Rank

⟹•◈•⟸

We are prepared, although in our *judicial infancy*, to advance to the front
rank in this warfare of principle against precedent. Beyond this we dare not
go. Judges cannot alter a law. . . . Their business is to declare what the law
is, and not what it ought to be.

Choice v. Marshall (1846)

When the Georgia Supreme Court met for the first time at Talbotton in January of 1846, it was fifty-eight years after Georgia was admitted to the Union
and just a month since Texas had become the twenty-eighth state. Development of jurisprudence in Georgia had lagged behind the twelve other original
states and many of the newer ones, but Lumpkin was determined to lead the
new court rapidly out of its judicial infancy into the front rank of state appellate courts. At the outset, his principal models for the Georgia court were in
New York, where he found that "the *Supreme Court . . .* is clothed with authority almost precisely similar to our own," in Massachusetts, which he called
"the morningstar of the bright constellation of States," and in South Carolina,
which he described in 1846 as "second perhaps to none in the Union for judicial
authority."[1]

In a number of his opinions, Lumpkin identified the federal and state judges
he most esteemed. Interestingly, he had praise for five out of the six antebellum judges whom Roscoe Pound counted among the "ten judges who must be
ranked first in American judicial history" in his influential 1938 book, *The Formative Era of American Law*. Those six were John Marshall (1755–1835), Chief
Justice of the United States Supreme Court for thirty-four years; James Kent
(1763–1847), who was on the New York law and equity benches for twenty-five
years; Joseph Story (1779–1845), a justice of the U.S. Supreme Court for thirty-
two years; John Gibson (1780–1853), thirty-seven years on the supreme court of

Pennsylvania, of which twenty-three years were served as chief justice; Lemuel Shaw (1781–1861), who was chief justice of Massachusetts for thirty-one years; and Thomas Ruffin (1787–1870), who spent nineteen of his thirty-five years on the bench as chief justice of the North Carolina Supreme Court.[2]

Many Georgians could not forgive John Marshall for his adverse rulings in the Cherokee cases, yet Lumpkin called him "a pure and spotless man, and eminent jurist." As he dealt with the widespread public opposition to the Georgia Supreme Court in its early years, Lumpkin probably felt a special affinity for the similar challenges that had been faced by Marshall in shaping the federal Supreme Court. He would certainly have welcomed the judgment of one Georgia historian: "What John Marshall was to the judiciary of the United States Joseph Henry Lumpkin was to the judiciary of the State."[3]

Ranked along with Marshall at the top of the hierarchy were Chancellor James Kent of New York and Judge Joseph Story. In his tribute to the memory of his friend, John Berrien, Lumpkin speculated that, had Berrien been appointed to the United States Supreme Court, "his judicial fame would have been measured by that of . . . Marshall and Kent, and Story." The most conclusive evidence for him of the correctness of his decision in one case was that "it has the sanction of . . . Chief Justice Marshall and Chancellor Kent, and many of the most eminent jurists at home and abroad." Elsewhere, he gave his highest accolade to James Kent and Joseph Story as "men unsurpassed for legal learning" and called Kent "the father and ornament of the American Bar."[4]

In paying tribute to Pennsylvania chief justice John Gibson, Lumpkin wrote: "No other on earth united the same originality, vigor, clearness, precision of thought with the same elegance and felicity of expression. He is unquestionably, for force and beauty of style, the ablest judicial writer this or any other country has produced." In *Moultrie v. Smiley and Neal* (1854), Lumpkin stated candidly, "I am constantly admonished to be brief," and then he proceeded to write a thirty-nine-page opinion. Four years later, in *Chance v. McWhorter*, he questioned his own writing skills and again confessed that "a friendly writer admonishes me that I weaken my opinions by making them too long." Although his opinions did become shorter in later years when the court's case load was greater, his colleague, Judge Iverson Harris, commented on Lumpkin's discursive style, noting, "This very abundance has subjected his printed decisions often to criticism neither tolerant nor appreciative, nor even apologetic." Harris went on to explain, "Judge Lumpkin's opinions were written out hastily, often a most irksome task, and when the impressions of the argument had faded from the memory, and almost always without revision . . . it was a great misfortune that the Court had not had connected with it an expert stenographer, so as to have taken down his decisions as delivered, that they, after having undergone his revision, might have been preserved to us."[5]

Lumpkin praised his fellow Princetonian Thomas Ruffin more than once and equated him on one occasion with Ambrose Spencer of New York and Spencer Roane of Virginia, saying, "Abler common law judges never presided in the Courts of this country." The sixth of Pound's stellar antebellum judges, Lemuel Shaw, does not appear to have gained any mention in Lumpkin's opinions, but Lumpkin cited the law of Massachusetts as precedent almost as often as the holdings in New York, especially in cases involving corporate and commercial legal issues. As conflicts over slavery and abolition intensified, however, his admiration for "the Bay State" declined so far that in 1858 he commented in one opinion, "I am glad to find something to commend in that ancient commonwealth."[6]

Lumpkin and his fellow judges wrote their opinions, of course, primarily for the lawyers and trial court judges in Georgia to guide them on substantive points of law as to what they "believe[d] the true rule to be . . . and that upon every consideration of reason, public policy and authority." He also continuously attempted in his opinions to persuade Georgia judges and lawyers to adopt better trial practices and procedures. In a case where, ironically, his colleague Judge Nisbet gave no opinion because he had been of counsel in the lower-court proceedings, Lumpkin wrote caustically, "The court does not feel called on to go at great lengths into all the questions arising out of this *chaotic record*. A more reprehensible example of vexatious litigation has not come under its review."[7]

He strongly condemned practices that undermined the jury system and criticized counsel in another case for undertaking "by a side wind, to get that in as proof which is merely conjecture, and thus to work a prejudice in the mind of the Jury." Showing that he could use both a carrot and a stick to make his point, however, he then wrote in the same opinion: "Is it, I ask, worthy of the noblest of professions thus to sport with the life, liberty, and fortune of a citizen? A profession which is the great repository of the first talents of the country, and to whose standard the most gifted habitually flock, as offering the highest inducements of reputation, wealth, influence, authority and power, which the community can bestow."[8]

Because of his twenty-five years as a practicing attorney he maintained great pride in the legal profession as well as a warm affinity for his fellow lawyers. In the period before a separate bar association was created in Georgia, lawyers who were admitted to practice before the supreme court constituted, in effect, a statewide bar, of which Lumpkin, as the chief justice, was the nominal head. It was his responsibility in that capacity to write many memorial tributes to recently deceased lawyers who had argued before the court. At the session at Atlanta in March of 1858, he wrote in one tribute, "I never approach a task like the present, but with mingled feelings of pleasure and pain. From my deep attachments to my brethren of the bar, I cheerfully contribute my mite on these melancholy occasions, in order that our names may live together when our earthly connection is dissolved. . . . But to portray the peculiarity of each, would be to overlook all which constitutes the distinction between men. . . . Would that I had the genius of Plutarch, that I might sketch properly the lives of those deceased worthies who have adorned, by their learning and eloquence, the jurisprudence of our State!"[9]

From these memorial tributes and from numerous comments in his opinions, it is possible to construct a composite picture of the ideal traits he valued in a lawyer. Of a Macon lawyer he wrote, "He never experimented upon the Bench or Jury-Box, by assuming positions manifestly untenable, or palpably contradictory. Nothing tends more to emasculate the vigor of the mind and dim the bright perceptions of intellectual truth, than to indulge habitually in sophistry. The age for using this once formidable weapon of scholastic gladiatorship, has passed away." He made a similar point less poetically in praising a lawyer appearing before the court who "has argued his case in a lawyer-like manner—that is to say, briefly, closely, earnestly, yet without declamation, and upon authority." He remembered one promising young lawyer as "another living refutation of the absurd idea, that it is impossible for a man to be a fine scholar and a thorough lawyer." Yet he extolled another as belonging "to that class of lawyers who rely more upon their clear perceptions of what is just and true, than upon books and cases—more upon principle than precedent."[10]

When counsel in one case complained that court rules were turning them into "absolute drudges," Lumpkin replied, "Let such appeals be addressed to those who lounge in castles of indolence. . . . Everybody must learn to labor. This is the fundamental law of the universe." Then, memorializing another member of the bar, whom he said was "no idler in the vineyard," and perhaps recalling his own courtroom style, he wrote with great feeling about "the voice, the look, the gesture, the impassioned feeling, the burning words, the searching thought, the soaring fancy, the scathing sarcasms, who can adequately portray these, for the admiration of posterity. And yet, these are the frail foundations of the lawyer's fame; born of, dying with the occasion that produced them; Digests and Form books will be cited by the names of their authors, when the lawyer, whose mind furnished the matter, will be forgotten."[11]

Lumpkin could be diplomatic in dealing with the sensibilities of trial judges, especially when reversing a lower court's opinion. In *Reynolds v. Reynolds* (1847), ruling that a defendant was improperly put on trial twice for the same offense, he wrote, "Far be it from us to intimate that the court below intended to oppress the prisoner. That judge is above reproach." However, reversing another verdict in *Monroe v. State* (1848) because of various judicial errors, Lumpkin took the occasion to comment, "We flatter ourselves, that since the organization of this court, short as its existence has been, something has been done to establish *trial* by *jury* in criminal prosecutions in this state, on a foundation so broad and deep, that it will not easily be shaken. On this vital subject, there should be no vacillation in the judicial mind."[12]

While Lumpkin's opinions were addressed primarily to lawyers and judges in Georgia, it appears that he frequently considered the state legislature almost as important an audience. In his earlier opinions, he took a conservative approach to statutory construction, calling himself in *Carey v. McDougald* (1849) "somewhat of a literalist in the interpretation of laws," and he made it clear the court recognized that "in the distribution of power, we are the *law-expounding* and not the *law-making* or *law-executing* department of the Government." Once he was moved to make the point even more strongly, writing in *Martin v. Broach* (1849), "I trust the period is passed for judicial legislation, under the pretext of *construction*. It is the monster mischief of the law, the prolific uncertainty with which it has so long and so deservedly been reproached."[13]

Such conservative statements may have been aimed at fostering good relations with the legislature in the period when it still harbored substantial opposition to the court. However, Lumpkin appears to have gradually adopted a more flexible

approach to statutory construction, depending on the issues involved. In a case
decided in 1850, *Worthy v. Johnson*, he wrote that "some of us think, that the
Courts should give a more liberal construction to Statutes authorizing the sale
of real estate and slaves, in Georgia, by executors and administrators." Yet only
a month later, in *Flournoy v. Newton*, he stated, "It is well known that we, as a
court, are not latitudinarian, but strict constructionists, as to the great rule of
evidence—that where a writing exists, it constitutes the best, if not the exclusive
medium of proving the facts to which it relates." When a major issue of public
policy was involved, such as the manumission of slaves, he deferred to the legislature, saying in *Cleland v. Waters* (1855), "It is not the province of the courts
to make public policy, but simply *to declare it*, as it exists. The policy of a state
is to be gathered from its Constitution and laws."[14]

If constitutional issues were involved, Lumpkin had no doubt as to the court's
responsibilities. In the case of *Flint River Steamboat Company v. Foster*, decided
in 1848, he wrote, "I will not stop at this late day to inquire whether the Courts
have the power, and if so, if it be not their duty to declare Acts of the Legislature
repugnant to the Constitution, void?" Despite his confidence in the court's constitutional role, he was sufficiently concerned about relations with the legislature
in 1850 that he wrote diplomatically in *Beall v. Beall*: "Should it ever become
our unpleasant task to do, what we are here importuned to do, namely, set aside
a Statute on account of its unconstitutionality, we have an abiding confidence
in the liberality of the Legislature, that they will do us the credit to believe, that
we acted only in obedience to the sternest convictions of duty."[15]

As Lumpkin's tenure on the court and judicial stature increased, he included
increasingly critical comments about the legislature in his opinions, calling on
them to enact or change particular statutes. In *Watson v. Tindall*, decided in
1858, referring to "that 'Pandora's Box' of evils, the New Trial Act of February,
1854," he complained, "This one Act has more than doubled the delay and cost
of litigation in Georgia, without possessing one redeeming feature of public benefit." The following year, in *Vanderzer v. McMillan*, he criticized a statutory rule
as "unreasonable and oppressive in the extreme" and called on the legislature,
as he had in his report on law reform, to "follow the lead of New York" and
merge the remedies of law and equity. It was probably not just coincidental that
his bolder attitude toward the legislature coincided with the passage of a law
in 1858 providing that a decision of the supreme court in which all three of the

judges concurred had the same effect as if it had been enacted by the General Assembly. The court had finally achieved full standing in the state government.[16]

His frustration with the legislature reached such an intensity in 1859 that he wrote, in *Bethune v. Hughes*, "A convention of the people, called by the people, I would most respectfully suggest, is imperiously needed to impose additional restraints upon the Legislature, now more unlimited, in the opinion of some of our ablest jurists, than those of the British Parliament. . . . Something should be done to arrest this evil. The dearest rights of the people are being jeopardized." This call for a popular convention to correct the legislature's excesses contrasts sharply with his assertion eight years earlier in *Beall v. Beall* that "the Legislature may pass laws the most absurd and unreasonable—if that not be disrespectful to suppose such a thing—still, if they be *constitutional*, the *people* have made *them* the sole and exclusive judges, whether or not they are '*for the good of the State*.' "[17]

Even though his views about the relative power of the legislature and court may have changed over the years, he steadfastly maintained that "the supreme power resides in the people." In order to keep ordinary citizens informed of the court's decisions, he declared in *Merritt v. Scott* (1849):

> It shall be my aim to popularize [opinions] as much as possible. For while I am not enthusiastic enough to believe that the time will come when every man will be his own lawyer, still I feel it a duty to accommodate our decisions, so far as we can, to the comprehension of those who are not lawyers by profession. . . . All men here are by birthright, hereditary law makers, and judges upon the reputations and lives, as well as arbiters of the property of their fellow citizens. . . . It is right, therefore, that every man should read and understand the decisions of the courts, and to enable him to do this, they should be divested as far as practicable, of all technicality and intricacy.

While he was prepared through his decisions to enlist public opinion in support of some legal, economic, and social reforms, he acknowledged in *State v. Lockhart* (1858) that "steps at legal, moral or any other species of reform, must not go too fast nor too far at once, otherwise the old and the timid are left behind and keep back a large part of the masses with them."[18]

CHAPTER TWELVE

Spirit of Improvement

━━━►◆◄━━━

> For myself, I will not be found fighting to the water's edge to uphold the
> tottering fabrics of superannuated systems. I believe the legislature is only
> keeping pace with the spirit of improvement, which so signally characterizes
> the age. Conservatism in law, as in politics, may be carried too far.
>
> *The Bank of St. Mary's v. Mumford & Tyson* (1849)

Anticipating his speech to the South-Carolina Institute the following year, Lumpkin wrote with conviction in *Young and Calhoun v. Harrison and Harrison* (1849): "Civilization must advance; the improvements of society, diffusing plenty and prosperity, knowledge and refinement and morality all around, must not, cannot be restrained; public opinion has willed it, decreed it, and there is no higher power to which to appeal—*Vox Populi, vox Dei*." Expanding that concept globally in *Haywood v. the Mayor* (1853), he predicted: "Free Trade is destined to become the permanent and paramount policy of the world. And I rejoice it is so. It is the forerunner, as well as the fruit, of the rapidly advancing civilization of the nineteenth century. It is the adjunct and handmaiden of Christianity."[1]

As an evangelical Christian, Lumpkin believed that an important aspect of his judicial role was to aid the advance of civilization through reform, at least from a southern perspective. To achieve that goal, he incorporated into his jurisprudence what legal historians have called "legal instrumentalism." Kermit Hall defines that term as "a pragmatic and utilitarian view of the law" that "competed with an older conception of it as precedent-bound rules that judges applied mechanically." According to Hall, antebellum judges of the instrumentalist school "continued to declare rights based on law, but in the emerging market economy affirming the rights of one party and denying those of another often amounted to mediating between competing visions of economic progress."[2]

Because of Georgia's traditional agricultural economy, the supreme court often had to resolve disputes between the competing interests of landowners. For example, in *Conyers v. Kenans and Hand* (1848), Lumpkin construed the statute of limitations liberally, stating, "Public policy dictates that even waste lands should be immediately settled and rendered productive by cultivation, in order that the power and resources of the State should be fully developed." Yet in *Beverly and McBride v. Burke* (1851), showing his own farming background, he expressed a somewhat contradictory view: "No man in this country cultivates his whole tract of land. . . . Good husbandry forbids that the whole should be planted."[3]

Lumpkin's pragmatic approach to balancing economic interests was particularly evident in cases involving issues of eminent domain and public nuisance. As he wrote in *Water-Lot Company of Columbus v. Bucks and Winter* (1848), deciding whether to enjoin the operation of a mine required "balancing the question between these two parties, and the extent of the inconvenience likely to be incurred on one side or the other." A series of cases in the northern states during the 1830s and 1840s had extended the power of eminent domain to private corporations in order to achieve a public use or benefit. The same doctrine of public use that had been developed for the benefit of milling, bridge, and ferry companies was later applied by a number of state courts to aid in the expansion of the railroads. These pro-business principles were so well established by 1849 that Lumpkin could write confidently in *Young and Calhoun v. Harrison and Harrison*:

> Suppose all Georgia were congregated together, and it should be determined that the public good made it expedient and highly advantageous, to erect every public work which now exists, and which gives us such a proud pre-eminence among our Southern sisters, who doubts the power of the people to construct these railroads, canals and bridges, and to seize appropriate private property for that purpose, allowing to the owner, if his injury exceeded his share of the common advantage, to be compensated by a Jury? If this State could do this directly, what is there to prevent it being done by contract?[4]

Mygatt v. Goetchins, decided in 1858, dealt with the law of nuisance and required balancing the right of a business owner to operate a gin versus the personal and property interests of an individual residing near the factory. In a short opinion, Lumpkin concluded that "the contemplated structure, *prima facie*, will not be a nuisance. It will neither work hurt, discomfort or damage. The only sense it will offend, is that of hearing. And we know of no sound, however discordant, that may not, by habit, be converted into a lullaby, except the braying of an ass or the tongue of a scold. . . . But be this as it may, as well attempt to stop up the mouth of Vesuvius as to arrest the application of steam to machinery at this day."[5]

As the author of a recent study of Georgia's early negligence law observes, "Steam power raised the likelihood of accidental injury and property destruction and posed a difficult issue in public policy. . . . Both before and after the Civil War, economic growth meant developing a commercial agricultural economy through the construction of railroads. As a result, the crucial problem of accident law was the extent to which new devices, especially railroads, would be required to pay for the injuries they caused."[6] In one accident, a train hit a carriage at a railroad crossing, killing a slave and three white children while injuring the mother and another child. In *Macon & W. R. R. v. Winn* (1856), one of several cases resulting from the accident, the supreme court had to weigh the comparative negligence of the carriage driver and the railroad. In his opinion, Lumpkin wrote, "Shall it be said that the steam-car, on account of its uncontrollable speed and power, requires super-added care of its management? The fact is admitted; but this very circumstance should induce greater caution and circumspection in those who approach them. This is the dictate of prudence." He then concluded, "Courts must not permit themselves to be carried away by feeling in these cases, but endeavor to administer the law, firmly and fearlessly, in favor of, as well as against corporations. Our State is, unquestionably, mainly indebted to railroads, for the proud pre-eminence which she occupies in the Union."[7]

Despite his inclination to rule in favor of manufacturing and commercial enterprises in order to support economic development in Georgia, Lumpkin was not prepared to stray from common-law precedent when he did not have the weight of authority on his side. He concluded in *Wade v. Johnson* (1858) that the rule governing real-estate fixtures was well established in the principal manufacturing states: "Seeing [that] New York, Connecticut, and other Northern States, which have the largest amount of machinery in operation, have not been persuaded as to the wisdom of changing the common-law rule, we may well pause before taking the step." Lumpkin was clearly on the side of competition versus exclusive franchises, and in *Shorter v. Smith and the Justices* (1851) he disagreed with the eminent Chancellor Kent of New York in finding that the doctrine of implied monopoly rights "is at war with the universally recognized principles of American constitutional law, and totally inapplicable to our local situation and change of circumstances." In support of his decision, Lumpkin cited the U.S. Supreme Court decision in the *Charles River Bridge* case, noting Chief Justice Taney's dictum that "while the rights of private property are sacredly granted, we must not forget, that the community, also, have rights."[8]

In the view of Timothy Huebner, Lumpkin's opinion in *Shorter* "demonstrated all at once his commitment to a dynamic view of property, his belief in unfettered competition, and his emphasis on the public interest over vested rights." This same philosophy underlay his general support of corporate charters providing limited liability, so long as they contained "suitable provisions for the protection of the community against fraud, as well as . . . reckless speculation." In *Franklin Bridge Co. v. Youngwood* (1853) Lumpkin upheld statutes permitting self-incorporation to all but banking and insurance companies, noting that "corporations have become the usual and favorite mode of conducting the industrial pursuits of the civilized world in modern times." In *Hightower v. Thornton* (1850) he stated even more emphatically, "I am no enemy of corporations. On the contrary, I look upon them as *proof*, and in no small degree the *cause* of the unparalleled advancement of modern civilization." With such support from Lumpkin and his colleagues on the supreme court, business corporations became well established in Georgia by the 1850s.[9]

Of all the corporate sectors participating in the dynamic economic development of antebellum Georgia, none was more challenging for the court than the emerging banking business. The panic of 1837, the effects of which continued well into the 1840s, resulted in numerous cases involving debtor-creditor and banking issues. Lumpkin commented on the difficult economic conditions in the early case of *Whitehead v. Peck* (1846), noting that "the plea of usury was rare in the South prior to the late revulsion in money matters." He then added, "I am satisfied it has operated beneficially . . . in driving capital into internal improvements, agricultural, manufacturing and industrial pursuits. Still, I see no reason for singling out money lenders . . . as the greatest culprits in the community." Lumpkin's comments show his understanding of how important available credit was for Georgia, along with other southern and western states. Because of the lack of contracts, however, many lawsuits arose out of bank failures, including twenty-six cases arising out of the collapse of just one bank, the Planter's and Mechanic's Bank of Columbus. Lumpkin, who owned shares in several banks over the years, made it clear in *Hightower v. Thornton* (1850) that he was "a friend of banks . . . [and] a friend of the credit system," but he also noted that "there is no business so liable to be *overdone*, because none which holds out more tempting prospect to grow suddenly rich—none has been managed in a more reckless and improvident manner." Recalling "the losses to the country within a few years, by the failure of banks," he warned that "we feel it a most solemn duty to guard with vigilance those checks which are designed . . . to secure for paper money a substantial basis to rest upon."[10]

While bank failures affected a broad cross-section of Georgians, most members of the planter and professional class, including Lumpkin and his family, were prospering by 1850. However, poor farmers and artisans were increasingly excluded from the benefits of economic expansion, and as Lumpkin noted in his speech to the South-Carolina Institute, "Thousands are now idle, and thousands who are engaged exclusively in planting, must be employed, in whole or in part, in mechanism and manufactures." In his humanitarian view, poor whites in the South required not only improved educational and economic opportunities but also additional protection under the law. In *Lane v. Morris* Lumpkin supported statutes that made bank shareholders personally liable for every bill or note issued by the bank, observing that, among others, "laborers of every class are exposed to risk, and those generally are the greatest sufferers by a bank failure, who are least able to bear the loss."

He saw a need for stricter regulation of the growing number of mutual building and loan associations, which were being promoted as the "poor man's exchequer," in order to protect the interest of borrowers and investors. He also called for a change, albeit belatedly, in the harsh common-law rules, which continued to favor the rights of creditors over debtors in Georgia. As late as 1856, he acknowledged in *Mims v. Lockett*: "In view of our State Constitution, to say nothing of the strong tendency in the public mind to abolish entirely imprisonment for debt, it would seem that our insolvent laws were entitled to a more liberal construction in favor of debtors than heretofore received at the hands of the Court." Despite his concern for protecting the poor from the abuses of banks and other corporate wrongdoers, his Protestant ethic made him a strong believer in the need for hard work and self-reliance. Upholding a conviction for vagrancy in *Waddel v. State* (1859) he wrote, "I am quite satisfied that a large portion of the population of our towns could be convicted on stronger proof than this. It is time, perhaps, to give them a scare."[11]

While Lumpkin often dealt progressively with economic issues that affected the larger community, he was more conservative when cases involved family relationships. In *Vance v. Crawford* (1848) he stated his fundamental view that "*families* are the original of all societies and contain the foundation and primitive elements of all other social institutions." In his evangelical and paternalistic concept of families, parents were accountable for the children's acts, while husbands and fathers were responsible for and had control of their wives and children. Unwilling to reverse a jury award of only $50 in damages for a young girl who had run into the path of a dray, he preached in *Flanders v. Meath* (1859): "The conduct of children must be controlled; the failure to do this is the curse and ruin of this country." In *Kendrick v. McCrary* (1852) he upheld another jury's damage award of $1,049 on behalf of a father against the seducer of his daughter on the grounds that the daughter's value to her father as a servant had been diminished by the seduction. However, he went much further in *Biggs v. State*, ruling that it was justifiable homicide when a husband killed his wife's seducer, for "in what has society a deeper concern than in the protection of female purity, and the marriage relation?"[12]

According to Chancellor Kent, the rules governing the property rights and duties of married women ("femmes coverts" in old English legal terminology) were derived mainly from one key "principle of the common law, by which the husband and wife are regarded as one person, and her legal existence and authority in a degree lost or suspended, during the continuance of the matrimonial union." By midcentury, however, some improvements in the property rights of women were beginning to occur, led by reformers such as Timothy Walker, who wrote in 1849: "I can see neither policy, justice, nor humanity, in many legal doctrines respecting married women. They bear every mark of a barbarous origin."[13]

Lumpkin's evangelical and paternalistic philosophy, however, made it difficult for him to advocate changes in women's legal rights. For him, it was fundamental that "by the Common Law and by the Bible, which is the foundation

of the Common Law, the union of man and wife was a junction of persons and
fortunes." Nonetheless, by 1851 he was ready to acknowledge in *Wylly v. Collins*
that "this link which bound them in one bond, for better and for worse, has been
broken, and, in the progress of civilization, a new principle has been introduced
from the Roman Law, viewing husband and wife as distinct persons, with distinct property and distinct powers over it. Time will test the propriety of this
innovation." As early as 1847 he supported marriage settlements that allowed
married women to enjoy separate property and income. In *Blake v. Irwin* he
observed, "This is an age of enterprise, of bold, reckless speculation, of refinement and increasing luxury. There are cases of frequent occurrence, in which
it is the duty of an affectionate parent to place at least a portion of his means
beyond the control of his daughter's husband." Thirteen years later he still felt
it was necessary to explain in *Hobgood v. Martin* that "the doctrine of a wife's
equity to a settlement, as against her husband, his creditors and assignees, is
comparatively modern in Georgia. Its enforcement was unknown in practice
when I came to the bar. The case before us is another step in the right direction;
hence, we desire to see it established upon a firm foundation." It was not until
1866, however, that Georgia enacted a law changing a married woman's status
with respect to property rights, making her a "femme sole," capable of inheriting
and holding property in her own name. Under the same law, a husband did not
acquire any ownership right in property belonging to the wife before or after
marriage.[14]

Dealing with cases of separation and divorce troubled Lumpkin and his fellow
judges much more than resolving disputes over marital property rights. In the
first supreme court case dealing with divorce, *Head v. Head* (1847), Judge Nisbet
commented on the ease with which divorces were granted in Georgia at the time
and called on the "patriot, the Christian and the Moralist" to "look about him for
some device to stay this swelling tide of demoralization." Similarly, in *Chapman
v. Gray* (1850), decided shortly after the legislature adopted new divorce laws,
Lumpkin declared, "For myself, I am inclined to believe, that policy and morality, if not religion itself, stand opposed to these voluntary separations," but, he
wrote, "I feel that I am not at liberty to act upon my own opinion in the matter,
but that the rule is binding upon the Judiciary, as part of the Common Law of
the land." To buttress his decision, he added: "A married woman very seldom
abandons the most sacred of her duties, unless driven to it by necessity." His

commitment to the sanctity of marriage and protection of the weaker sex were no less strong ten years later when he condoned a Georgia marriage law because he felt it would save a woman's honor, explaining in *Askew v. Dupree* (1860) that "this is worth more than everything, even life itself. All other contracts may be rescinded, and the parties restored to their former condition; marriage cannot be undone."[15]

Occasionally, he was able to depart from his pious and moralistic views about marriage and women. When he was in an unusually cynical mood, he posed the question, in *Brown v. Westbrook* (1859), "Do mercenary marriages never take place, in this, our day and generation, except among the insane? Such a conclusion, I regret to say, would almost stultify our race. Love matches! They exist only in the creation of novelists. They are rarely known in actual life." In *Cason v. Cason* (1854) he recounted in a similar but more humorous vein: "Instead of 'sweet seventeen, with the bloom of a plum, unbroken, upon her cheek, and all the blossoms of youthful innocence, flowering and flourishing around her,' the testimony shows, that this much injured wife, was a buxom young widow . . . who allied herself to the defendant, a hoary and dilapidated octogenarian of eighty-four! Her own evidence shows . . . that in the only fight they ever had, *she fell on top*." In a very personal tone, he concluded, "We speak as an *old* man, and not as a judge. Our friend, the Major, has well stigmatized these meretricious marriages, as the conjunction of December and May. From such unnatural unions, domestic comfort and conjugal felicity need not be expected. And eloquence bestowed on such family broils, is mere *Arcadian fancy*—painting from the scenes of one's early reading."[16]

When cases involved women who were victims of sexual offenses, Lumpkin usually relied on Victorian terms such as "chastity," "dishonor," and "debauched" in composing his decisions, but he was capable of using surprisingly explicit language, if necessary, to make his point. For example, in the case of *Smith v. State* (1857), where a man had been convicted of "incestuous bastardy," he first explained that a charge of rape was no longer nullified by pregnancy, as had once been the rule in England; instead, it was then recognized that "impregnation may take place where there is great repugnancy on the part of the female, amounting even to a virtuous recoil or a sense of honor at the time." Confessing that "we shall probably never know what is necessary to cause conception," he was still "willing to concede that the law of constitutional orgasm or the excitation of the sexual passion may be such that females may conceive without their knowledge, while under the influence of narcotics, intoxication or asphyxia, or even while asleep." He concluded, "Still we apprehend the case is rare where a virgin has been begotten with child," quoting from the trial testimony for emphasis that it had occurred on "the coldest day of the winter," "with snow on the ground," "in a room without fire," and "when there was only a single *coitus*, seated in the lap of her ravisher or seducer, with her back to him . . . yet, such is the mode and manner of the illicit intercourse which took place between Miss Sears and her uncle, as sworn to by herself."[17]

Although Lumpkin must have enjoyed including some wit and spice in his decisions from time to time, he was much more likely to embellish his opinions with classical allusions and biblical references. In *Boon v. State* (1846) he discussed the ideal of impartiality in a jury but acknowledged, "for jurors to come into the box without any impression, with minds as pure as the unsoiled snow on the virgin lap of Diana, such a jury could not be obtained unless it was to fall directly from heaven." Praising the Judiciary Act of 1799 as the "forerunner and model of all Law Reform," he said effusively in *Van Buren v. Webster* (1853), "As Minerva, the Goddess of Wisdom, was generated full grown, from the brain of Jupiter, so I revere this statute as the embodiment and personification of judicial perfection." The memorials he wrote for deceased lawyers and judges were often fertile ground for his classicisms, as in his tribute to John Berrien: "We shall no more listen to the silvery eloquence of those lips, 'upon which the bees of Hybla might have rested.'"[18]

"There is scarcely a book from the entire Bible from which he has not drawn illustration or authority," one of Lumpkin's admirers wrote. In *Dean v. Traylor* (1850), in which a slave mother and her children were found after their sale to be suffering from tuberculosis, Lumpkin held that the jury had erred in awarding damages to the buyer with respect to the children. After discussing conflicting medical theories about hereditary diseases, he concluded, "I deem it altogether useless to spend more time in establishing physiological fact, which appears to have passed into a proverb among the Jews. . . . 'The fathers have eaten sour grapes, and the children's teeth are set on edge.'" Affirming a judgment of slander in favor of a woman in *Richardson v. Roberts* (1857) he recalled, "The SAVIOUR of the world, who said to one taken in adultery, 'go and sin no more,' would have covered her fault with a mantle of his silence." With equal solemnity, he stated in the *Flint River Steamboat* case (1848) that "even God himself did not pass sentence upon Adam before he was called on to make his defense." Despite his frequent use of biblical references to buttress his opinions, he stated clearly in *Neal v. Crew* (1852): "I would not intermeddle with the natural and indispensable right of all men, to worship God, or not, according to the dictates of their own consciences. The State should compel no one to erect, attend or support a place of public worship or maintain any ministry against his consent." [19]

As indicated by only a small sample of his opinions, Lumpkin was an intelligent and complex individual with wide-ranging interests, who frequently had to reconcile his fundamental religious and cultural values with his commitment to many social and economic reforms. Along with Marshall, Gibson, and others in Pound's judicial pantheon, Lumpkin was a representative of the "Grand Style" of judicial decision-making, which Karl Llewellyn defined as "a functioning harmonization of vision with tradition, of continuity with growth." In a thoughtful summary of his judicial career, Timothy Huebner wrote recently: "In short, Lumpkin's conception of law and the economy was dynamic. His adherence to market principles in determining the use and value of property promoted development, while his Taney-like repudiation of exclusive rights upheld the interest of the community and furthered technological progress. Underlying Lumpkin's decisions were deeply held values: a firm belief in the moral advantages of economic advancement and confident assurance that only a competitive environment would serve the public interest." [20]

CHAPTER THIRTEEN

From Slavery to Secession

⟹•◆•⟸

> Lumpkin's evangelical moral sense caused him to view the issues of slave-
> holding and southern independence in stark, uncompromising terms. Ulti-
> mately convinced of the social benefits of slavery, Lumpkin viewed an inde-
> pendent southern nation as a morally superior civilization blessed by God.
> As a judge and a reformer, Lumpkin did his best to make this vision a reality.
>
> TIMOTHY S. HUEBNER, *The Southern Judicial Tradition*

Although Joseph Henry Lumpkin was not selected by Roscoe Pound as one of
the ten greatest judges of the antebellum era, his slavery opinions have probably
received more attention from legal scholars and historians in the past thirty years
than any other southern jurist, with the possible exception of Thomas Ruffin.
He did not attract such academic interest because of a lack of other candidates,
as there were nearly two hundred judges on the southern state appellate courts
during the antebellum period, according to one scholar's count. Included in
that number were such distinguished judges as Spencer Roane of Virginia and
Thomas Ruffin of North Carolina (both on Pound's list), John O'Neall of South
Carolina, John Catron of Tennessee, and John Hemphill of Texas. There are
undoubtedly many reasons why Lumpkin's slavery opinions have generated
so much interest, but for one legal historian, John Philip Reid, "Lumpkin is
especially interesting because his perception of best policy changed over the
years, and he recorded this change in his opinions." Moreover, Reid found that
"Lumpkin and his colleagues were remarkably frank. There was no hypocrisy
in their arguments; they favored slavery and they said so."[1]

Paul Finkelman, one of the leading writers on the legal history of slavery, described Lumpkin as an "important southern judge" while praising Reid for his
"superb analysis of Lumpkin's decisions relating to the political issues of slavery
and secession." However, not everyone has viewed Lumpkin and his colleagues

on the Georgia Supreme Court with such equanimity. One writer called him "the most polemical of southern judges," while another wrote that "the Georgia supreme court, from its creation in 1845, had the solitary distinction of being the only continuously pro-slavery, 'fire-eating' state supreme court."[2]

A comprehensive analysis of Lumpkin's slavery opinions is contained in a law-review article by Mason W. Stephenson and D. Grier Stephenson entitled " 'To Protect and Defend': Joseph Henry Lumpkin, the Supreme Court of Georgia, and Slavery." The central thesis of this article, according to the authors, is that "the Georgia Supreme Court while under the dominance of Justice Lumpkin was not a neutral forum which heard disputes and applied even-handed justice in the factual and legal situations presented, but was an active arm of government, committed to the preservation of the slave system. In effect, Lumpkin's personal beliefs and attitudes were a positive force in the resolution of disputed issues, thus contributing to the development of his court as one of policy, not merely one of law." In a more recent article, Reid strongly criticized this statement, contending, "The Supreme Court of Georgia was an active arm of government; all courts are." "Lumpkin, who believed that he was applying neutral standards and not personal predilections," Reid added, "understood the state's public policy in the matter of slavery and did not hesitate to explain, expound, or promulgate it."[3]

From 1846 through 1866, 330 of the nearly 3,800 Georgia Supreme Court cases involved some aspect of slavery, as recorded in the comprehensive research study, *Judicial Cases Concerning American Slavery and the Negro*. Approximately 60 of these cases dealt with important issues affecting the legal status of slaves and slavery, and it is significant that Lumpkin authored more than half of those opinions. In assigning himself a disproportionate share of such key opinions, he was clearly deviating from his normal practice of evenly dividing the caseload among the three members of the court. This change in his policy could have been motivated by many factors, including a recognition of the greater expertise in slavery law he had gained from his long continuity on the court, but it certainly indicates that he had a strong interest in shaping Georgia's law as well as its public policy on slavery issues.[4]

There was no uniform law of slavery among the southern states. Instead, as one scholar wrote recently, "There were many incompatible *laws* of slavery, which can be understood only through close attention to the biographies of individual lawmakers and the socioeconomic and political forces at work in individual jurisdictions." That insight might well have been drawn directly from Lumpkin's opinion in an 1853 case (*Bryan v. Walton*), in which he noted that "the condition of the African race is different in every slave State; and is less favorable in the extreme Southern, than in the more Northern slave States; and that consequently, whenever a question is made relative to a free person of color, we must have recourse to our own local laws, to find a rule for our determination, and to such principles as are dictated by the peculiar genius of our people, and policy of our institutions."[5]

Lumpkin's duties on the supreme court kept him from playing an active role in state and national politics, but his comments in *Bryan v. Walton* make it clear that he intended to keep the court's decisions on slavery issues in tune with the political climate of Georgia. Because of his earlier statements at Boston in favor of emancipation, he may also have felt a need to demonstrate how solid his support for the institution of slavery had become, both personally and in his judicial capacity. In January of 1848 he wrote to Howell Cobb, who was then a leader of the Georgia delegation in Congress, expressing great concern about the attempts in Congress to pass the Wilmot Proviso, which was intended by its supporters to prohibit slavery in any territory acquired during the war with Mexico. He told Cobb,

> I never for the moment believed that the North would take the responsibility of dissolving the American Union upon a *false issue*, even when slavery was the subject. And I believe at this very moment that the institution stands upon a firmer basis than it ever has since the formation of the Republic. Had the Abolitionists let us alone we should have been guilty, I verily believe, of political and social suicide by emancipating the African race, a measure fatal to them, ourselves, and to the best interests of the Confederacy and of the whole world. The violent assaults of these fiends have compelled us in self defense to investigate this momentous subject in all its bearings, and the result has been a firm and settled conviction that duty to the slave as well as to the master forbids the relation should be disturbed.[6]

The debates in Washington over the Wilmot Proviso had escalated into a serious sectional conflict by November of 1849 when the Georgia legislature convened in Milledgeville. At the start of the session, Governor George Towns advocated that Georgia take a strong stand against the northern antislavery movement while also calling for improvements in local slavery laws. When Lumpkin delivered his report on law reform in late 1849 he included some strongly worded proposals to guide the legislators in making slavery law changes, advising:

> In the present state of the union and of the world, the law of slavery should undergo the most thorough examination, and its various details and provisions, be made to conform to the exigencies of the times. If duty to ourselves, as well as our slaves require increased severity, by way of security, let it be imposed, regardless of the hypocritical cant and clamor of the fanatics of our own and other countries. If on the other hand, it shall be found that existing enactments may be relaxed or ameliorated, without prejudice to our safety or rights of property, let us not be deterred from doing what is right and just, as Christian masters.[7]

Hiram Warner, one of Lumpkin's initial associates on the supreme court, was as concerned as Lumpkin that the Wilmot Proviso threatened the rights of Georgia and other slave states. In his letter of January 21, 1848, to Howell Cobb, Lumpkin wrote, "Even Judge Warner, Massachusetts man as he is, declared to me a few days since that dearly as he is attached to the Union, he would not hesitate a moment to advocate dissolution should the principle of the Wilmot Proviso be engrafted upon our system." Lumpkin's own commitment to states' rights dated back to his years in the Georgia legislature when he supported Governor Troup in the state's fight with the federal government over the Creek Indian lands. It is, therefore, not surprising to read in a letter written in July of 1850 by his nephew, John Henry Lumpkin, to Howell Cobb (his political mentor) that "prominent individuals I have met with are in favor of a dissolution of the Union *per se* (as I understand uncle Jos. H. Lumpkin has written to you he is)."[8]

Of Lumpkin's early supreme court colleagues, there was no more ardent proponent of secession than Henry L. Benning, who joined the court in 1853. In 1849, while he was still a young lawyer in Columbus, Benning was one of the leaders of a group advocating not only secession but also establishment of a southern confederacy. At a convention of slaveholding states held in Nashville in June of 1850, a number of Benning's radical resolutions were adopted, including one directly opposed to the Wilmot Proviso. However, the secessionist movement in Georgia was overcome at that point by growing support for the compromise proposed by Henry Clay, which included amendments to tighten enforcement of the Fugitive Slave Act. Resolutions approved at a convention in December of 1850, which became known as the "Georgia Platform," declared that Georgia would abide by the compromise so long as none of the platform's conditions was violated. Just as he had sided in the early 1830s with his brother Wilson and the Unionists to oppose Nullification, Lumpkin chose this time to support the compromise rather than side with the old Whigs or new Southern Rights party. In February of 1851, he wrote to Howell Cobb, urging him to lead the compromise cause in the upcoming elections; Lumpkin assured him, "You can be Governor, if you desire it." Cobb and his fellow candidates of the new Constitutional Union party decisively defeated their Southern Rights opponents, including Henry Benning, who was running for Congress. In the view of one historian, "The decision of Georgia to hold to the Union in 1850 was one of the outstanding events of the national crisis of that year. This decision was indeed a cardinal factor in the salvation of the Union then, and perhaps later, in that it gave check to both the northern and southern extremists."[9]

Although by 1850 Lumpkin was ready to back compromise rather than secession, he had also by then become a staunch supporter of slavery, because of his conviction that the institution was divinely sanctioned. In his law reform report to the Georgia legislature, he warned, with Old Testament rhetoric: "The conscience of the whole South, after having been thoroughly aroused, to the most earnest and intense investigation of the subject by the merciless and unremitting assaults of our relentless foes, has become thoroughly satisfied, that this institution—like government itself—is of God. That being recognized and regulated by the Decalogue, it will, we have every reason to believe, be of perpetual duration. That it subserves the best interests of both races, and that we will preserve and defend it at any and all hazards." Lumpkin's associate, Judge Eugenius Nisbet, who was also known as a devout Christian, shared his conviction that there was a biblical justification for slavery. In *Neal v. Farmer* (1851) Nisbet contended, "Christ . . . recognizing the relation of master and servant . . . ordained it an *institution of christianity*. It is the crowning glory of this age and this land, that our legislation has responded to the requirements of the New Testament in great part, and if left alone, the time is not distant, when we, the slaveholders, will come fully up to our obligations as such, under the christian dispensation."[10]

These and other "Christian" slavery beliefs are explored by Eugene Genovese in his recent book, *A Consuming Fire*. Genovese argues, "For pro-slavery spokesmen, 'Christian' slavery offered the South—indeed, the world—the best hope for the preparation for the kingdom, but they acknowledged that, from a Christian point of view, the slavery practiced in the South left much to be desired. For them, the struggle to reform or, rather, transform social relations was nothing less than a struggle to justify the trust God placed in them when he sanctioned slavery." Lumpkin's participation in that struggle is well documented in a number of his slavery opinions. One of the best examples is his decision in *Scudder v. Woodbridge* (1846), the first case in a slave state to determine whether the "fellow servant rule" should be applied to slaves. That rule, which had been established by Chief Justice Shaw of Massachusetts in the landmark case *Farwell v. Boston & Worcester Railroad* (1842), held that industrial workers assumed the risks incident to their employment. In deciding not to follow the rule in *Farwell*, Lumpkin made it clear that the "restriction of this rule is indispensable to the welfare of the slave." He conceded that the general doctrine "may be correct" as it was laid down in *Story on Agency* and applied by the courts of South Carolina, Massachusetts, and New York. However, he concluded that "interest to the owner and humanity to the slave, forbid its application to any other than *free white agents*," explaining that "a large portion of the employees at the South are either slaves or free persons of color, wholly irresponsible, *civiliter*, for their neglect or malfeasance."[11]

The fellow-servant rule was not directly involved in the subsequent case of *Gorman v. Campbell* (1853), in which the death of a hired slave was attributed to the negligence of a steamboat captain, but Lumpkin reached a similar conclusion in favor of the owner. He decided that "humanity to the slave as well as a proper regard for the interests of the owner, alike demand that the rules of law regulating this contract should not be relaxed." The wording of this opinion has generated controversy among some legal historians. Paul Finkelman observes that what "Lumpkin meant by 'humanity to the slave' was unclear," but he disagrees with another historian, Mark Tushnet, who, he says, "appears to overstate the case in asserting that 'the rule adopted in *Gorman* can be justified in the end only because humanity demands it.' " That same phrase, "humanity to the slave," has been cited by one critic as an example of "the judicial muddle-headedness of Judge Lumpkin" as well as a "rationale for the greatest barbarism, not to mention the greatest economic incoherence."

In contrast to the ambiguous reasoning for which Lumpkin is criticized, the language of Judge Ruffin in the North Carolina case *State v. Mann* (1829) has been noted by legal scholars as an example of a clear, albeit cold-blooded, state-ment of the legal and economic realities of slavery. Deciding that an owner was not culpable in wounding his disobedient slave, Ruffin wrote, "With slavery . . . [t]he end is the profit of the master, his security and the public safety; the subject, one doomed in his own person, and his posterity, to live without knowledge and without the capacity to make things his own, and to toil that another may reap the fruits . . . The power of the master must be absolute, to render the submission of the slave perfect." It is likely that one reason Ruffin is held in such high esteem is because of this honest statement in *State v. Mann*: "I most freely confess my sense of the harshness of this proposition, I feel it as deeply as any man can. And as a principle of moral right, every person in his retirement must repudiate it. But in the actual condition of things, it must be so. There is no remedy. The discipline belongs to the state of slavery."[12]

In the 1860 case of *Johnson v. Lovett*, Lumpkin allowed that "when insults are given personally by a slave, it is right to punish instantly," but he went on to criticize the defendant for inflicting a beating on a slave which "both as to its extent and the mode of inflicting, is alike revolting to the feelings of decency and humanity." Although the defendant in that case was neither the owner nor the employer, Lumpkin indicated that he was not willing to concede that whites held absolute power over slaves. However, there was only a fine line in his mind between absolute and conditional dominion, as shown in the 1855 case *Moran v. Davis*, in which a runaway slave drowned while being pursued by trackers and their dogs. Interpreting the Georgia statutes, Lumpkin held that "if a capture of the slave could not be accomplished but by the use of dogs . . . a pursuit in this mode would be justifiable, provided it were made with such dogs as would not lacerate or otherwise materially injure the slave." As if he needed a higher authority to confirm his decision, he ended the opinion by exhorting his fellow southerners "willingly or otherwise, to redouble our vigilance and to tighten the chords that bind the negro to his condition of servitude—a condition which is to last, if the Apocalypse be inspired, until the end of time."[13]

In his law reform report to the legislature, Lumpkin had based his case for the "perpetual duration" of Negro slavery on the Old Testament, and in *Moran v. Davis* he pointed to wording in the New Testament Book of Revelation as additional proof that the institution would last until the end of time. He shared these convictions with many southern Presbyterians, who have been described by Jack Maddex as "postmillennialists" because they believed that "Christianity was improving the world as well as saving souls. . . . Its advance would gradually usher in the thousand happy years which would prepare humanity for Christ's subsequent return." Maddex also explained that for postmillennialists the words of Revelation provided proof to northerners and southerners alike that the system of slavery was neither sinful nor temporary.[14]

Lumpkin was joined in these evangelical Christian beliefs by his son-in-law Thomas Cobb, whose work on the history and law of slavery was published in 1858 to widespread acclaim. Even if Lumpkin was too busy to read the manuscript, as Cobb's biographer contends, the book, which Cobb dedicated to his father-in-law, undoubtedly reflected their many discussions on the subject. At the opening of the first part of the book, titled "Historical Sketch of Slavery," Cobb traced the origins of slavery "at least to the deluge." Then, referring to Noah's curse that his youngest son would become a "servant of servants," he noted that "in the opinion of many the curse of Ham is now being executed upon his descendants, in the enslavement of the negro race."[15]

Many white southerners during the antebellum period subscribed to what Eugene Genovese calls the ideology of the "Noahic curse and the black descent from Ham." In the 1849 case *Giles v. State*, Lumpkin mentioned in his opinion, without relevance to the decision, that, because Ham had mocked Noah for his drunkenness, "he and his descendants, to the present generation, have been deservedly punished for this contempt of his father." Eugenius Nisbet, writing for the court in *Neal v. Farmer* two years later, stated more optimistically: "The curse of the Patriarch rests still upon the descendants of Ham. The negro and his master are but fulfilling a divine appointment. Christ came not to remove the curse; but recognizing the relation of master and servant, he prescribed the rules which govern, and the obligations which grow out of it, and thus ordained it an *institution of christianity*." Lumpkin took up the theme again in *Bryan v. Walton* (1853), in which, indulging his taste for both classical and biblical references, he declared with more venom that "the social and civil degradation, resulting from the taint of blood, adheres to the descendants of Ham in this country like the poisoned tunic of Nessus."[16]

Shortly after authoring that opinion, he wrote his daughter Callie that he had "just finished reading a most interesting Book—a work on negro slavery—by a man named Priest. . . . I took it up to aid me in writing out my opinion on the status or condition of a free negro in Georgia. . . . It should be in the house and hands of every southern slave holder. It agrees with and fully confirms all my previous notions as to the Bible doctrine of slavery. Which in short are neither more nor less than this—that the tribe of Ham are cursed. That they are judicially condemned to perpetual bondage." It is curious that this tract, which was written in 1843 by a New York harness maker, Josiah Priest, made such a favorable impression on Lumpkin. Priest was one of a number of pro-slavery writers who argued the case for divine sanction of the enslavement of blacks while also popularizing racist stereotypes of black behavior. Priest asserted in his book that the word Ham in Hebrew meant "dark, hot and black" and signified, among other uncivilized tendencies, "beastly lusts, and lasciviousness," speculating even that Ham was guilty of incest with his mother. Indicating the effectiveness of these arguments, Lumpkin told Callie in his letter that Priest had proved to him "incontestably" that Jezebel, one of the most notorious Old Testament characters, was "a negro wench with a black skin and wooly head." Cobb echoed this theme in his "Historical Sketch of Slavery" when he noted that "an evil attributed to slavery, and frequently alluded to, is the want of chastity in female slaves."[17]

In *Mayor v. Howard* (1849) Lumpkin combined both racist and paternalistic arguments in concluding, "The want of discretion in our slave population is notorious. They need a higher degree of intelligence than their own, not only to direct their labor, but likewise to protect them from the consequences of their own improvidence." However, he rejected claims of some southerners that blacks did not belong to the Christian human family, affirming in *Cleland v. Waters* (1855), "True, slaves are property—*chattels*, if you please; still they are rational and intelligent beings. Christianity considers them such, and our municipal law, in many of its wise and humane provisions, has elevated them far above the level of the brute."

Consistent with that statement, he ruled in *Bailey v. Barnelly* (1857) that the business records of a black artisan were admissible in evidence, or otherwise they "would not be able to collect their accounts—a startling proclamation to make to the country." Cobb stated in his book that the mental development of the slave population "has advanced very considerably" and that "they are frequently exemplary Christians." Yet he contended, nonetheless, "The great Architect had framed them both physically and mentally to fill the sphere in which they were thrown, and His wisdom and mercy combined in constituting them thus suited to the degraded position they were destined to occupy. Hence, their submissiveness, their obedience, and their contentment." As submissive dependents, slaves then fit into what Cobb described as "a patriarchal, social system. The master is the head of his family. Next to his wife and children, he cares for his slaves. He avenges their injuries, protects their persons, provides for their wants, and guides their labors. In return, he is revered and held as protector and master."[18]

It was to those masters and hirers who were not "protectors" that Lumpkin addressed his repeated calls for "humanity to the slaves." While not denying that he was appealing to benevolent as well as racist and paternalistic motivations among his fellow Georgians, some historians, like Finkelman, have concluded that, primarily, "Lumpkin was concerned about the life and death of slaves because they were valuable property." There is no doubt that economic factors were important in many of his slavery decisions. In *Moran v. Davis* (1853), dealing with the question of whether it was lawful to track runaway slaves with dogs, he noted, "The South has lost, already, upwards of 60,000 slaves, worth between 25 and 30 millions of dollars," and in *Cleland v. Waters* (1855) he acknowledged that "slaves constitute a portion of the vested wealth and taxable property of the State; that without them, a large portion of our most productive lands would be worthless." While his slavery opinions certainly reflected his sense of the prevailing social and economic imperatives, it is unlikely that he intentionally favored the interests of slaveowners over those of hirers, as some have argued. Two of his decisions that have been cited as evidence of his favoring owners are *Latimer v. Alexander* (1853), in which he ruled that a slave's medical expenses should be imposed on the hirer, and *Lennard v. Boynton* (1852), in which he decided that rent should not be abated where a hired slave died before the end of the term, even through no fault of the hirer. He acknowledged in *Brooks v. Smith* (1857) that the result in *Lennard* was so unpopular that "hirers, who constitute a large class, especially in towns, cried out against the decision." Because it would have been known that he was the owner of a small number of slaves, he even commented in *Brooks*: "I have no interest in this class of contracts, either individually or representatively."[19]

Initially, small-business owners and artisans were the principal employers of hired slaves, but industries (particularly steamboats and railroads) and

municipalities were increasingly in the market to hire slaves for construction
and other projects. It has also been suggested that Lumpkin's decision in *Scudder* shows that he was less willing to support the interests of industrialists over
slaveowners than Thomas Ruffin, who was the only southern judge to apply the
fellow-servant precedent of *Farwell* to slaves. However, Lumpkin's speech to
the South-Carolina Institute in 1850 clearly demonstrated his strong commitment to the cause of industrialization. David Langum has suggested that these
decisions can be understood by applying Lawrence Friedman's instrumentalist
explanation of legal development, which, Langum noted, "has moved far beyond economic analysis. The historian is urged to look to the people with the
power and their demands and not simply to their objective economic interests."
From that perspective, it is apparent that Lumpkin's primary consideration was
not the competing economic interests of owners versus hirers or planters versus industrialists but rather the broader strategic objective of finding the best
way to preserve the institution of slavery. As Lumpkin explained in *Lennard
v. Boynton* (1852), "Humanity to this dependent and subordinate class of our
population requires, that we should remove from the hirer or temporary owner
all temptation to neglect them in sickness, or expose them to situations of unusual peril and jeopardy. . . . Every safeguard, consistent with the stability of
the institution of slavery, should be thrown around the lives of these people. For
myself, I verily believe, that the best security for the permanence of slavery, is
adequate and ample protection to the slave, at our own hands."[20]

As the decade of the 1850s progressed, Lumpkin's opinions expressed increasing concern about the threats to slavery both from within and outside the
system. In the 1848 case *Vance v. Crawford* he had written of the "impropriety
of tolerating domestic manumission," which, he believed, "cannot fail greatly to
corrupt the other slaves of the country, and to render them dissatisfied with the
condition of their servitude." Five years later, in *Bryan v. Walton*, he expressed
doubt about "ejecting our free negroes upon the free states. They will not only
become troublesome allies in the unconstitutional and unholy work of inveigling
off our slaves, and assisting them to escape; but their constant effort and aim will
be to create discontent among our slaves; and in case of intestine war, which may
Heaven in its mercy avert, such a population would be in a situation to do us
much mischief." By 1855, even though Georgia law still permitted foreign manumission, Lumpkin reported in *Cleland v. Waters* that he had become "fully

persuaded that the best interests of the slave, as well as a stern public policy, resulting from the whole frame-work of our social system, imperatively demand that all *post mortem* manumission of slaves should be absolutely and entirely prohibited." One reason he gave for his change of mind was that there were "in our midst large gangs of slaves who expected emancipation by will of their owners" and who were "likely to sow the seeds of insubordination, perhaps of revolt, amongst the slaves in their neighborhood."[21]

He acknowledged another change of mind in the 1857 case *American Colonization Society v. Gartrell*, when he decided against the society and stated forcefully, "I was once a friend . . . of this enterprise. I now regard it as a failure." Then, showing the level of his frustration, he went on in that opinion to ridicule the "women and old men, and persons of weak and infirm minds" who believed that "slavery is sinful, and that they will peril their souls if they do not disinherit their offspring by emancipating their slaves." In the 1858 case *Sanders v. Ward*, he called once again on the legislature to prohibit all post-mortem manumission of slaves, reiterating his concern about "colonization of our negroes upon our northwestern frontier. . . . In case of civil war, they would become an element of strength to the enemy." Finally, in 1859 the legislature heeded Lumpkin's advice and changed the law.[22]

Despite the references in *Sanders* to the possibility of a "civil war" where freed slaves might support the "enemy," Lumpkin's slavery opinions are remarkably free of inflammatory comments about the northern states and their growing conflict with the South. Even when he referred to a Massachusetts decision that freed slaves in transit as a "fungus . . . engrafted upon their Codes by the foul and fell spirit of modern fanaticism," he went on to note that "the Legislatures of many of the free States passed laws securing to citizens of the slave States, who came within their territories, upon business or pleasure, and brought slaves with them, means and facilities to take those slaves back to their domicil." Lumpkin believed that he could legitimately use his judicial position to influence public policy on slavery issues, but despite his personal conviction that the South should withdraw from the Union, he was not prepared to lead the court further onto the secessionist battlefield.[23]

CHAPTER FOURTEEN

A Flaming Sword

> Manumission is not only a *two-edged* sword, but like the flaming sword
> placed at the East of the garden of Eden, at Adam's expulsion, *turning every*
> *way* towards the community.
>
> *Riley v. Martin* (1866)

Despite occasional periods of poor health, Lumpkin's energy reached a peak
during 1859 and 1860, just as he turned sixty. The supreme court heard appeals
in 733 cases in those two years, and he authored 271 of the opinions, almost as
many as he had written in his first six years on the court. He also had to assume
a greater workload when three judges left the court in a period of fifteen months.
The first to go was Judge McDonald, who resigned in May of 1859 because of
failing health. His successor, Linton Stephens, who was only age thirty-five at
the time, had graduated at the head of his class from the law school at the University of Virginia and then studied under Judge Joseph Story at Harvard Law
School. While less successful in politics than his older half-brother, Alexander
H. Stephens, a future vice president of the Confederacy, Linton Stephens had
served in both houses of the Georgia legislature and had built a successful law
practice prior to joining the court. Writing his brother about his appointment
to the court by Governor Joseph Brown, Linton Stephens noted, "Tom Cobb
was greatly pleased by it. This rather confirms me in what I told you about Tom
Cobb's having a hand in it. . . . I think it will be particularly acceptable to Judge
Lumpkin. I have heard of his saying more than once, in the most unqualified
terms, that I had the best legal mind in Georgia."[1]

Even though they were nearly twenty-five years apart in age, it appears that
a close bond developed quickly between Lumpkin and the younger Stephens.
In one letter he told his brother of taking breaks from court sessions to swim
in a spring-fed pond outside of Macon where "Judge Lumpkin . . . went into

the water, but didn't swim, for he knew not how. The company had some sport out of my efforts to teach him. He went into the frolic with the spirit of a boy." In another letter he gave a witty description of how Lumpkin, who had been distracted by a surprise visit from his wife and one of his sons, apologized in the courtroom for the desultory manner in which he delivered an opinion, explaining that "circumstances beyond his control broke in upon him." Stephens went on to recount how at supper that evening he had "told Mrs. Lumpkin, who had sat right opposite me at the supper-table, that she ought to haul the Judge 'over the coals . . . because he had called her a *circumstance*.' The Judge's reply to me was 'Ain't you ashamed to report me so? I said nothing about a *circumstance*; I said *circumstances*.' 'So you did,' said I; 'but . . . as I knew nothing had broken in upon you except your wife and your son, I took Mrs. Lumpkin to be one *circumstance* and Miller another.' "[2]

These moments of fun and fellowship for the two judges ended soon thereafter when Linton Stephens resigned from the court after only fifteen months of service, ostensibly because of poor health. In a letter dated July 23, 1860, he told his brother, Alexander: "The place has worn me out. I should like it if I could be the *sole* judge, but I do not relish a divided sceptre." He seemed relieved when he reported to his brother that "Judge Lumpkin . . . had not a word to say in opposition" to his resignation.[3]

When Henry Benning failed to be reelected to a second term in November of 1859, his seat on the court was filled by Richard F. Lyon, an able and industrious attorney who was then age fifty-two and had once been a law student of Lumpkin. The third addition to the court in this fifteen-month period was Charles J. Jenkins, successor to Linton Stephens. At age fifty-five, Jenkins had enjoyed a generally successful career in state politics, although he had narrowly lost the race for governor in 1853. The personnel changes on the court created substantial administrative work for Lumpkin in his capacity as presiding judge, in addition to his assuming a higher than usual share of the opinion writing.

At the same time, he was actively involved in establishing the new law school at the University of Georgia. As recorded in the trustees' minutes of August 4 and November 3, 1859, the board approved a plan to enlarge the university by establishing several new "University Schools, each independent of each other, and also of the College proper, so far as such schools can be made self-sustaining." The first of these was to be a "Law School with three professors . . . in which facilities for the best legal education shall be offered." Specifically, the trustees committed to dedicate one story of a new fire-proof three-story building to lecture rooms for the law school and other university schools. The minutes also note, "The Law School will probably be furnished with the use of Judge Lumpkin's and Mr. T. R. R. Cobb's valuable libraries, and this part of the University will be self-sustaining."[4]

The board also approved awarding the "Degree of Bachelor of Law, to all Law Students, who have attended the lectures of the professors and secured their approbation." To provide a further attraction to prospective students, the trustees agreed to propose legislation that would admit graduates of the law school to practice before any superior court or the supreme court "by the presentation of the Diploma, without examination, upon payment of the usual fee." That legislation, which officially chartered the institution as the Lumpkin Law School, was not passed by the Georgia General Assembly until December 19, 1859, but the law school opened for classes on October 1 of that year. For Lumpkin, it was the fulfillment of a plan he had begun in the early 1840s when he briefly held a professorship of law at the university but was unable to continue because of his duties with the newly established supreme court.

The announcement of the law school's opening stated: "Our object shall be, as far as in us lies, to teach law, not as a collection of arbitrary rules, but as a collected logical system, founded on principles, which appeal for their sanction to eternal truth. We shall endeavor to train and develop those faculties that make up what we call a 'legal mind,' and so send out our pupils, prepared to apply to every case as it arises, the test of controlling principles, which power, as we all know, is what makes the true lawyer, as distinguished from the mere legal quibbler."[5]

The prospectus describing the law school disclosed that Thomas Cobb and William Hope Hull, the two other co-founders and lecturers, would be in regular attendance, but "Judge Lumpkin will give to the School such attention as is in his power, consistent with the duties of his judicial position." The fourteen original students had a daily regimen of three lectures as well as weekly moot court competitions. One of the early students recalled in his memoirs that "Judge Joseph Henry Lumpkin . . . once a week gave the Senior Class, of which I was a member, lectures on the Constitution of the United States. The Judge was a strong Secessionist, and delighted and enthused our young hearts with his word pictures of the glorious South, cut loose from the Union, with Cotton as King and free trade with the world."[6]

There is no evidence from the letters of Lumpkin or other sources to confirm if and when he became a "strong secessionist." However, it is likely that his views remained closely aligned with Thomas Cobb's as they had on many issues over the years. Cobb appears to have finally embraced secession when he wrote his wife in October of 1860 about the "Black Republicans," saying, "I can see no earthly hope of defeating them in November, and their success then, whether we will it or not, is inevitable disunion. . . . Separation is desirable, peaceably if we can, forcibly if we must." While Lumpkin may have shared his secessionist views with his law students, he seldom referred to the growing sectional crisis in his supreme court opinions. However, in *Choice v. State*, decided in August of 1860, he denounced the "moral insanity doctrine" as "an offshoot from that upas of humanism, which has so pervaded and poisoned the northern mind of this country, and which, I fear, will cause the glorious sun of our union to sink soon in the sea of fratricidal blood." At the same August session, he wrote an opinion in *McGinnis v. State* dealing with a Georgian who had killed one of a group of South Carolinians in a fight. Rather than treat the incident as just part of the longstanding rivalry between residents of the neighboring states, he chose to view it in a broader context, observing, "Here the spirit of the partizan had got mastery over all the personal likes and dislikes; and this is no new phase of human nature—with all associations it is enacted daily before our eyes. The Democrat and the American will each forget, in a day, the friendship of a long lifetime, so soon as his party blood is boiling."[7]

These unusual political comments indicate how concerned Lumpkin had become in August of 1860 about the partisan split that left Democrats in Georgia and elsewhere backing two different candidates for president, namely, Stephen A. Douglas of Illinois and John C. Breckinridge of Kentucky. His frustration was undoubtedly aggravated by the failure of efforts by Thomas Cobb and himself to have Howell Cobb nominated as a candidate that would be acceptable to both factions within the Democratic Party. When the newly formed Constitutional Union Party nominated John Bell of Tennessee as its candidate, the divisions among the three opponents of the Republicans helped to make election of Abraham Lincoln almost inevitable.

Shortly after the election results confirmed that the Republicans had won,

Governor Brown sent a message to the legislature urging Georgia's immediate secession and the appropriation of one million dollars for the state's defense. Although the secession proposal was defeated, the legislature passed the defense appropriation as well as a law authorizing the governor to call a state convention to determine whether and how long Georgia would remain in the Union. The law provided for delegates from each county to be elected on January 2, 1861, and for the convention to meet in Milledgeville on January 16. Before taking this unprecedented step, the legislature consulted a committee of eighteen distinguished citizens, which included Joseph Henry Lumpkin and such ardent secessionists as Thomas Cobb and Henry Benning as well as unionists like Alexander and Linton Stephens.[8]

Even though Breckinridge, who was the candidate of most secessionists, had won the greatest number of votes in Georgia, his failure to win a plurality indicated that a vote for secession was not a foregone conclusion in early January when the convention delegates were elected. However, in the weeks leading up to the convention, a growing number of influential leaders were actively endorsing the case for immediate secession, including Howell Cobb, who resigned his position in President Buchanan's cabinet to promote the cause, and even Wilson Lumpkin, who came out of political retirement at age seventy-seven to add his support. By the time the convention met, South Carolina, which was the first state to secede, had been joined by Alabama, Florida, and Mississippi, putting further pressure on the delegates as they assembled in Milledgeville on January 16. Although they were not delegates, Governor Brown and Howell Cobb occupied seats of honor on the convention floor along with Lumpkin and the other members of the supreme court. Numerous speeches were made in support of immediate secession or of postponement, but in the opinion of Alexander Stephens, Thomas Cobb carried the day when he argued, "We can make better terms out of the Union than in it." Ultimately, a committee headed by Eugenius Nisbet, a former supreme court judge, proposed an ordinance of secession, which was passed by a vote of 208 to 89, thereby repealing Georgia's ratification of the federal Constitution in 1788 and asserting her full rights of state sovereignty. According to Michael Johnson's detailed account of the convention, "As all the delegates lined up to sign the ordinance of secession at noon on Monday, January 21, it became clear that the tactic of immediate secession had deftly eviscerated any organized resistance. . . . Where was the man who was disloyal to Georgia, his home? Asking these questions allowed secessionists to avoid the disturbing question of who was disloyal to slaveholders. Immediate secession had smoothly translated the defense of slavery into the defense of the state."[9]

Following the secession vote, Lumpkin left for Macon to preside at the January term of the supreme court. It remained for Thomas Cobb and other leaders among the convention delegates to implement Georgia's new status and deal with her role in the emerging Confederacy. Cobb was named chairman of the Committee on the Constitution of the State and the Constitution and Laws of the United States and was also elected as one of ten Georgia delegates to a convention of seceding states, which met in Montgomery, Alabama, on February 4. With Howell Cobb presiding, the convention delegates, who were acting simultaneously as the Confederate Congress, began the process of forming the Provisional Government of the Confederate States of America by electing Jefferson Davis as president and Alexander H. Stephens as vice president. Lumpkin managed to keep abreast of the proceedings in Montgomery through contact with Thomas Cobb directly and from letters that Cobb wrote to his wife, Marion. According to Cobb's biographer, William McCash, one of the proposals that Cobb made to his fellow Congressmen was "a 'cotton scheme' suggested by his father-in-law, Judge Joseph Henry Lumpkin, a scheme which involved export restrictions on the chief staple crop of the lower South." Although the proposed plan was ultimately enacted into law, it was McCash's opinion that "both as a tool of diplomacy and as a means of financing the war, the 'King Cotton' concept was a dismal failure."[10]

During this period of extraordinary change, Lumpkin and his supreme court colleagues maintained their regular circuit schedule. However, the routines of most other Georgians were far from normal as military mobilization became a state-wide priority following the attack on Fort Sumter on April 12 and Lincoln's call for volunteers. On April 24 the Troup Artillery left Athens for coastal defense duty in Savannah with a unit of seventy-four men, including three of Joseph Henry's sons: Third Lieutenant Edward P. Lumpkin and Privates Charles M. and Frank Lumpkin. Describing the occasion, Augustus Longstreet Hull recalled that "the company was escorted to the Georgia Railroad by the Athens Guards, Oconee Cavalry and the Fire Companies. At the depot then across the river two thousand citizens had assembled to say goodbye, and Chancellor

Lipscomb addressed the departing company with characteristic eloquence and in a strain of the highest patriotism." When the Athens Guards left for Virginia five days later, Private Miller G. Lumpkin was on its rolls.[11]

Even though his congressional duties kept Thomas Cobb tied down in Montgomery, he took an active interest in Georgia's military developments, including the assignments of friends and family members. He was able not only to secure a commission for his brother-in-law, Charles Lumpkin, but also to arrange for the Troup Artillery to be transferred from Savannah to the front lines in Virginia. After his brother, Howell, received approval to raise and command a regiment, Thomas Cobb set about raising his own regimental unit, which he proposed to call the "Georgia Legion." By the end of August he had received a commission as a colonel in the Confederate Army, and all but one of the units under his command had assembled at a camp near Richmond. The latest unit to arrive was the Mell Rifles, which was originally formed as the Lumpkin Law School Cadets and was then composed of both former law students and older men from Athens, including William Wilberforce Lumpkin. Still to join the legion's ranks was the Troup Cavalry, which was then in western Virginia. Cobb repeatedly tried to arrange for its transfer, but, among other problems, he had to contend with interference from Lumpkin, who, according to McCash, "objected to the removal of the Troup Artillery from West Virginia while there was a possibility of a battle, apparently on the ground that such a withdrawal would weaken the Confederate position in that region."[12]

After appealing directly to Robert E. Lee, Cobb was finally able to arrange for the Troup Artillery to join his command in November of 1861. By that time, the Georgia Legion had taken up a position at a site near Yorktown, which Cobb named "Camp Marion" after his wife. On November 6, he wrote his sister-in-law, Callie, from Camp Marion thanking her for the present of blue socks she had sent him and telling her:

> I think and talk of nothing here but speculations about the war and the daily alarms about the enemy below us in this Peninsula. . . . It will be terrible . . . for Georgians and Alabamians to have to stay here defending a country for people the majority of whom are barely loyal and a large portion of whom are miserable Tories. When the news comes that the invaders' feet are triumphantly treading the soil of our own States, the truth is I cannot and I will not do it. If Georgia is invaded, I shall manage some way to meet the scoundrels there.

In closing he reported, "The boys with me are all well. The Artillery Company I think I shall soon get and then I shall have Wilby, Miller, Charley, Ed and Frank and Joe Gerdine. These with my own kin make up more than a corporal's guard."[13]

With the Confederate government in Richmond and his troops not yet engaged in battle, Thomas Cobb managed to participate in the debates of the Provisional Congress at its fifth session in January and February of 1862. At the same time, the legislature in Georgia was holding its first session since the establishment of the Confederacy. One of its highest priorities was the election of two individuals to represent Georgia in the Confederate Senate. Ben Hill won a majority of the votes for the full-term seat on the first ballot, but it took five ballots before Robert Toombs was chosen for the other Senate seat. Governor Brown notified Toombs, who had recently resigned his position as the Confederate secretary of state to take a general's commission in the army. When Brown learned that Toombs might not accept the Senate seat, he wrote Lumpkin,

> After mature reflection I can say in all candor that my mind rests upon no one of the many distinguished sons of Georgia whose appointment would be as appropriate as your own to fill the senatorial position when vacated by Genl. Toombs. It is no flattery to say that you have the full confidence of all men of all parties in the state to the fullest extent, that your known ability, profound statesmanship and lofty patriotism would inspire all with firm reliance that the interests of the State and the Confederacy would be secure in your hands. . . . I know that your retirement from the bench of the Supreme Court would be an irreparable loss to that branch of the public service; but I beg you to remember that our courts must remain closed to the end of the war, and we cannot say when the end will be.[14]

Brown's relationship with Lumpkin had not always been so warm, as indicated by a letter he wrote to a supporter during his gubernatorial campaign of 1859: "I do not think Judge Lumpkin or Mr. Cobb or their friends will continue any war upon me." Despite Brown's strong appeal to his ego and patriotism, however, Lumpkin declined the offer, so Brown turned to his longtime friend and early benefactor, Dr. John Lewis, to fill the seat. Lumpkin may have decided against serving in the Senate because of a lack of confidence in the Confederate leadership. In a letter to his daughter in March of 1862, he wrote, "O God Callie—that such a cause and such a people should fail through the incompetency and inefficiency of our Public men—with Jeff Davis at the head. They have systematically ignored from the beginning every principle upon which Revolutions succeed." Whatever was his reason for not wanting to leave the supreme court, Lumpkin chose to ignore Brown's curious contention that the Georgia courts "must remain closed till the end of the war." Certainly the war greatly disrupted proceedings in the Georgia courts in various ways, but primarily because many members of the bar as well as litigants and witnesses were in the military or otherwise unavailable for trials. In many sections of the state the superior and inferior courts sat infrequently, if at all, during the war, but the supreme court continued to hold two terms a year at Milledgeville, Savannah, Macon, Atlanta, and Athens throughout 1861 and 1862. In April of 1863 the legislature passed a law reducing the sessions for the duration of the war from ten to three a year, with sessions held thereafter at Macon in March, Atlanta in July, and Milledgeville in November. [15]

The first case involving a war-related issue was heard by the supreme court in August of 1861. In his opinion, Lumpkin noted that the plaintiffs, who were New York residents, had become "alien enemies" after the lawsuit was begun, and therefore had no standing to sue Georgia citizens in a Georgia court. Although he acknowledged that Massachusetts precedents seemed to support the plaintiffs' argument for "renewing the action at the termination of hostilities," he upheld the lower court's dismissal, concluding that it was up to "the Legislature to direct what disposition shall be made of this and similar cases." In the very next case, however, he chose not to apply the same rule against a Tennessee corporation, even though that state was not a member of the Confederacy on April 16, 1861, when the case arose. He first noted that, "I will not stop to inquire whether the bombardment of Fort Sumter, and other facts which had transpired up to that date, showed the existence of such a war as, by the law of nations, would subject the citizens of two countries to this recognized disability. But we utterly repudiate the idea that the State of Tennessee was, at that time, or at any other time, a party to any such war." He rationalized his decision by explaining,

President Lincoln may wage an unnatural and unconstitutional war upon a portion of the States; but if Tennessee, Kentucky, or any other sovereign State, refuse, by men or money, to sanction his war, the citizens of these non-concurring States are not to be considered and treated as alien enemies, outlawed by our courts.

True, Tennessee refused at first, to secede; but she had many difficulties, peculiar to her geographical situation, to encounter. But in a few short months, by an
overwhelming popular vote, she linked her destiny with that of Georgia and the
other Confederate States. She is entitled to our warmest sympathy. She has never
aided and abetted in this unholy war upon human rights, or given comfort to our
enemies.[16]

With five sons and a son-in-law risking their lives on the battlefront, Lumpkin
was moved in June of 1862 to donate $1,000 of his judicial salary to help defray
the expenses of sick and wounded soldiers who were in transit from the front
lines. In March of 1862, he was elected President of the Bible Society of the
Confederate States of America, but he never resigned as a vice president of the
northern-dominated American Bible Society. An obituary published by the latter organization in 1867 noted that when Lumpkin was elected a vice president
in 1853, "His letter of acceptance [was] fragrant with the spirit of ardent love for
the Bible and of this Institution." The same spirit of benevolence moved him
to pay tribute in November of 1862 to the Georgia women who were providing
aid to returning soldiers, saying that, "One of the regrets of my declining years
is, that in the course of nature so short a time remains to me to love and honor
these legitimate successors of the Apostolic women—the Marys and Marthas of
the New Testament. Their charities shall be remembered as a sweet memorial
of them to the end of time."[17]

A month later, Lumpkin and his family felt the full impact of the war when they
received the news that Thomas Cobb had been killed in battle at Fredericksburg
on December 13, 1862. He had assumed command of a brigade from his brother
Howell the previous October and, with backing from Robert E. Lee, had been
promoted to the rank of brigadier general just a month before his death. When
the train bearing his body arrived in Athens on December 18, the military escort
included his brothers-in-law, Charles and Edward Lumpkin. At the First Presbyterian Church, where he had followed in Joseph Henry Lumpkin's footsteps
as one of the leading laymen, the funeral service was conducted by the Reverend
Nathan Hoyt, who had officiated at his marriage to Marion Lumpkin in 1844.
He was buried as a Confederate war hero in a grave in the Oconee Hill Cemetery
in Athens, next to the Lumpkin family plot.[18]

When the supreme court met in Savannah in January of 1863, Judge Charles
Jenkins assumed the duty of delivering a tribute to the memory of Thomas

Cobb. However, on the next occasion for such a memorial in March of 1864, Lumpkin had an opportunity to voice his own sense of loss. With great pathos he wrote,

> This is not the time to inscribe epitaphs on the monuments of the mighty dead. We propose only to turn aside for a moment to plant the tribute of affection on the graves of our brethren of the bar—to pause for a while to pay honor to the memory of those by whose blood the heritage of liberty will be bequeathed to us. The aching anxieties and afflictions of these times are hardly endurable. It seems to be the very jubilee of death. More than twenty members of the bar of this Court, in this district alone, have fallen since the war commenced. The world has never yielded a harvest so rich and so horrible. Look at the Army! The noble men who have fallen in this wicked struggle would have made a nation for numbers, and the most glorious nation yet known for worth of every kind. . . . We stretch out the sympathizing hand to the thousands who mourn in the country, and we weep with those who weep, yet while we do this we say, all honor to the heroes who have won for us so glorious a name—who have vindicated us and our cause in the opinion of mankind—who have elevated Southern character, in this greatest of modern wars, to the highest pinnacle of fame. [19]

In July and August of 1864 there were skirmishes between the Athens home guard and Union troops on the outskirts of the city. On one of these occasions, the Wilson Lumpkin Artillery, commanded by Captain Edward Lumpkin, was credited with saving Athens from invasion. Fortunately for the Lumpkin family and other residents of Athens, the city was spared the fate of Atlanta. In an opinion written by Judge Iverson Harris in 1866, there is a graphic account of what Georgians faced when confronted by war on their home ground. Reversing the dismissal of a lawsuit, he explained that

> the then condition of the Western and Southwestern portion of the State was such as to excuse all persons, Judge, jurors, parties, witnesses, and attorneys, from attendance. War was existing. At the very hour that Court was being held, a Federal army of sixteen thousand men, under General Wilson, was in possession of the City of Columbus, which had been captured after an ineffectual resistance. This army was of mounted men. They were moving with rapidity on Macon— a portion above, a part below, Columbus. They spread over a wide extent of country, inspiring terror and meeting with no resistance. War raged everywhere; there was no personal security—travel broken up—one could scarce look within

his horizon by day without seeing the ascending column of smoke, or at night, the lurid flames of burning dwellings or gin houses of our people. [20]

Even though the residents of Athens did not experience the worst ravages of the war, they suffered shortages of food and other essentials as the economic conditions deteriorated throughout the state. Their problems were particularly aggravated in all aspects of commerce and finance by the rapid depreciation of Confederate currency. The accounts of an Augusta broker that appeared as evidence in a supreme court case of 1866 show that on January 1, 1861, one dollar in gold was worth $1.05 in Confederate currency but was worth $20.00 on December 1, 1863, and climbed to $50.00 on December 31, 1864. By May 1, 1865, it took $1,200 in Confederate treasury notes to acquire one gold dollar. In the midst of all the negative developments, Lumpkin and his family must have received some satisfaction when they learned he had finally received the official title of chief justice. Provision was made in the Georgia Code of 1863 that "the oldest Judge in commission is the Chief Justice, or President thereof, but without greater powers than his associates." When he presided for the first time as Chief Justice at Milledgeville in November of 1864, the only significant change for Lumpkin was that he could finally sign his opinions as "Lumpkin, C.J." [21]

The end of the war finally came on April 9, 1865, when Lee surrendered to Grant at Appomattox Courthouse, although it was not until May 5 that Governor Brown surrendered the Georgia militia to General James Wilson, putting the state under military rule. As Lumpkin described the general situation in *Armstrong v. Jones* (1866), "The Confederacy itself was extinguished, as completely as if its last champion had perished when Stonewall Jackson fell. Submission to the authority of the victorious North was absolute . . . throughout the whole region which had been designated as in insurrection." When Brown was arrested and transported to a federal prison in Washington, his wife destroyed a number of his personal papers including, as he later wrote, "a great many letters from such men as Governor Towns, Gov. McDonald, Judge Warner, Judge Lumpkin, and a great number of the leading men of Georgia that I prized highly." Released from prison in June, Brown resigned as governor and in his farewell address advised his fellow Georgians to support the Constitution and make every effort to return to the Union as quickly as possible. Judge Jenkins was elected governor in the 1865 election with Brown's active support, and shortly after he resigned, Lumpkin lost his other associate on the court, Judge Lyon, who failed to win another six-year term. Thus, he was joined at the supreme court session in January of 1866 by two new judges, bringing to ten the number of judges who served with Lumpkin during his more than twenty years on the court. Dawson A. Walker had been chosen over both Lyon and another former member of the court, Henry Benning, despite his service in the Confederate army, while Iverson L. Harris had defeated three other candidates, including Hiram Warner, who was one of the original members of the court.[22]

Although Lumpkin's health was deteriorating during 1866, he still managed to write more than his usual one-third share of the seventy-one opinions issued by the court that year. Yet a growing pessimism caused him to write in *Heard v. State* (1866): "In this age of recklessness and terrible demoralization, if men sew to the wind, they cannot expect the Courts and juries to interpose and prevent them from reaping the whirlwind. . . . This is an age of Cains, and the voices of murdered Abels come up at every court, crying aloud to the ministers of the law for vengeance." His spirits were buoyed, however, by an invitation from Joseph Brown in January of 1867 to join him and Judge Dawson Walker on a trip to Washington to assess the repercussions for Georgia after it failed to ratify the Fourteenth Amendment. Although his health was not up to the trip, Lumpkin said in his reply to Brown on January 25, 1867: "Having finished my opinions (27 in number), allotted to me in the division of labor at the late session of the court at Milledgeville, I should like very much to accompany you to Washington to see and talk with some of the men there as regards the situation. Our people should learn to appreciate their condition; and bad as it is, if we could have peace by a general pardon and negro suffrage, I am inclined myself to accept it. If you can spare the time whilst in Washington, I should like very much to hear from you."[23]

Brown wrote a lengthy letter to Lumpkin reporting on his meetings with "many prominent men on both sides" and concluded that the South's only choice was to accept the terms of the Republican Congress along the lines Lumpkin had conceded in his letter. In conclusion, Brown wrote, "If you think it best for our people that I make these views public, send me back this letter written in much haste and I will revise and publish it, whatever may be its effect upon me personally." By the time the letter reached Athens, Lumpkin was suffering a paralysis, which his doctor attributed to a kidney condition, and had become too ill to reply. His son James read him Brown's letter and returned it with a message that his father "says your sagacity and opportunities of judgment are so much better than his—even if capable of mental exertion—he begs you will give that direction to your views which you may think best for our people & the country. That for himself—whether his time be long or short—he sees nothing but gloomy future before him."[24]

When the supreme court next met in Milledgeville on the first Monday in June, Lumpkin was too ill to attend, and he died the next day, June 4, at his home in Athens. His funeral service was held the following day at the Presbyterian Church, where he had long served as a ruling elder. One of the Athens newspapers reported that the "sermon was preached by Chancellor Lipscomb and was worthy of the occasion. All places of business were closed, and almost the entire population followed his remains to Oconee Cemetery. . . . Thus has passed away one of Georgia's noblest sons."[25]

The surviving members of the supreme court convened that same Wednesday in Milledgeville long enough to adjourn the session as a token of respect to their deceased colleague. They then joined with members of the supreme court bar, led by former governor Joseph Brown, in electing a committee to prepare a suitable memorial for Lumpkin. As reported in volume 36 of the *Georgia Reports*, that committee, headed by Governor Charles Jenkins, delivered an eloquent *in memoriam* tribute at the supreme court session on June 24. Assuming the role so often performed on such occasions by Lumpkin as chief justice, his successor, Hiram Warner, responded to the tribute. In summation, he stated, "His high intellectual attainments, his great professional learning, his strong sense of justice, his polished manners, added to his moral worth and Christian charity, deeply impressed those of us who have been the witnesses and companions of his judicial labors, with the irreparable loss which this Court and the Bar have sustained in his death."[26]

The last public ceremony in Lumpkin's memory was held at the University of Georgia on August 5, 1867, when W. T. Brantly delivered "An Oration on the Life and Character of Joseph Henry Lumpkin" before the Phi Kappa Society, which he had helped to found nearly fifty years earlier. Lumpkin would certainly have approved of the Presbyterian Church, the supreme court, and the University of Georgia as the venues for his memorial services, for they were his principal interests, outside of his family, as well as the custodians of his major legacies. He had found within each of those institutions the stimulation and resources he needed, fueled by his intellect, imagination, and energy, to make lasting contributions as a judge, educator, and evangelical reformer.

Twenty-five years after his death Lumpkin was lauded as a reformer by Georgia's then chief justice, Logan E. Bleckley, who wrote, "It would be difficult to imagine a finer specimen of physical, intellectual and moral manhood than was Joseph Henry Lumpkin." Fifteen years later, he was described in *Reminiscences of Famous Georgians* as "the great chief justice" of Georgia and compared to John Marshall. In more recent years, Lumpkin's fame has faded, along with the reputations of other state appellate court judges who achieved eminence during the antebellum era.[27]

However, Timothy Huebner's recent book, *The Southern Judicial Tradition*, has led the way in exploring the accomplishments of six influential southern jurists, including Lumpkin. Following Huebner's lead, I have sought to examine the life of Lumpkin, especially as manifested through his judicial opinions and letters, and to reveal that, among the many facets of his complex personality, he was intelligent and emotional, pious and witty, principled and pragmatic, urbane and domestic.

As a champion of state sovereignty and southern culture, including the institution of slavery, he was solidly rooted in the planter and professional aristocracy. Yet Lumpkin was also a leading proponent of legal, social, and economic reforms: "Civilization must advance," he wrote in *Young and Calhoun v. Harrison and Harrison* (1849); "the improvements of society, diffusing plenty and prosperity, knowledge and refinement and morality all around, must not, cannot be restrained."[28]

In his speeches as well as his judicial opinions he promoted reduction of the South's dependence on agriculture and development of a more balanced economy by encouraging manufacturing and commerce. In the view of Neill H. Alford Jr., a former dean of the University of Georgia Law School, the industrial development of the South can be traced in part to "Judge Lumpkin's astute molding of the business and banking law of this state [Georgia] in accordance with sound economic principles. Just as Chief Justice John Marshall laid the basis for centralized Federal power and interstate commerce, Judge Lumpkin cleared the way through the thicket of antiquated doctrine which threatened to strangle in their infancy banking and business in corporate form."[29]

To achieve the types of legal reform cited by Alford, Lumpkin took a pragmatic and utilitarian approach to the law in his decision-making, a view that in recent years has been termed "legal instrumentalism." In one of his earliest opinions, *Choice v. Marshall* (1846), he stated, "We are prepared, although in our *judicial infancy*, to advance to the front rank in this warfare of principle against precedent." He encouraged the growth of corporations in order to achieve economic independence in Georgia and throughout the South, writing in *Hightower v. Thornton* (1850) that they were the "proof, and in no small degree the cause of the unparalleled advancement of modern civilization." Yet Lumpkin aimed for a balancing of interests, and recognized a responsibility to protect the poor and uneducated from the abuses of corporate powers. Therefore, Lumpkin appears to fit within a narrower definition of "instrumentalist" suggested by Peter Karsten in his recent book, *Heart versus Head: Judge-made Law in Nineteenth-Century America*: namely, those whose "instrumentalism, their use of law as a purposive instrument to achieve a goal, was 'far kinder and gentler' to those suing a corporation, or being sued by creditors, than the reigning paradigm has maintained."[30]

Even though Lumpkin's opinions cover a wide range of legal issues, including such important areas as contracts, negligence, property, and constitutional law, most of the academic commentary about his jurisprudence has thus far focused on his opinions dealing with slavery. Writing as a biographer rather than as a legal historian, I have focused on his slavery opinions mainly in the context of his religious, political, and cultural views on the subject as they evolved over time. As a young politician in the 1820s, he was a strong advocate of states' rights and criticized northern interference with the institution of slavery, yet in 1833 he gave a remarkable speech in Boston in which he spoke strongly in favor of emancipation. It is likely that he then supported colonization of freed blacks as well, although there is no record of such endorsement until 1847, when he became a national vice president of the American Colonization Society. Ten years later, however, he had rejected colonization as a solution and wrote in *American Colonization Society v. Gartrell* (1857) that he "was once a friend . . . of this enterprise" but "now regard[ed] it as a failure." By then, he had also become convinced that the slavery was divinely sanctioned, claiming in his report on law reform to the Georgia legislature: "Being recognized and regulated by the Decalogue, it will, we have every reason to believe, be of perpetual duration." It was this kind of candor that caused one legal historian to write that the Georgia Supreme Court members "were as willing as any Southerners to state their mind about slavery, and they were remarkably articulate," adding, "The most outspoken as well as the most influential judge in Georgia was Joseph Henry Lumpkin."[31]

Lumpkin achieved that influence through his steadfast dedication to building the stature of the supreme court. He and his judicial colleagues not only had to overcome the entrenched bias in Georgia against a centralized court but also had to endure a grueling circuit over hundreds of miles each year in order to hold sessions in as many as nine cities around the state. Ten judges served on the court with him, some of whom resigned for health reasons while others failed to be reelected for partisan reasons, but Lumpkin managed to win four consecutive terms on the court. His political independence and leadership skills guided the court toward the front rank and earned him the highest respect from his fellow Georgians. As the introduction to a 1948 history of the Georgia Supreme Court observed, "How remote and Jove-like Joseph H. Lumpkin looms until we catch a glimpse of the great Chief Justice, in the letters of Linton Stephens, while on circuit at Savannah, swapping miserable puns with his colleagues. . . . These may be little things. Yet they are the sauce of history. They bring the dead past back to life on the printed page."[32] At the end of the Civil War, Lumpkin might well have chosen to end his long career in public life and assume a Jovian retirement. Instead, he remained dedicated to his role as chief justice, which not only gave him pride of place but also allowed him to continue serving the people of Georgia during the difficult early years of the postwar period. Putting behind him the years of sectional strife, near the end of his life he advised Joseph Brown to seek not just what was best for their fellow Georgians but for the United States as a whole.[33]

NOTES

Unless otherwise indicated, letters to and from Lumpkin are in the Joseph Henry Lumpkin Papers at Hargrett Rare Book and Manuscript Library, University of Georgia Libraries, including letters on loan to Hargrett from the Alexander Campbell King Law Library at the University of Georgia School of Law.

Introduction

1. Pound, *The Lawyer*, 185; Karsten, *Heart versus Head*, 2; Pound, *Formative Era*, 4, 30, 447–448.

2. Tocqueville, *Democracy in America*, 2:184–185.

3. Alford, speech.

4. Thomas R. R. Cobb, *Negro Slavery*, 1.

5. Huebner, *Southern Judicial Tradition*, 9.

6. *Bryan v. Walton*, 14 Ga. 185, 199 (1853).

One. The Early Years

1. Wise, *Story of Oglethorpe*, 23–26.

2. Webb, *1676*, 3–165. For Lumpkin family genealogy, see L. L. Cody, *The Lumpkin Family of Georgia*; Ben Gray Lumpkin and Martha Neville Lumpkin, eds., *The Lumpkin Family of Virginia, Georgia, and Mississippi*; Bryan H. Lumpkin, *Lumpkin Family History*; Sam and Eloise Lumpkin, *The Alabama Family of Lumpkin*. Some of the Lumpkin family genealogists contend that Jacob Lumpkin was the first American ancestor while others believe that distinction belongs to Dr. Thomas Lumpkin, as was stated in Wilson Lumpkin, *Removal*, 9–10.

3. Cody, *Lumpkin Family*, 6–8; *History of Oglethorpe*, 110.

4. *History of Oglethorpe*, 110–111; Coleman, *American Revolution*, 217; Mohr, *Oglethorpe County*, 19–20; Heath, *Constructive Liberalism*, 84.

5. Bartram, *Travels*, 30.

6. Wilson Lumpkin, *Removal*, 9–11; Coulter, *Old Petersburg*, 13.

7. Warren, *The Supreme Court*, 392–399.

8. Wilson Lumpkin, *Removal*, 6.

9. Brantly, *Life and Character*, 11.

10. Coulter, "Francis Meson," 26.

11. Wise, *Story of Oglethorpe*, 44–45.

12. Coulter, "Meson Academy," 125, 131; Borgher, *Secondary Education*, 101.

13. Mohr, *Oglethorpe County*, 174; Coulter, "Meson Academy," 134.

14. Sparks, *Memories*, 175; Hill, *The Hills of Wilkes County*, 2:631; the prize list also shows that Thomas Lumpkin trailed his older brother with third honors in composition, similar to their relative academic rankings when they graduated together from Princeton five years later.

15. *Savannah Georgian*, July 22, 1826.

16. Wilson Lumpkin, *Removal*, 7.

17. Faz, *Salem Baptist Church*, 151–152.

18. Coulter, "Francis Meson," 4.

19. Mohr, *Oglethorpe County*, 46, 57, 136; Paschal, *Ninety-four Years*, 31, 65–66.

20. Wilson Lumpkin, *Removal*, 5; Faz, *Salem Baptist Church*, 151; Coleman, *American Revolution*, 215–216; Mohr, *Oglethorpe County*, 133–134.

21. Joseph Henry Lumpkin to Callender Grieve, February 4, 1821; Joseph Henry Lumpkin, *South-Carolina Institute*, 35. Unless otherwise indicated, letters to and from Lumpkin are in the Joseph Henry Lumpkin Papers at Hargrett Rare Book and Manuscript Library, University of Georgia Libraries.

22. Joseph Henry Lumpkin, *South-Carolina Institute*, 38.

Two. Bright College Days

1. Wood, *A Unique*, 3.

2. Hull, *Annals*, 21.

3. Hull, *Annals*, 28; Coulter, *College Life*, 1–22.

4. Brown, *Memoirs*, 116–117; Coulter, *College Life*, 15–16, 28.

5. Brown, *Memoirs*, 128–129.

6. Edgar W. Knight, *Documentary History*, 46–47.

7. Wilson Lumpkin, *Removal*, 13.

8. Wertenbaker, *Princeton*, 167, 169.

9. Wertenbaker, *Princeton*, 170–172.

10. Princeton Faculty Minutes, 1812–1820.

11. Williams, *Cliosophic Society*, 1–10.

12. Cliosophic Society Archives, box 3, "Final Minutes."

13. Jones, *Ashbel Green*, 422; Collins, *Princeton Past and Present*, 133–134.

14. Wertenbaker, *Princeton*, 210. According to the Princeton alumni records, John Stuart became editor of the *Charleston Mercury* and Abraham Venable later represented North Carolina in both the U.S. Congress and the Confederate Congress.

Three. Making His Mark

1. Andrews, *Reminiscences*, 41.

2. Warren, *History of the American Bar*, 336–338; Reese, "Reminiscences," 330–331.

3. Warren, *Harvard Law School*, 1:339.

4. Cody, *Lumpkin Family*, 33–34.

5. Paschal, *Ninety-four Years*, 118; *Savannah Georgian*, July 22, 1826.

6. Coulter, *College Life*, 56.

7. Hynds, *Antebellum Athens*, 78; Coulter, *College Life*, 104–105.

8. Sparks, *Memories*, 176.

9. Phillips, *Georgia and State Rights*, 96–97.

10. Reports of Georgia House of Representatives, Extra Session, May–June 1825, 68.

11. Joseph Henry Lumpkin to John M. Berrien, May 27, 1825; *The Antelope* 10 Wheat. 66 (1825); Warren, *The Supreme Court*, 584–586; Harden, *Life of George M. Troup*, 302–308.

12. Beeson, *History Stories*, 2; Harris, "In Memoriam," 30.

13. Bonner, *Milledgeville*, 45, 77.

14. Phillips, *Georgia and State Rights*, 111.

Four. Riding the Circuit

1. Reese, "Reminiscences," 331; Brantly, *Life and Character*, 13–14.

2. Custer, "The Golden Age," 70; Andrews, *Reminiscences*, 20; Mohr, *Oglethorpe County*, 115.

3. Custer, "The Golden Age," 71–72; Grice, *Georgia Bench and Bar*, 237.

4. Lucian Lamar Knight, *Georgia and Georgians*, 684–685.

5. Miller, *Life of the Mind*, 109.

6. Dudley, *Reports of the Decisions*, v–vi.

7. 36 Ga. 34–36 (1867).

8. Jean V. Matthews, *Toward a New Society*, 123.

9. Brantly, *Life and Character*, 31; Johnston, *Autobiography*, 106, 109–112.

10. Johnston, *Autobiography*, 103–106.

11. Reese, "Reminiscences," 331–332.

12. Reese, "Reminiscences," 331; Milledgeville, Georgia newspaper clippings, vol. 3, 9.

13. Andrews, *Reminiscences*, 100–102; Johnston, *Autobiography*, 103.

14. Andrews, *Reminiscences*, 103; Brantly, *Life and Character*, 16. The Clarke County, Georgia, Probate Court records show that Lumpkin's estate was valued at $33,797.

Five. Evangelical Benevolence

1. Campbell, *Georgia Baptists*, 309–310; Paschal, *Ninety-four Years*, 158–161; *History of Oglethorpe*, 112.

2. Donald G. Matthews, *Religion*, xvi; Samuel S. Hill, *Encyclopedia of Religion in the South*, 243–244.

3. Heyrman, *Southern Cross*, 7–9.

4. Smith, *Methodism in Georgia*, 80–84.

5. Coleman and Gurr, *Dictionary of Georgia Biography*, 2:797–798; Sparks, *Memories*, 62–63.

6. *Savannah Republican*, January 15, 1825.

7. Miller, *Life of the Mind*, 3; Jean V. Matthews, *Toward a New Society*, 29–32; McGloughlin, *Revivals*, 131–138.

8. McGloughlin, *Revivals*, 114.

9. Goulding, *Thomas Goulding*, 181–187; Joseph Henry Lumpkin, diary entitled "Notes and Reflections."

10. Morton H. Smith, *Studies*, 107–109; LaMotte, *Colored Light*, 37–38.

11. Brantly, *Life and Character*, 45.

12. Miller, *Life of the Mind*, 32.

13. Hardman, *Charles Grandison Finney*, 234, 239.

14. McGloughlin, *Revivals*, 128–129; for an explanation of doctrinal and governance disputes between "Old School" and "New School" Presbyterians, see Hill, *Encyclopedia of Religion*, 570–572.

15. Pegram, *Demon Rum*, 21.

16. Scomp, *King Alcohol*, 237–245, 271; Tyrrell, *Sobering Up*, 5.

17. Article reprinted in *Southern Watchman*, May 17, 1860; Loveland, *Southern Evangelicals*, 135; Cory, *Temperance*, 21.

18. Paschal, *Ninety-four Years*, 206–207.

19. Brantly, *Life and Character*, 37.

20. Scomp, *King Alcohol*, 263–264.

21. King, *Augustus Baldwin Longstreet*, 12–13.

22. Scomp, *King Alcohol*, 278–280; Tyrell, "Drink and Temperance," 485–510.

23. Scomp, *King Alcohol*, 300–301; *Southern Banner*, July 13, 1833; *Milledgeville Federal Union*, July 18, 1833.

24. Scomp, *King Alcohol*, 299, 301; *Southern Banner*, August 3, 1833.

25. Tyrell, "Drink and Temperance," 490; the American Temperance Society changed its name to the American Temperance Union in 1836.

26. Tyrell, "Drink and Temperance," 488–489; Josiah Flournoy to Joseph Henry Lumpkin, May 20, 1839, and August 30, 1839.

27. Coulter, *College Life*, 95.

28. Murray, *Whig Party in Georgia*, 107; *Savannah Daily News and Herald*, June 7, 1867.

29. Scomp, *King Alcohol*, 448–451; John M. Berrien to Joseph Henry Lumpkin, January 12, 1850.

30. *Southern Banner*, June 29, 1854; McCash, *Thomas R. R. Cobb*, 74; Pegram, *Demon Rum*, 40–41.

31. Scomp, *King Alcohol*, 449.

Six. Sounding the Trumpet

1. Foster, *Errand of Mercy*, 52–53; Barnes, *Anti-Slavery Impulse*, 30; Wyatt-Brown, *Lewis Tappan*, 6.

2. Foster, *Errand of Mercy*, 52.

3. *Boston Courier*, June 21, 1833, reprinted in *Milledgeville Federal Union*, July 18, 1833.

4. *Southern Banner*, July 13, 1833.

5. *Southern Banner*, July 13, 1833; *Milledgeville Federal Union*, July 18, 1833.

6. *Northampton Courier*, July 10, 1833, reprinted in *Southern Banner*, August 3, 1833; references are to Senator Robert Y. Hayne of South Carolina and to the debate between Hayne and Webster.

7. Phillips, *Georgia and State Rights*, 127; Coulter, "Nullification," 35.

8. *Milledgeville Federal Union*, July 18, 1833; Debats, *Elites and Masses*, 71–75.

9. *Savannah Georgian*, January 20, 1834.

10. Coulter, "Nullification," 1.

11. *Niles Register*, October 5, 1853, 85–86.

12. *Cleland v. Waters*, 16 Ga. 496, 514 (1854).

13. Scarborough, *Opposition to Slavery,* 179–180, 198–199; Sydnor, *Southern Sectionalism,* 222–223.

14. Staudenraus, *African Colonization,* 26–29.

15. Cresson, *James Monroe,* 336; Gifford, *African Colonization in Georgia,* 222.

16. Report of Joint Committee, December 5, 1827, 9–11.

17. *Niles Register,* October 5, 1853, 85–86; Gifford, *African Colonization in Georgia,* 222; Joseph Henry Lumpkin to the Rev. William McLain, published in *The African Repository and Colonial Journal,* vol. 23 (1847), 158–159. On page 94 of the same issue, the list of officers of the American Colonization Society elected in 1847 included sixty-seven vice presidents, of which number sixty-six was listed as "H. L. Lumpkin, Esq., Athens, Geo." In each subsequent annual listing through 1858, the same name was used, although it was changed to "Hon. H. L. Lumpkin."

18. Staudenraus, *African Colonization,* 186, 245; *Cleland v. Waters,* 16 Ga. 496, 513 (1854).

19. Fredrickson, "A Man But Not a Brother," 48, 49.

20. *Bryan v. Walton,* 14 Ga. 185, 206 (1853).

21. *American Colonization Society v. Gartrell,* 23 Ga. 448, 464 (1857).

22. *Southern Banner,* August 3, 1833; Genovese, *A Consuming Fire,* 24–25.

23. Myers, *The Children of Pride,* 1599.

24. *Slave Narratives, Georgia Narratives,* 155.

25. Russell and Thornbery, "William Finch of Atlanta: The Black Politician As Civic Leader," in Rabinowitz, ed., *Southern Black Leaders,* 309–332.

26. *Dudley v. Mallery,* 4 Ga. 52, 65–66 (1848).

27. Joseph Henry Lumpkin, *South-Carolina Institute,* 12–13.

Seven. Aristocracy of Talent

1. *Tribute to Major Kelly,* 6 Ga. 114, 116 (1849); Oakes, *Slavery and Freedom,* 122.

2. Gilmer, *Sketches,* 345; Orr, *History of Education,* 84–85.

3. Joseph Henry Lumpkin to Gov. George R. Gilmer, October 8, 1830, Georgia State Archives and History Department.

4. Orr, *History of Education,* 118.

5. Coulter, "A Georgia Educational Movement," 16.

6. McCash, *Thomas R. R. Cobb,* 113–116.

7. Coulter, *College Life,* 218.

8. Phi Kappa Society to Joseph Henry Lumpkin, April 2, 1838; for an interesting biography of Pettigru, see Pease, *James Louis Pettigru*.

9. LaBoone, *Library*, 44.

10. Catalogue of the Demosthenian Society Presented by Bennett Harris, July 1828, Hargrett Library; LaBoone, *Library*, 46.

11. Joseph Henry Lumpkin, *Address on Natural History*, 17.

12. Stacy, *Presbyterian Church in Georgia*, 111–112.

13. Joseph Henry Lumpkin, *Address before Hopewell Presbytery*, 11.

14. McPherson, "Wilson Lumpkin," 164–165; the Calhoun quote is taken from a historical marker standing in downtown Atlanta entitled "The Prophecy of John C. Calhoun."

15. "Atlanta's Godmother," *The Literary Digest*, April 21, 1917; Garrett, *Atlanta and Its Environs*, 185, 202, 225–226.

16. Shyrock, "Early Industrial Revolution," 115.

17. Lander, *Charleston*, 349; Joseph Henry Lumpkin, *South-Carolina Institute*, 26, 35.

18. Joseph Henry Lumpkin, "Industrial Regeneration of the South," 41–50; Huebner, "Joseph Henry Lumpkin," 273.

Eight. Paterfamilias

1. "Memoir of Joseph Henry Lumpkin, Chief Justice of Georgia," *United States Law Magazine*, July and August 1851, 36; Thomas R. R. Cobb, *The Temperance Crusader*, 1860.

2. Rogers, *Housing of Oglethorpe*, 58–59; the Lumpkin children and birth order were Marion (1822), Lucy (1823), Joseph Troup (1824), Callie (1826), Thomas Miller (1827), William Wilberforce (1829), Chalmers (1831), Miller (1832), Edward (1834), James (1836), Charles (1839), Robert (1840), and Frank (1842).

3. Historic Oglethorpe County, Inc., "Historic Oglethorpe County, A Guide to Historic Resources and Points of Interest."

4. Callie Lumpkin to Howell Cobb, January 1844 (copy of original in private ownership).

5. Thomas Cobb to Marion Lumpkin, December 14, 1843, quoted in McCash, *Thomas R. R. Cobb*, 22.

6. Materials of the Joseph Henry Lumpkin Foundation, Inc.

7. Hargrett, "Student Life," 49; Koch, "The View from Chalky Level," 44; Hardee, "Notes and Documents," 175.

8. Joseph Henry Lumpkin to Callie Lumpkin King, August 5, 1853.

9. Coulter, *College Life*, 148.

10. James Lumpkin to Callie Lumpkin King, August 14, 1854.

11. Coulter, "Madison Springs," 390–395; "Madison Springs Furnished Frolic, Food and Fashion," *Athens Banner Herald*, May 7, 1964.

12. Joseph Henry Lumpkin to Callie Lumpkin King, August 10, 1854; James Lumpkin to Callie Lumpkin King, August 14, 1854.

13. Marion Lumpkin to Mary Ann Cobb, January 2, 1842, Howell Cobb Collection, Hargrett Library.

14. *Slave Narratives*, interviews with Anna Parkes, 159, and with Susan Castle, 181.

15. *Slave Narratives*, 156.

16. Coulter, *College Life*, 48–49; Joseph Henry Lumpkin to Callie Lumpkin King, September 7, 1856; Coleman and Gurr, *Dictionary of Georgia Biography*, "Mary Bryan Thomas Lumpkin," 643–644. The association of Athens and the Lumpkin family with flowers was continued in 1891 when the first garden club in the country was founded at the home of Mrs. Edwin K. Lumpkin, whose husband was a grandson of Joseph Henry and Callender Lumpkin.

17. McCash, *Thomas R. R. Cobb*, 76, 86; James Lumpkin to Callie Lumpkin King, June 6, 1854; Joseph Henry Lumpkin to Callie Lumpkin King, December 10, 1855.

18. Washington Irving, preface to *Bracebridge Hall* (1821), quoted in Bradbury, *Dangerous Pilgrimages*, 68.

19. Samuel Miller to Rev. Dr. Thomas Chalmers, May 5, 1845; Shepperson, "Thomas Chalmers," 517, 526; Joseph Henry Lumpkin, *South-Carolina Institute*, 8, 42–43; *Johnson v. State*, 14 Ga. 55, 67 (1853).

20. Joseph Henry Lumpkin to Callie Lumpkin King, April 26, 1857; "Memoir of Joseph Henry Lumpkin, Chief Justice of Georgia," *United States Law Magazine*, 35.

Nine. Establishing the Court

1. 6 Ga. 114, 115–116 (1849).

2. Act of February 16, 1799, sec. LIX.

3. *Georgia v. Brailsford*, 2 Dall. 402 (U.S. 1792); *Chisholm v. Georgia*, 2 Dall. 419 (U.S. 1793); Lamar, "Establishment of the Supreme Court of Georgia," 88; Surrency, *Creation of a Judicial System*, 234; Warren, *The Supreme Court*, 100–104.

4. *Worcester v. Georgia*, 6 Pet. 515 (U.S. 1832); Warren, *American Bar*, 398, 415.

5. Norgren, *The Cherokee Cases*, 122–130.

6. *Senate Journal 1839*, 24. A detailed account of the legislative history appears in John B. Harris, *Supreme Court of Georgia*.

7. 68 Ga. 847, 855 (1881).

8. John MacPherson Berrien to Allen F. Owen, January 26, 1846, quoted in Miller, *Bench and Bar of Georgia*, 1:75–76.

9. John B. Harris, *Supreme Court of Georgia*, 36; Joseph Henry Lumpkin to Hon. George W. Crawford, October 6, 1846, Telamon Cuyler Collection, Hargrett Library.

10. Surrency, *Creation of a Judicial System*, 254; *Thornton v. Lane*, 11 Ga. 459, 490–491 (1852).

11. *Nunn v. State*, 1 Ga. 243, 250–251 (1846); Amar, "The Bill of Rights," 1193, 1211–1212; Robert Dowlut, "Constitutional Guarantees to Arms," 59, 67.

12. *Senate Journal 1847*.

13. Wilson Lumpkin to Joseph Henry Lumpkin, December 15, 1847; "Judge Lumpkin's Report on Law Reform," *Southern Recorder*, December 4, 1849; Haar, *Golden Age*, 211–213.

14. Ingersoll, "Confusion of Law and Equity," 58; Story, *Equity Jurisprudence*, 1:27; Henry L. McClintock, *Handbook*, 12–17.

15. "Judge Lumpkin's Report on Law Reform" in Hall, *The Magic Mirror*, 126; Cook, *American Codification Movement*, 197–198.

16. McCash, *Thomas R. R. Cobb*, 59, quoting Almond, "Code of 1863," 164.

17. Coulter, *College Life*, 198–203; McCash, *Thomas R. R. Cobb*, 123–125.

Ten. First among Equals

1. Warren, *Harvard Law School*, 168–174.

2. American Bible Society, *Testimony*, 60–62; J. C. Bingham to Joseph Henry Lumpkin, October 20, 1852.

3. John B. Harris, *Supreme Court of Georgia*, 48–51; Deen and Henwood, *Georgia's Appellate Judiciary*, 15, 17; Coleman and Gurr, *Dictionary of Georgia Biography*, 71–72; James C. Cobb, "The Making of a Secessionist," 313–323.

4. *Gray v. Gray*, 20 Ga. 804, 821 (1856).

5. Surrency, *History of the Federal Courts*, 310–312.

6. "Bulletin of the University of Georgia Alumni," October 1906 Catalogue of Trustees, Officers and Alumni of University of Georgia 1785–1906; University of Georgia Trustees Minutes, vol. 3, 1835–1857.

7. Coulter, *College Life*, 202–203.

Eleven. The Front Rank

1. *Johnson v. Holt*, Ga. 117, 119 (1847); *Tucker v. Harris*, 13 Ga. 1, 20 (1853); *Smith v. Simms*, 9 Ga. 418, 423 (1851); *Bostwick v. Perkins*, 1 Ga. 136, 139 (1846).

2. Pound, *Formative Era*, 4, 30. Lemuel Shaw is the only one of the six judges who does not appear to have been mentioned in Lumpkin's opinions.

3. *The State v. K. P. Boon*, 1 Ga. 618, 626 (1846); Lucian Lamar Knight, *Reminiscences of Famous Georgians*, 358.

4. *Cappell v. Causey*, 11 Ga. 25, 31 (1852); Tribute to Judge Berrier 19 Ga. 202; *Rogers v. Atkinson*, 1 Ga., 12, 24 (1846).

5. *Chance v. McWhorter*, 26 Ga. 315, 318 (1858); Llewellyn, "Theory of Appellate Decision," 395, 396; *In Memoriam*, 36 Ga. 37–38 (1867).

6. *Tucker v. Harris*, 13 Ga. 1, 20 (1853); *Martin v. The State*, 25 Ga. 494, 514 (1858).

7. *Sealy v. The State*, 1 Ga. 213, 217 (1846); *Evans v. Rogers*, 1 Ga. 463, 466 (1846).

8. *Berry v. The State*, 10 Ga. 511, 522 (1851).

9. *Obituary of Judge James H. Stark*, 25 Ga. 290 (1858).

10. Tribute to Richard K. Hines, 11 Ga. 134 (1852); *Moody v. Threlkeld*, 13 Ga. 55, 60 (1853); Tribute to R. S. Hall, 17 Ga. 240 (1855).

11. *Dacey v. The State*, 17 Ga. 430, 443 (1855); *Tribute to Judge Cone*, 28 Ga. 624 (1859).

12. *Reynolds v. Reynolds*, 3 Ga. 53, 74 (1847); *Monroe v. State*, 5 Ga. 85, 148 (1848).

13. *Carey v. McDougald*, 7 Ga. 84, 86 (1849); *Martin v. Broach*, 6 Ga. 21, 36 (1849).

14. *Worthy v. Johnson*, 8 Ga. 236, 243 (1850); *Flournoy v. Newton*, 8 Ga. 306, 311 (1850); *Cleland v. Waters*, 19 Ga. 35, 49 (1855).

15. *The Flint River Steamboat Co. v. Foster*, 5 Ga. 194, 204 (1848); *Beall v. Beall*, 8 Ga. 210, 228 (1850).

16. *Watson v. Tindal*, 24 Ga. 494, 505 (1858); *Vanduzer v. McMillan*, 28 Ga. 339, 342 (1859).

17. *Bethune v. Hughes*, 28 Ga. 560, 564 (1859); *Beall v. Beall*, 8 Ga. 210, 217 (1850).

18. *Merritt v. Scott*, 6 Ga. 563, 569 (1849); *State v. Lockhart*, 24 Ga. 420 (1858).

Twelve. Spirit of Improvement

1. *Young and Calhoun v. Harrison and Harrison*, 6 Ga. 130, 149 (1849); *Haywood v. the Mayor*, 12 Ga. 404, 411 (1853).

2. Kermit Hall, *Magic Mirror*, 106.

3. *Conyers v. Kenans and Hand*, 4 Ga. 308, 318–319 (1848); *Beverly and McBride v. Burke*, 9 Ga. 440, 448 (1851).

4. *Water-Lot Company of Columbus v. Bucks and Winter*, 5 Ga. 315, 327 (1848); *Young and Calhoun v. Harrison and Harrison*, 6 Ga. 130, 148 (1849).

5. *Mygatt v. Goetchins*, 20 Ga. 350, 358 (1856).

6. Hunt, "Law, Business and Politics," 266.

7. *Macon & W. R. R. v. Winn*, 19 Ga. 440, 446 (1856).

8. *Wade v. Johnston*, 25 Ga. 331, 336 (1858); *Charles River Bridge Company v. Warren Bridge Company*, 11 Peters (36 U.S.) 420 (1837): *Shorter v. Smith and Justices of the Inferior Court of Floyd County*, 9 Ga. 517, 526 (1851).

9. Huebner, *Southern Judicial Tradition*, 83; Joseph Henry Lumpkin, *South-Carolina Institute*, 33–34; *Franklin Bridge Co. v. Youngwood*, 14 Ga. 80, 85–86 (1853); *Hightower v. Thornton*, 8 Ga. 486, 501, 505 (1850); Heath, *Constructive Liberalism*, 310.

10. *Whitehead v. Peck*, 1 Ga. 140, 144 (1846); *Hightower v. Thornton*, 8 Ga. 486, 501, 505 (1850). Lumpkin did not participate in the case of *Carey v. Rice*, 2 Ga. 406 (1847), because he was a shareholder in Bank of Columbus, one of the parties in interest.

11. Joseph Henry Lumpkin, *South-Carolina Institute*, 14; *Mims v. Lockett*, 20 Ga. 474, 477 (1856); *Waddel v. State*, 27 Ga. 262, 263 (1859).

12. *Vance v. Crawford*, 4 Ga. 445, 460 (1848); *Flanders v. Meath*, 27 Ga. 358, 363 (1859); *Kendrick v. McCrary*, 11 Ga. 603, 605 (1852); *Biggs v. State*, 29 Ga. 723, 729 (1860).

13. Kent, *Commentaries*, 2nd ed., 2:129, quoted in Friedman, *A History of American Law*, 184; Walker, "The Legal Condition of Women," 145.

14. *Vance v. Crawford*, 4 Ga. 445, 460 (1848); *Wylly v. Collins & Co.*, 9 Ga. 225, 237 (1851); *Hobgood v. Martin*, 31 Ga. 62, 68 (1860); *Blake v. Irwin*, 3 Ga. 345, 370 (1847).

15. *Head v. Head*, 2 Ga. 191 (1847); *Chapman v. Gray*, 8 Ga. 337, 348–349 (1850); *Askew v. Dupree*, 30 Ga. 173, 190 (1860).

16. *Brown v. Westbrook*, 27 Ga. 102, 107 (1859); *Cason v. Cason*, 15 Ga. 405, 407–408 (1854).

17. *Smith v. The State*, 23 Ga. 297, 305–306 (1857).

18. *Boon v. State*, 1 Ga. 618, 624 (1846); *Van Buren v. Webster*, 12 Ga. 615, 617 (1853).

19. *Dean v. Traylor*, 8 Ga. 169, 171 (1850); *Richardson v. Roberts*, 23 Ga. 215, 221 (1857); *The Flint River Steamboat Co. v. Foster*, 5 Ga. 194, 204 (1848); *Neal v. Crew*, 12 Ga. 93, 94–95 (1852).

20. Huebner, *Southern Judicial Tradition*, 85.

Thirteen. From Slavery to Secession

1. Pound, *Formative Era*, 4; Reid, "Lessons of Lumpkin," 571, 593.

2. Finkelman, "Slaves As Fellow Servants," 290; Flanigan, "Criminal Procedure," 547; Nash, "The Texas Supreme Court," 622, 624 n.11.

3. Stephenson, "To Protect and Defend," 579–608; Reid, "Lessons of Lumpkin," 591.

4. Catterall, *Judicial Cases*, 1–94; see also "Lessons of Lumpkin," 582.

5. Fisher, "Ideology and Imagery," 45; *Bryan v. Walton*, 14 Ga. 185, 199 (1853).

6. Joseph Henry Lumpkin to Howell Cobb, January 21, 1849, reprinted in the "Correspondence of Robert Toombs, et al.," 94–95.

7. *Southern Recorder*, December 4, 1849; Shyrock, *Georgia and the Union*, 218.

8. John Henry Lumpkin to Howell Cobb, July 29, 1950, reprinted in the "Correspondence of Robert Toombs, et al.," 208–209.

9. Potter, *The Impending Crisis*, 128–129; James C. Cobb, "Making of a Secessionist," 318–319; Joseph Henry Lumpkin to Howell Cobb, Feb. 10, 1851, reprinted in "Correspondence of Robert Toombs, et al.," 227; Shyrock, *Georgia and the Union*, 8.

10. *Southern Recorder*, December 4, 1849; *Neal v. Farmer*, 9 Ga. 555, 582–583 (1851).

11. Genovese, *A Consuming Fire*, xiv; *Scudder v. Woodbridge*, 1 Ga. 195, 198–199 (1846); *Farwell v. Boston & Worcester Railroad*, 45 Mass. (4 Met.) 49 (1842).

12. *Gorman v. Campbell*, 14 Ga. 137, 143 (1853); Finkelman, "Slaves As Fellow Servants," 269–293; *State v. Mann*, 13 N.C. (1 Dev.) 263, 265–267 (1829).

13. *Johnson v. Lovett*, 31 Ga. 187, 190–191 (1860); *Moran v. Davis*, 18 Ga. 722, 723–724 (1855).

14. Maddex, "Proslavery Millennialism," 46, 48–50.

15. Thomas R. R. Cobb, *Negro Slavery*, xxxv–xxxvi.

16. Genovese, *A Consuming Fire*, 81; *Giles v. State*, 6 Ga. 276, 283 (1849); *Neal v. Farmer*, 9 Ga. 555, 582 (1851); *Bryan v. Walton*, 14 Ga. 185, 198 (1853).

17. Joseph Henry Lumpkin to Callie Lumpkin King, October 13, 1851; Thomas R. R. Cobb, *Negro Slavery*, 219.

18. *Mayor v. Howard*, 6 Ga. 213, 220 (1849); *Cleland v. Waters*, 19 Ga. 35, 41 (1855); *Bailey v. Barnelly*, 23 Ga. 582 (1857); Thomas R. R. Cobb, *Negro Slavery*, 207, 218.

19. Finkelman, "Slaves As Fellow Servants," 292; *Latimer v. Alexander*, 14 Ga. 259, 265 (1853); *Lennard v. Boynton*, 11 Ga. 109, 113 (1852); *Brooks v. Smith*, 21 Ga. 261, 265 (1857).

20. Langum, "The Role of Intellect," 1, 2; *Lennard v. Boynton*, 113.

21. *Vance v. Crawford*, 4 Ga. 445, 459 (1848); *Bryan v. Walton*, 14 Ga. 185, 206 (1853); *Cleland v. Waters*, 19 Ga. 35, 43 (1855).

22. *American Colonization Society v. Gartrell*, 23 Ga. 448, 465 (1857); *Sanders v. Ward*, 25 Ga. 109, 124 (1858).

23. *Cleland v. Waters*, 19 Ga. 35, 42 (1855).

Fourteen. A Flaming Sword

1. Linton Stephens to Alexander H. Stephens, May 18, 1859, Manhattanville College collection (hereafter abbreviated MCC).

2. Linton Stephens to Alexander H. Stephens, July 10, 1860, and July 15, 1860 (MCC).

3. Linton Stephens to Alexander H. Stephens, July 13, 1860 (MCC).

4. Coulter, *College Life*, 39; University of Georgia Trustees Minutes, 1857–1877.

5. Gwen Wood, *A Unique*, 6–13. Wood states that the Lumpkin Law School "was finally incorporated into the University structure within the first year of operation," but the trustees' minutes make it clear that it was an integral part of the university from the outset.

6. McCash, *Thomas R. R. Cobb*, 126; Thomas, *Memoirs of a Southerner*, 32.

7. McCash, *Thomas R. R. Cobb*, 184; *Choice v. State*, 31 Ga. 424, 475 (1860); *McGinnis v. State*, 31 Ga. 256, 259 (1860).

8. Avery, *State of Georgia*, 130–131.

9. Avery, *State of Georgia*, 138–142; Johnson, *Patriarchal Republic*, 120.

10. McCash, *Thomas R. R. Cobb*, 216–217.

11. Hull, *Annals of Athens*, 222, 226.

12. McCash, *Thomas R. R. Cobb*, 244, 254, 260, 265–266.

13. Thomas R. R. Cobb to Callie Lumpkin King, November 6, 1861.

14. Parks, *Joseph E. Brown*, 180–181; Joseph E. Brown to Joseph Henry Lumpkin, January 28, 1862, Joseph E. Brown Papers, Hargrett Library.

15. Joseph Henry Lumpkin to Callie Lumpkin King, March 15, 1862.

16. *Howes, Hyatt & Co. v. Chester & Co.*, 33 Ga. 89, 90 (1861); *Edmonson v. Union Bank of Tennessee*, 91, 93 (1861).

17. Coulter, *Confederate States*, 76, 417.

18. McCash, *Thomas R. R. Cobb*, 321–322.

19. *In Memoriam*, 33 Ga. Supp. 199, 201–203 (1864).

20. Coleman, *Confederate Athens*, 171–172; Hull, *Annals of Athens*, 241; *Darracott v. Pennington and Stapleton*, 34 Ga. 388, 392 (1866).

21. *McLaughlin & Co. v. O'Dowd*, 34 Ga. 485, 487 (1866). The "Program of the Unveiling of Busts of Four Chief Justices of the Supreme Court of Georgia," dated January 7, 1963, states that Lumpkin "was recognized as the President or Presiding Officer of the Court till the office of Chief Justice was created in 1866, at which time he became the Chief Justice of the Court."

22. *Armstrong v. Jones*, 34 Ga. 309, 312 (1866); Talmadge, "Missing Correspondence," 411, 413.

23. *Heard v. State*, 35 Ga. 158, 168 (1866); Joseph Henry Lumpkin to Joseph E. Brown, quoted in Parks, *Joseph E. Brown*, 365.

24. Parks, *Joseph E. Brown*, 366–367.

25. *Southern Watchman*, June 12, 1867.

26. 36 Ga. 20, 41–42 (1867).

27. Bleckley, "Joseph Henry Lumpkin," 633–635; Lamar, *Reminiscences of Famous Georgians*, 358.

28. *Young and Calhoun v. Harrison and Harrison*, 6 Ga. 130, 149 (1849).

29. Alford, speech.

30. *Choice v. Marshall*, 1 Ga. 97, 106 (1846); *Hightower v. Thornton*, 8 Ga. 486, 501 (1850); Karsten, *Heart v. Head*, 5.

31. *American Colonization Society v. Gartrell*, 23 Ga. 448, 464 (1857); Reid, "Lessons of Lumpkin," 578–579.

32. John B. Harris, *Supreme Court of Georgia*, viii.

33. Parks, *Joseph E. Brown*, 367.

BIBLIOGRAPHY

Alford, Neil H. Speech commemorating transfer of deed to Lumpkin House in Athens, November 14, 1975. Box 8. Administrative Archives, School of Law, University of Georgia.

Almand, Bond. "The Preparation and Adoption of the Code of 1863." *Georgia Bar Journal* 14 (1951–52).

Amar, Akhil Reed. "The Bill of Rights and the Fourteenth Amendment." *Yale Law Journal* 101 (April 1992).

Andrews, Garnett. *Reminiscences of an Old Georgia Lawyer*. Atlanta: Franklin Steam Printing House, 1870.

Avery, I. W. *History of the State of Georgia*. New York: Brown & Derby, 1881.

Barnes, Gilbert Hobbs. *The Anti-Slavery Impulse, 1830–1844*. New York: Harcourt Brace & World, Harbinger edition, 1964.

Bartram, William. *The Travels of William Bartram: Francis Harper's Naturalist Edition*. Athens: University of Georgia Press, 1998.

Beeson, Leola Selman. *History Stories of Milledgeville and Baldwin County*. Macon, Ga.: The J. W. Burke Company, 1943.

Bleckley, Logan E. "Joseph Henry Lumpkin: First Chief Justice of Georgia." *The Green Bag* 19 (1907), 633–635.

Bode, Frederick A. "A Common Sphere: White Evangelicals and Gender in Antebellum Georgia." *Georgia Historical Quarterly* 79 (1995).

Bonner, James C. *Milledgeville, Georgia's Antebellum Capital*. Athens: University of Georgia Press, 1977.

Borgher, Elbert W. G. *Secondary Education in Georgia, 1732–1858*. Camden, N.J.: I. F. Hontzinger & Co., 1933.

Bradbury, Malcolm. *Dangerous Pilgrimages, Transatlantic Mythologies and the Novel*. London: Secker & Warburg, 1955.

Brantly, W. T. *Life and Character of Joseph Henry Lumpkin, An Oration delivered in Athens, Ga. before the Phi Kappa Society*. Savannah, Ga.: News and Herald, 1867.

Brown, Isaac V. *Memoirs of the Rev. Robert Finley, D.D., Late Pastor of the Presbyterian Congregation of Basking Ridge, New-Jersey and President of Franklin College, Located in Athens, in the State of Georgia, with Brief Sketches of Some of His Contemporaries and Numerous Notes.* New Brunswick, N.J.: Terhune & Letson, 1819.

Campbell, J. H. *Georgia Baptists: Historical and Biographical.* Macon, Ga.: J. W. Burke & Co., 1874.

Cardozo, Benjamin. *The Nature of the Judicial Process.* New Haven: Yale University Press, 1921.

Catterall, Helen Tunncliff, ed. *Judicial Cases.* Vol. 3. New York: Negro Universities Press, 1968.

Cobb, James C. "The Making of a Secessionist: Henry L. Benning and the Coming of the Civil War." *Georgia Historical Quarterly* 60 (1976).

Cobb, Thomas R. R. *An Inquiry into the Law of Negro Slavery in the United States of America to which is prefixed, An Historical Sketch of Slavery.* Athens: University of Georgia Press, 1999.

Cody, L. L. *The Lumpkin Family of Georgia.* Macon, Ga.: n.p., 1928.

Coleman, Kenneth. *American Revolution in Georgia 1763–1789.* Athens: University of Georgia Press, 1958.

———. *Confederate Athens.* Athens: University of Georgia Press, 1968.

Coleman, Kenneth, and Charles Stephen Gurr, eds. *Dictionary of Georgia Biography.* Vol. 2. Athens: University of Georgia Press, 1983.

Collins, V. L. *Princeton Past and Present.* Princeton: Princeton University Press, 1945.

Cook, Charles M. *The American Codification Movement: A Study in Antebellum Legal Reform.* Westport, Conn.: Greenwood Press, 1981.

"Correspondence of Robert Toombs, Alexander H. Stephens and Howell Cobb." *2 Ann. Rep. Am. Hist. Ass'n for Year 1911.*

Cory, Earle Wallace. "Temperance and Prohibition in Ante-bellum Georgia." M.A. thesis, University of Georgia, 1961.

Coulter, E. Merton. *College Life in the Old South.* Athens: University of Georgia Press, 1983.

———. *The Confederate States of America 1861–1865.* Baton Rouge: Louisiana State University Press, 1950.

———. "Francis Meson, an Early Georgia Merchant and Philanthropist." *Georgia Historical Quarterly* 42 (1958).

———. *Georgia, a Short History.* Chapel Hill: University of North Carolina Press, 1960.

———. "A Georgia Educational Movement." *Georgia Historical Quarterly* 9 (1925).

————. "Madison Springs, Georgia Watering Place." *Georgia Historical Quarterly* 47 (1963).

————. "Meson Academy, Lexington, Georgia." *Georgia Historical Quarterly* 42 (1958).

————. "The Nullification Movement in Georgia." *Georgia Historical Quarterly* 5 (1921).

————. *Old Petersburg and the Broad River Valley of Georgia: Their Rise and Decline.* Athens: University of Georgia Press, 1965.

Cresson, William Penn. *James Monroe.* Chapel Hill: University of North Carolina Press, 1964.

Custer, Lawrence B. "The Golden Age of the Circuit Rider." *Georgia State Bar Journal* 29, no. 2 (1992).

Debats, Donald Arthur. "Elites and Masses: Political Studies, Communication and Behavior in Ante-Bellum Georgia." Ph.D. diss., University of Wisconsin, 1973.

Deen, Braswell D., Jr., and William Scott Henwood. *Georgia's Appellate Judiciary, Profiles and History.* Norcross, Ga.: The Harrison Company, 1987.

Dowlut, Robert. "Federal and State Constitutional Guarantees to Arms." *Dayton Law Review* 15 (1989).

Dudley, G. M. *Reports of the Decisions made by the Judges of the Superior Courts of Law and Chancery of the State of Georgia.* New York: Collins, Keese & Co., 1837.

Faz, Carolyn Bryant. *The History of Salem Baptist Church, 1789–1989.* Katy, Tex.: C. B. Faz, 1989.

Finkelman, Paul. "Exploring Southern Legal History." *North Carolina Law Review* 64 (1985–86).

————. *An Imperfect Union.* Chapel Hill: University of North Carolina Press, 1981.

————. "Slaves as Fellow Servants: Ideology, Law, and Industrialization." *American Journal of Legal History* 31 (1987).

————"Southern Slavery at the State and Local Level." In *Articles in American Slavery*, ed. Finkelman. Vol. 7. New York: Garland Publishing, 1989.

Fisher, William W., III. "The Ideology and Imagery in the Law of Slavery." In *Slavery and the Law*, ed. Paul Finkelman. Madison, Wis.: Madison House, 1997.

Flanigan, Daniel J. "Criminal Procedure in Slave Trials in the Ante-bellum South." *Journal of Southern History* 4 (1974).

Foster, Charles I. *An Errand of Mercy, The Evangelical Front, 1790–1837.* Chapel Hill: University of North Carolina Press, 1960.

Fredrickson, George M. "A Man but Not a Brother: Abraham Lincoln and Racial Equality." *Journal of Southern History* 41 (Feb. 1975).

Friedman, Lawrence M. *A History of American Law*. New York: Simon and Schuster, 1973.

Garrett, Franklin M. *Atlanta and Its Environs: A Chronicle of Its People and Events*. Athens: University of Georgia Press, 1969.

Genovese, Eugene D. *A Consuming Fire: The Fall of the Confederacy in the Mind of the White Christian South*. Athens: University of Georgia Press, 1998.

Gifford, James M. "The African Colonization Movement in Georgia, 1817–1860." Ph.D. diss., University of Georgia, 1977.

Gilmer, George R. *Sketches of Some of the First Settlers of Upper Georgia*. Reprint, Americus, Ga.: Americus Book Company, 1926.

Goulding, Rev. F. R. "Memorial of Thomas Goulding, D.D." In *Memorial Volume of the Semi-Centennial of the Theological Seminary at Columbia, South Carolina*. Columbia, S.C.: Presbyterian Publishing House, 1884.

Grice, Warren. *The Georgia Bench and Bar*. Vol. 1. Macon, Ga.: J. W. Burke & Co., 1931.

Haar, Charles M., ed. *The Golden Age of American Law*. New York: George Braziller, 1965.

Hall, Kermit L. *The Magic Mirror, Law in American History*. New York: Oxford University Press, 1989.

Hardee, Charles Seton Henry. "Notes and Documents." *Georgia Historical Quarterly* 12 (1928).

Harden, Edward Jackson. *The Life of George M. Troup*. Savannah: E. J. Purse, 1859.

Hardman, Keith J. *Charles Grandison Finney, 1792–1875*. Syracuse: Syracuse University Press, 1987.

Hargrett, Lester. "Student Life at the University of Georgia in the 1840s." *Georgia Historical Quarterly* 18 (1924).

Harris, Iverson. "In Memoriam." *Georgia Reports* 36 (1867).

Harris, John B., ed. *A History of the Supreme Court of Georgia, A Centennial Volume*. Macon, Ga.: J. W. Burke & Co., 1948.

Heath, Milton Sydney. *Constructive Liberalism: The Role of the State in the Economic Development in Georgia to 1860*. Cambridge: Harvard University Press, 1954.

Heyrman, Christine Leigh. *Southern Cross: The Beginnings of the Bible Belt*. Chapel Hill: University of North Carolina Press, 1997.

Hill, Lodowick Johnson. *The Hills of Wilkes County, Georgia, and Allied Families*. Danielsville, Ga.: Heritage Papers, 1987.

Hill, Samuel S., ed. *Encyclopedia of Religion in the South*. Macon, Ga.: Mercer University Press, 1984.

Historic Oglethorpe County, Inc. *Historic Oglethorpe County, A Guide to Historic Resources and Points of Interest.* Athens: Piedmont Impressions, n.d.

Huebner, Timothy S. "Joseph Henry Lumpkin and Evangelical Reform in Georgia: Temperance, Education and Industrialization, 1830–1860." *Georgia Historical Quarterly* 75, no. 2 (1991).

———. *The Southern Judicial Tradition: State Judges and Sectional Distinctiveness, 1790–1890.* Athens: University of Georgia Press, 1999.

Hull, Augustus Longstreet. *Annals of Athens, Georgia, 1801–1901.* Danielsville, Ga.: Heritage Papers, 1978.

Hunt, James L. "Law, Business and Politics: Liability for Accidents in Georgia, 1846–1880." *The Georgia Historical Quarterly* 84 (2000).

Hynds, Ernest C. *Antebellum Athens and Clarke County.* Athens: University of Georgia Press, 1974.

Ingersoll, Henry J. "Confusion of Law and Equity." *Yale Law Journal* 21 (1911).

Johnson, Michael P. *Toward a Patriarchal Republic—The Secession of Georgia.* Baton Rouge, La.: Louisiana State University Press, 1977.

Johnson, William R. *Schooled Lawyers: A Study in the Clash of Professional Cultures.* New York: New York University Press, 1978.

Johnston, Richard Malcolm. *Autobiography of Col. Richard Malcolm Johnston.* Washington: The Neale Company, 1901.

Jones, Joseph H. *The Life of Ashbel Green, V.D.M.* New York: Robert Carter and Brothers, 1849.

Karsten, Peter. *Heart versus Head: Judge-made Law in Nineteenth-Century America.* Chapel Hill: University of North Carolina Press, 1997.

Knight, Edgar W., ed. *A Documentary History of Education in the South before 1860.* Vol. 3. Chapel Hill: University of North Carolina Press, 1952.

Knight, Lucian Lamar. *Centennial Oration: The Voices of the Past, Delivered in the Chapel of the State University of Georgia at Athens, Ga., Tuesday Evening, June 15, 1920 at the Centennial Exercises of the Phi Kappa Society, Founded by Chief Justice Joseph Henry Lumpkin.* n.p.

———. *Georgia and Georgians.* Vol. 1. Chicago: The Lewis Publishing Co., 1917.

———. *Reminiscences of Famous Georgians.* Atlanta: Franklin-Turner Co., 1907.

Koch, Mary Levin. "The View from Chalky Level: Francina Elizabeth Greer and the Plantation World of Clarke County." *Georgia Historical Quarterly* 80 (1996).

LaBoone, Elizabeth. "History of the University of Georgia Library." M.A. thesis, University of Georgia, 1954.

Lamar, Joseph R. "History of the Establishment of the Supreme Court of Georgia." *Report of the Georgia Bar Association* 24 (1907).

LaMotte, Louis A. *Colored Light, The Story of the Influence of Columbia Theological Seminary, 1828–1936.* Richmond: Presbyterian Committee of Education, 1937.

Langum, David J. "The Role of Intellect and Fortuity in Legal Change: An Incident from the Law of Slavery." *The American Journal of Legal History* 28 (1984).

Llewellyn, Karl N. "Remarks on the Theory of Appellate Decision and the Rules or Canons about How Statutes Are to Be Construed." *Vanderbilt Law Review* 3 (1950).

Loveland, Anne C. *Southern Evangelicals and the Social Order, 1800–1860.* Baton Rouge: Louisiana State University Press, 1980.

Lumpkin, Ben Gray, and Martha Neville, eds. *The Lumpkin Family of Virginia, Georgia, and Mississippi.* Clarksville, Tenn.: n.p., 1973.

Lumpkin, Bryan H. "Lumpkin Family History." Typed document. Georgia State Archives, 1936.

Lumpkin, Joseph Henry. *Address before Hopewell Presbytery, the Board of Trustees of Oglethorpe University, March 31, 1837.* Georgia Journal, 1837.

———. *An Address before the South-Carolina Institute at Its Second Annual Fair on 19th November, 1850.* Charleston, S.C.: Walker and James, 1851.

———. *Address on Natural History Delivered before the Phi Delta and Ciceronian Societies on the 1st day of July, 1836 at the Mercer Institute.* Washington, Ga.: Christian Index, 1836.

———. "Industrial Regeneration of the South." *DeBow's Review* 12 (January 1852).

Lumpkin, Sam, and Eloise Lumpkin. *The Alabama Family of Lumpkin.* Georgia State Archives, n.d.

Lumpkin, Wilson. *Removal of the Cherokee Indians from Georgia 1827–1838.* Vol. 1. New York: Dodd, Mead, and Co., 1907.

Maddex, Jack C., Jr. "Proslavery Millennialism: Social Eschatology in Antebellum Southern Calvinism." *American Quarterly* 31 (1971).

Matthews, Donald G. *Religion in the Old South.* Chicago: University of Chicago Press, 1977.

Matthews, Jean V. *Toward a New Society: American Thought and Culture 1800–1830.* Boston: Twayne Publishers, 1991.

McCash, William B. *Thomas R. R. Cobb: The Making of a Southern Nationalist.* Macon, Ga.: Mercer University Press, 1983.

McClintock, Henry L. *Handbook of the Principles of Equity.* St. Paul: West Publishing Co., 1946.

McGloughlin, William G. *Revivals, Awakenings, and Reform.* Chicago: University of Chicago Press, 1978.

McPherson, Robert G. "Wilson Lumpkin." In *Georgians in Profile*, ed. Horace Montgomery. Athens: University of Georgia Press, 1958.

"Memoir of Joseph Henry Lumpkin, Chief Justice of Georgia." *United States Law Magazine*, July and August 1851.

Miller, Perry. *The Life of the Mind in America from the Revolution to the Civil War.* New York: Harcourt, Brace & World, 1965.

Miller, Stephen F. *Bench and Bar of Georgia.* Vol. 1. Philadelphia: J. B. Lippincott, 1858.

Mohr, Clarence Lee. "Oglethorpe County, Georgia, During the Formative Period, 1773–1830." M.A. thesis, University of Georgia, 1970.

Morris, Thomas. *Southern Slavery and the Law, 1619–1860.* Chapel Hill: University of North Carolina Press, 1996.

Murray, Paul. *The Whig Party in Georgia, 1825–1853.* Chapel Hill: University of North Carolina Press, 1948.

Myers, Robert Manson, ed. *The Children of Pride, A True Story of Georgia and the Civil War.* New Haven: Yale University Press, 1972.

Nash, A. E. Keir. "Negro Rights, Unionism, and Greatness of the South Carolina Court of Appeals: The Extraordinary Chief Justice John Belton O'Neall." *South Carolina Law Review* 21 (1969).

———. "The Texas Supreme Court and Trial Rights of Blacks 1845–1860." *Journal of American History* 58 (1971).

Norgren, Jill. *The Cherokee Cases: The Confrontation of Law and Politics.* New York: McGraw-Hill, 1966.

Oakes, James. *Slavery and Freedom, An Interpretation of the Old South.* New York: Alfred A. Knopf, 1990.

Orr, Dorothy. *History of Education in Georgia.* Chapel Hill: University of North Carolina Press, 1950.

Parks, Joseph H. *Joseph E. Brown of Georgia.* Baton Rouge: Louisiana State University Press, 1977.

Paschal, George W. *Ninety-four Years, Agnes Paschal.* 1871. Reprint, Spartanburg, S.C.: The Reprint Company, 1974.

Pease, William H., and Jane H. Pease. *James Louis Pettigru: Southern Conservative, Southern Dissenter.* Athens: University of Georgia Press, 1995.

Pegram, Thomas R. *Battling Demon Rum: The Struggle for a Dry America, 1800–1933.* Chicago: Ivan R. Dee, 1998.

Phillips, Ulrich B. *Georgia and State Rights.* Yellow Springs, Ohio: The Antioch Press, 1968.

Potter, David M. *The Impending Crisis, 1848–1861.* New York: Harper & Row, 1976.

Pound, Roscoe. *The Formative Era of American Law.* Gloucester, Mass.: Peter Smith, 1960.

———. *The Lawyer from Antiquity to Modern Times.* St. Paul: West Publishing Co., 1953.

Reed, Alfred Z. *Training for the Public Profession of Law, Historical Development and Principal Contemporary Problems of Legal Education in the United States.* New York: The Carnegie Foundation for the Advancement of Teaching, 1921.

Reese, Wm. M. "Reminiscences: A Paper by Judge Wm. M. Reese of Washington, Ga., read before the Fourteenth Annual Session of the Georgia Bar Association." *Report of Georgia Bar Association* 14 (1897).

Reid, John Philip. "Lessons of Lumpkin: A Review of Recent Literature on Law, Comity, and the Impending Crisis." *William and Mary Law Review* 23 (1982).

Robinson, William M., Jr. *Justice in Grey: A History of the Judicial System in the Confederate States of America.* Cambridge: Harvard University Press, 1941.

Rogers, Ava D. *Housing of Oglethorpe County, Georgia, 1790–1860.* Tallahassee: Florida State University Press, 1971.

Russell, James M., and Jerry Thornbery. "William Finch of Atlanta: The Black Politician as Civic Leader." In *Southern Black Leaders of the Reconstruction Era,* ed. Howard N. Rabinowitz. Urbana: University of Illinois Press, 1982.

Ryman, Dean E. *Joseph Henry Lumpkin, An Unintentional Autobiography.* Privately published.

Scarborough, Ruth. *The Opposition to Slavery in Georgia prior to 1860.* New York: Negro Universities Press, 1968.

Scomp, H. A. *King Alcohol in the Realm of King Cotton.* Chicago: The Blakely Printing Co., 1888.

Shepperson, George, ed. "Thomas Chalmers: The Free Church of Scotland and the South." *Journal of Southern History* 17 (1951).

Shyrock, Richard Harrison. "The Early Industrial Revolution in the Empire State." *Georgia Historical Quarterly* 40 (1927).

———. *Georgia and the Union in 1850.* New York: AMS Press, 1968.

Slave Narratives, Georgia Narratives. Part 3, vol. 13. St. Clair, Mich.: Scholarly Press, 1976.

Smith, George G., Jr. *A History of Methodism in Georgia.* Washington, Ga.: Wilkes Publishing Company, 1970.

Smith, Morton H. *Studies in Southern Presbyterian Theology*. Phillipsburg, N.J.: Presbyterian and Reformed Publishing Company, 1987.

Sparks, W. H. *The Memories of Fifty Years*. Philadelphia: Claxten, Remsen & Haffelfinger, 1870.

Stacy, Rev. James. *A History of the Presbyterian Church in Georgia*. Elberton, Ga.: Press of the Star, 1912.

Staudenraus, P. J. *The African Colonization Movement 1816–1865*. New York: Columbia University Press, 1961.

Stephenson, Mason W., and D. Grier Stephenson. " 'To Protect and Defend': Joseph Henry Lumpkin, the Supreme Court of Georgia and Slavery." *Emory Law Journal* 25 (summer 1976).

Story, Joseph. *Commentaries on Equity Jurisprudence*. 14th ed. Vol. 1. Boston: Little, Brown and Company, 1918.

Streifford, David M. "The American Colonization Society: An Application of Republican Ideology to Early Antebellum Reform." *Journal of Southern History* 45 (1979).

Surrency, Erwin C. "The Creation of a Judicial System, the History of the Georgia Courts, 1753 to Date." Unpublished manuscript, 2000.

———. *History of the Federal Courts*. New York: Oceana Publications, 1987.

Sydnor, Charles. *Development of Southern Sectionalism, 1819–1848*. Baton Rouge: Louisiana State University Press, 1948.

Talmadge, John E. "Joseph E. Brown's Missing Correspondence." *Georgia Historical Quarterly* 44 (1960).

Thomas, E. J. *Memoirs of a Southerner, 1840–1923*. Savannah: n.p., 1923.

Tocqueville, Alexis de. *Democracy in America*. 2nd ed. 1836.

Tushnet, Mark V. *The American Law of Slavery, 1810–1860: Considerations of Humanity and Interest*. Princeton: Princeton University Press, 1981.

Tyrell, Ian R. "Drink and Temperance in the Antebellum South: An Overview and Interpretation." *Journal of Southern History* 68 (1982).

———. *Sobering Up*. Westport, Conn.: Greenwood Press, 1979.

Wade, John Donald. *Augustus Baldwin Longstreet: A Study of the Development of Culture in the South*. New York: The MacMillan Company, 1924.

Walker, Timothy. "The Legal Condition of Women." *Western Law Journal*. 1849.

Walther, Erich H. *The Fire-Eaters*. Baton Rouge: Louisiana State University Press, 1992.

Warren, Charles. *A History of the American Bar*. New York: Howard Fertig, 1966.

———. *History of the Harvard Law School and of Early Legal Conditions in America*. New York: Lewis Pub. Co., 1908.

————. *The Supreme Court in United States History*. Vol. 1. Boston: Little, Brown & Company, 1926.

Webb, Stephen Saunders. *1676, the End of American Independence*. New York: Alfred A. Knopf, 1984.

Wertenbaker, Thomas Jefferson. *Princeton 1746–1896*. Princeton: Princeton University Press, 1946.

Williams, Charles Richard. *The Cliosophic Society, Princeton University*. Princeton: Princeton University Press, 1916.

Wise, Lena Smith. *History of Oglethorpe County*. n.p.

————. *The Story of Oglethorpe County*. Lexington, Ga.: Historic Oglethorpe County, 1980.

Wood, Gwen Y. *A Unique and Fortuitous Combination*. Athens: University of Georgia Law School Association, 1998.

Wyatt-Brown, Bertram. *Lewis Tappan and the Evangelical War Against Slavery*. Cleveland: Press of Case Western Reserve University, 1969.

Zainadin, Jamil S. *Law in Antebellum Society: Legal Change and Economic Expansion*. New York: Knopf, 1983.

INDEX

Adams, John, 40

Adams, John Quincy, 27

Alford, Neill, 3, 150–51

Almand, Bond, 91–92

American Bible Society, 98, 145

American Colonization Society, 15, 56–60, 135, 151

American Colonization Society v. Gartrell, 59–60, 135, 151

American Temperance Society, 42–45, 157 (n. 25)

American Whig Society, 19, 21

Andrews, Garnett, 30–31, 36

Antelope, 27

Armstrong v. Jones, 147

Askew v. Dupree, 121

Athens, Georgia, 13, 57, 66, 81, 91; Lumpkin's move to, 76–77; in Civil War, 141, 146–47

Bacon's Rebellion, 5–6

Bailey v. Barnelly, 132

Baldwin, Abraham, 14

Bank of St. Mary's v. Mumford & Tyson, 114

Baptists, 10, 37, 39, 67–68

Bartram, William, 6

Beall v. Beall, 112–13

Beecher, Lyman, 42–43

Bell, John, 139

Benning, Henry L., 100, 127–28, 140, 148

Berkeley, Sir William, 5

Berrien, John MacPherson: Princeton graduate, 17; as important lawyer, 23; as senator, 27, 48; as head of moderates in State Rights party, 54; as dinner guest in Lumpkin's home, 77; turns down job as Georgia's chief justice, 90; Lumpkin's tribute to, 108, 122, 162 (ch. 11, n. 4)

Berry v. The State, 162 (n. 8)

Bethune v. Hughes, 113

Beverly and McBride v. Burke, 115

Biggs v. State, 119

Blackford, Isaac N., 104

Blackstone, Sir William, 23

Blake v. Irwin, 120

Bleckley, Logan E., 150

Boon v. State, 122

Bostwick v. Perkins, 161 (ch. 11, n. 1)

Brantly, W. T., 8, 16, 29, 149

Braxton, Carter, 6

Breckinridge, John C., 139–40

Brooks v. Smith, 133

Brougham, Lord Henry, 67

Brown, Rev. John, 15–16

Brown, Joseph E., 2, 136, 140, 143, 147, 149, 152

Brown v. Westbrook, 121

Bryan v. Walton, 3, 59–60, 126, 131

Buchanan, James, 140

Caldwell, Elias B., 56–57

Calhoun, John, 2, 22, 25, 54, 69, 159 (n. 14)

Camp meetings, 38–40

Cappel v. Causey, 162 (ch. 11, n. 4)

Cardozo, Benjamin, 98

Carey v. McDougald, 111

Carey v. Rice, 163 (n. 10)

Cason v. Cason, 121

Catron, John, 124

Chalmers, Rev. Thomas, 75, 83–84

Chance v. McWhorter, 108

Chapman v. Gray, 120

Charles River Bridge Company v. Warren Bridge Company, 117

Charlton, R. M., 31, 80–81

Charlton, T. U. P., 31

Cherokees, 6, 26–27

Chestnut, John, 18

Chestnut, Mary Boykin, 18

Choate, Rufus, 1, 98

Choice v. Marshall, 107, 151

Choice v. State, 139

Church, Alonzo, 77, 105–6

Clapham Sect, 51

Clark party, 26, 54, 58

Clay, Henry, 33, 47, 57, 59, 127

Cleland v. Waters, 56, 59, 112, 132–34

Cliosophian Society, 19–21, 25

Cobb, Howell, 2, 25, 75, 100, 103, 105, 139; Lumpkin's letter to, regarding

Wilmot Proviso, 126–28; role in Georgia's secession from United States, 140–42

Cobb, Marion Lumpkin, 24, 43, 74–75, 79, 82, 96, 142

Cobb, Thomas R. R., 2, 25, 77, 79, 101, 136; opinions about Joseph Henry Lumpkin, 33, 43, 74–75; and school reform with J. H. Lumpkin, 65; and sicknesses in family, 82; as court reporter, 96–97; as University of Georgia trustee, 105; views and writings on slavery, 3, 131–33; role in Georgia's secession from United States, 138–42; death of, in Civil War, 145–48

Cobb, Thomas W., 22, 74

Colquitt, Walter T., 18, 33

Columbia Theological Seminary, 41, 45

Compromise of 1850, 127–28

Conyers v. Kenans and Hand, 115

Coulter, E. Merton, 5, 7, 8, 25, 55, 77

Crawford, George W., 18, 86, 89, 91

Crawford, William, 2, 9, 25, 57–58, 74

Creeks, 6, 26–27

Cushing, Caleb, 55

Dacey v. The State, 162 (n. 11)

Darracott v. Pennington and Stapleton, 165 (n. 20)

Davis, Jefferson, 141, 144

Dean v. Traylor, 122

Democratic party, 139

Demosthenian Society, 16, 24, 66

Dickens, Charles, 83

Douglas, Stephen A., 59, 139

Dudley, G. M., 31–32
Dudley v. Mallory, 62

Edmondson v. Union Bank of Tennessee, 165 (n. 16)
Edwards, Rev. Justin, 42–43
Emory College 45, 67
Eustis, George, 98
Evans v. Rogers, 162 (ch. 11, n. 7)

Farwell v. Boston & Worcester Railroad, 129, 134
Field, David Dudley, 96
Fillmore, Millard, 59
Finch, Bill, 61
Finkelmann, Paul, 3, 124, 129, 133
Finley, Rev. Robert, 15–17, 56
Finney, Charles Grandison, 32, 41
Flanders v. Meath, 119
Fletcher v. Peck, 8, 88
Flint River Steamboat Company v. Foster, 112, 123
Flournoy, Josiah, 46–47, 49
Flournoy v. Newton, 112
Forsyth, John, 7, 31, 57
Franklin Bridge Co. v. Youngwood, 117
Franklin College. *See* University of Georgia
Frelinghuysen, Theodore, 47, 58
Friedman, Lawrence, 134
Fugitive Slave Law, 98, 128

Garrison, William Lloyd, 46, 48, 53
Genovese, 60, 128, 131
Georgia Platform, 128
Georgia Supreme Court: early history, 86–89; formation, 89–97; enhanced

stature, 104, 112; historians' views on, 125
Georgia Temperance Society, 43–44, 46
Gerdine, Lucy Lumpkin, 24, 74, 75, 79, 82
Gerdine, William L. C., 75, 82
Gibson, John, 107–8, 123
Gilchrist, John J., 104
Giles v. State, 131
Gilmer, George, 23, 63, 74, 89, 105
Gorman v. Campbell, 129
Goulding, Thomas, 40–41, 45
Gray v. Gray, 100
Greeley, Horace, 88
Green, Ashbel, 18–21, 37
Grieve, Miller, 10, 24

Haar, Charles, 95
Hall, Kermit, 114
Hall, R. S., 162 (n. 10)
Harris, Iverson, 32, 34, 108, 146, 148
Harvard Law School, 1, 23, 98–99
Hayne, Robert, 54, 65, 157 (n. 6)
Haywood v. the Mayor, 63, 114
Head v. Head, 120
Heard v. State, 148
Hemphill, John, 124
Heyrman, Christine, 38
Hill, Ben, 143
Hines, Richard K., 162 (n. 10)
Hightower v. Thornton, 117–18, 151
Hobgood v. Martin, 120
Howes, Hyatt & Co. v. Chester & Co., 165 (n. 16)
Hoyt, Nathan, 145
Huebner, Timothy, 1, 3, 72, 117, 124, 150
Hull, Augustus Longstreet, 141

Hull, William Hope, 138

Irving, Washington, 83
Iverson, Alfred, 18

Jackson, Andrew, 17, 88, 90
Jackson, James, 90
Jay, John, 88
Jefferson, Thomas, 7, 40
Jenkins, Charles, 100, 103, 137, 145, 147, 148
Johnson, Herschel, 100, 105
Johnson, Michael, 140
Johnson v. Holt, 161 (ch. 11, n. 1)
Johnson v. Lovett, 130
Johnston, Richard Malcolm, 34–35
Jones, Rev. Charles Colcock, 61

Karsten, Peter, 1, 151
Kelly, James M., 63, 86
Kendrick v. McCrary, 119
Kent, James, 1, 23, 31, 45, 107–8, 117, 119
Key, Francis Scott, 27, 57
King, Callie Lumpkin, 2, 28, 73–105
    passim, 131, 142
King, Porter, 78, 82

Lafayette, General, 28
Lane v. Morris, 118
Langum, David, 134
Latimer v. Alexander, 133
Lee, Robert E., 142, 145
Lennard v. Boynton, 133–34
Lewis, John, 143
Lewis, Meriwether, 7
Lexington, Georgia, 5, 11–13, 29, 39, 41, 57, 66, 74–76

Lincoln, Abraham, 59, 139, 144
Litchfield Law School, 19, 22, 23, 44
Llewellyn, Karl, 123
Longstreet, Augustus Baldwin, 25, 44–45
Lumpkin, Callender Grieve, 10–12, 23, 36, 73–74, 81, 83–84, 137
Lumpkin, Chalmers, 75
Lumpkin, Charles, 141–42, 145
Lumpkin, Edward, 78, 141, 145–46
Lumpkin, Frank, 104, 141
Lumpkin, George, 5–6
Lumpkin, Jacob, 5–6
Lumpkin, James, 78, 82, 149
Lumpkin, John, 5–9, 25, 88
Lumpkin, John Henry, 74, 127
Lumpkin, Joseph Henry: childhood, 5–13; at University of Georgia, 14–17; at Princeton, 17–21; law studies 22–23; founds Phi Kappa Society, 24–25, 66; state legislator, 25–28; law practice, 29–36; early religious experience, 39–41; temperance work, 43–50; Boston speech on emancipation, 46, 49, 51–56, 68; involvement in American Colonization Society, 56–60; interest in education, 63–68; economic reform, 68–72; family life, 73–85; European travel, 82–85; election to Supreme Court, 89–90; law reform, 94–96, 127; court of claims appointment, 104; University of Georgia trustee, 104–6; decisions on constitutional, economic and family issues, 111–18; slavery opinions, 124–35; founding of law school, 137–38; views on secession, 138–39;

Confederate senate seat declined, 143; death, 149

Lumpkin, Joseph Troup, 28, 51, 74, 82

Lumpkin, Lucy Hopson, 6, 10

Lumpkin, Martha, 70

Lumpkin, Miller, 137, 142

Lumpkin, Robert, 104

Lumpkin, Samuel, 74

Lumpkin, Dr. Thomas, 153 (ch. 1, n. 2)

Lumpkin, Thomas, 74, 75

Lumpkin, Thomas Jefferson, 17–19, 154 (n. 14)

Lumpkin, William Wilberforce, 51, 75, 97, 142

Lumpkin, Wilson, 2, 5, 16, 25–26, 74, 95, 128; as governor, 46, 53, 69; as University of Georgia trustee, 105; support of Georgia's secession from United States, 140

Lumpkin Law School. *See* University of Georgia Law School

Lyon, Richard F., 137, 148

Macon & W. R. R. v. Winn, 116

Maddex, Jack, 131

Madison, James, 17, 19, 58

Madison Springs, 77–78

Marshall, John, 1, 8, 58, 88, 107–8, 123, 150

Martin v. Broach, 111

Masonry, 67

Matthew, Father Theobold, 48–50

Matthews, Donald, 37–38

Mayor v. Howard, 132

McAllister, Matthew, 18, 89

McCash, William B., 96–97, 141

McDonald, Charles, 100, 103, 136, 147

McDowell, William, 45

McGinnis v. State, 139

McLaughlin & Co. v. O'Dowd, 165 (n. 21)

Meigs, Josiah, 14

Mercer University, 67

Merritt v. Scott, 113

Meson, Francis, 9

Meson Academy, 9–10, 17, 24, 75

Methodists, 10, 38–39, 67–68

Miller, Perry, 31

Miller, Rev. Samuel, 84

Mims v. Lockett, 118

Monroe, James, 9, 57–58, 65

Monroe v. State, 111

Moody v. Threlkeld, 162 (n. 10)

Moore, Clement, 79

Moran v. Davis, 130, 133

Moultrie v. Smiley and Neal, 108

Mygatt v. Goetchins, 115

Neal v. Crow, 123

Neal v. Farmer, 128, 131

Nisbet, Eugenius A., 64, 90–91, 99, 100, 109, 120; opinions on slavery, 128, 131; role in Georgia's secession from United States, 140

Nullification, 2, 46, 53–55, 88, 128

Nunn v. State, 94

Oglethorpe County, 5, 7–8, 11–12, 25, 29–30, 75

Oglethorpe University, 67

O'Neall, John Belton, 44, 47, 124

Parkes, Anna, 61

Paschal, George, 43, 51

Pettigru, James L., 65

Phi Kappa Society, 24–25, 47, 65–66, 149
Phillips, Ulrich, 28, 54
Pierce, Franklin, 103–4
Pierce, Lovick, 38–40
Pound, Roscoe, 1, 107, 123–24
Presbyterians, 11, 17–18, 41–42, 61, 67,
   149, 156 (ch. 5, n. 14)
Priest, Josiah, 131–32
Princeton, 11, 13, 17–22, 25–26, 33,
   89–90, 98–99

Reese, William, 34–35
Reeve, Tapping, 19, 22
Reid, John Philip, 124
Reynolds v. Reynolds, 111
Richardson v. Roberts, 122
Riley v. Martin, 136
Roane, Spencer, 109, 124
Ruffin, Edmund, 71
Ruffin, Thomas, 1, 107, 109, 124, 129–30,
   134

Sanders v. Ward, 135
Scarburgh, George P., 104
Schley, William, 35, 77
Scott, General Winfield 58, 103
Scudder v. Woodbridge, 129
Sealy v. The State, 162 (ch. 11, n. 7)
Second Great Awakening, 40–41
Shaw, Lemuel, 1, 98, 107, 109, 129
Shorter v. Smith and the Justices, 117
Smith v. Simms, 161 (ch. 11, n. 1)
Smith v. State, 121
Smyth, Thomas, 84
South-Carolina Institute, 12, 70–72, 84,
   98, 114, 118
Southern Rights party, 128

Spencer, Ambrose, 109
Stark, James H., 162 (n. 9)
Starnes, Ebenezer, 99–100, 103
State Rights party, 54–55, 103
State v. K. P. Boon, 162 (ch. 11, n. 3)
State v. Lockhart, 113
State v. Mann, 129–30
Stephens, Alexander, 33–34, 103, 136–37,
   140–41
Stephens, Linton, 136–37, 140
Stephenson, D. Grier, 125
Stephenson, Mason W., 125
Story, Joseph, 1, 23, 88, 96, 98, 106–7,
   136
Story Association, 98–99, 107
Stuart, John, 21, 155 (ch. 2, n. 14)

Taney, Roger, 117
Tappan, John, 45, 68
Tocqueville, Alexis de, 2
Toombs, Robert, 34, 77, 101, 103, 143
Towns, George, 126, 147
Troup, George M., 2, 17, 25–28, 31, 51,
   54–55, 57, 89
Tucker v. Harris, 161 (ch. 11, n. 1), 162
   (ch. 11, n. 6)
Turner, Nat, 56, 60
Tushnet, Mark, 129

Union party, 54–55, 103
University of Georgia, 13, 24, 43, 76, 81,
   104–6
University of Georgia Law School, 13,
   14, 138–39, 142, 149, 150
Upson, Stephen, 23, 74

Van Buren v. Webster, 122

Vance v. Crawford, 73, 119, 134
Vanderzer v. McMillan, 112
Venable, Abraham, 155 (ch. 2, n. 14)

Waddel, Moses, 24–25, 65
Waddel v. State, 119
Wade v. Johnson, 116
Walker, David, 56
Walker, Dawson, 148
Walker, Timothy, 96, 119
Walworth, Reuben, 45
Warner, Hiram, 88–89, 99–101, 127, 147–49
Warren, Charles, 87, 98
Washington, Bushrod, 57
Washington, George, 5, 57
Water-Lot Company of Columbus v. Bucks and Winter, 115
Watson v. Tindall, 112
Wayne, James M., 17, 59

Webster, Daniel, 1, 33, 54, 59, 65, 157 (n. 6)
Wertenbaker Thomas J., 18, 22
Whig party, 47, 103, 128
Whitehead v. Peck, 117
Whitney, Eli, 12
Wilberforce, William, College of, 51–52, 67
William and Mary, 22, 104
Wilmot Proviso, 126–27
Wilson, James, 146–47
Wisner, Benjamin, 45
Worcester v. Georgia, 88
Worthy v. Johnson, 112
Wylly v. Collins, 120

Yale, 14, 99
Yazoo Land Fraud, 7–8, 88
Young and Calhoun v. Harrison and Harrison, 114, 115, 150